9 95

W9-DHJ-204

Counseling
A Guide to Helping Others
Volume 2

Counseling
A Guide to Helping Others
Volume 2

Edited by R. Lanier Britsch/Terrance D. Olson

Deseret Book

Salt Lake City, Utah

©1985 Deseret Book Company
All rights reserved
Printed in the United States of America

No part of this book may be reproduced in any
form or by any means without permission in writing
from the publisher, Deseret Book Company,
P.O. Box 30178, Salt Lake City, Utah 84130

First printing August 1985

Library of Congress Cataloging in Publication Data
(Revised for volume 2)
Main entry under title:

Counseling : a guide to helping others.

    Includes bibliographies and indexes.
    1. Peer counseling in the church—Addresses, essays,
lectures. I. Britsch, R. Lanier. II. Olson, Terrance D.
BV4409.C68 1983   253.5   83-72396
ISBN 0-87747-960-7 (v. 1)
ISBN 0-87747-737-X (v. 2)

Contents

Preface

We have been gratified with the warm acceptance *Counseling: A Guide to Helping Others* has received. It is evident that it has filled a need for information among individuals who do lay counseling. Professionals, too, have expressed confidence in its usefulness. And many readers have used it as a self-help manual.

Even before we sent the first volume to Deseret Book for editing and publication, we were aware of a number of significant omissions. Before the volume was in print we began inviting potential authors to write the chapters that are included in this book. We have maintained the same editorial philosophy in this volume as in volume 1. It is not necessary to read volume 1 to benefit from the chapters contained herein. Each chapter is independent of all others. You may begin reading in any chapter and gain from the experience.

Each chapter is written by a Latter-day Saint scholar or therapist who is thoroughly familiar with his subject. We have made every effort to eliminate jargon and specialized words. Our goal has been to present up-to-date professional concepts in lay terms. We believe that knowledge is a blessing and that it contributes to inspiration.

Because all of our authors are committed Latter-day Saints, these books reflect certain assumptions regarding the nature of man and his ability to change that similar secular books do not. We believe that people have the ability to determine their own mental attitudes, and that they have the power within them to change, to grow, to seek, and to find those ideas and patterns of behavior that can bring peace and happiness. The counselor, trained or lay, can only suggest and encourage and set the appropriate example. People themselves must create the mental, spiritual, and physical environments that can bring them to the level of joy and the absence of remorse that they desire.

Happiness is difficult to define. Some people see it more as the absence of negative things than as a positive state of being. But joy and happiness can also be seen in a positive sense, of having appropriate attitudes toward life and of enjoying life's experiences as they occur.

Happy people have many attitudes that set them apart from unhappy people. That people should keep the Lord's commandments and repent of their sins is fundamental to being happy. Three attitudes are especially pertinent:

1. Recognize that life includes opposition and difficulty. People must mature to the point where they are not unduly surprised at accidents, pain, sickness, and other difficulties. They must realize that they were not put here on earth to spend their time in everlasting comfort. Life is a place for gaining experience, and some of the most valuable experience is the difficult kind.

2. Recognize that life is uncertain. There is no other way to live it and still have the blessing of agency. We must walk by faith. We do not know from one moment to the next whether we will live or die, or if our loved ones will remain with us. We cannot know whether the world will be blown away, and we cannot know if our investments will remain sound. Happy people recognize these facts of life and go on anyway.

3. Recognize that life includes injustice and unfairness. The Savior promised us peace if we embrace his gospel, but he did not assure us that this life will always be fair. It is not fair because the Lord has turned us over to ourselves and other humans and to the elements of a mortal world. Good men and women sometimes get sick and have serious accidents. Good men and women are sometimes defrauded by

dishonest people. And good men and women sometimes see their children fall away from activity in the Church. It is not fair, we say. Nobody who understands this life and the gospel ever said it would be.

Happy people recognize that life is difficult, uncertain, and unfair. But they do not take offense. Having confronted these realities, they go on their way living life fully. Because they know the realities of life and have resolved the difficult issues, they are free to help others instead of brooding about their own problems. Happy people invariably give of themselves in the service of others.

As editors we express gratitude to a group of happy people, the authors who so generously contributed their time, talents, knowledge, and training to these books. We realize that their contributions have been made in a spirit of service to the members of the Church and also as a manifestation of personal friendship to us. The authors have done a great service for those among us who are troubled and who seek sound direction for their lives.

We also thank the many fine people who have worked with us at Deseret Book. We extend special gratitude to Jack Lyon, who edited these volumes. He has handled his labors with competence, skill, and a warm spirit. We also thank the word-processing technicians who have processed parts of these manuscripts, especially those who serve in the Faculty Support Center of the College of Family, Home, and Social Sciences at Brigham Young University. Finally, we again thank our wives and families who have encouraged and supported our efforts.

As with volume 1, the contents of the various chapters are the thoughts and contributions of the various authors, but we would not have included them if we did not agree with their contents.

1

The Gospel, Emotions, and Being Human

Terrance D. Olson

When we are angry, frustrated, sorrowful, happy, or filled with remorse, where do our feelings come from? Sometimes the emotions we experience seem totally authentic to the situation. Often, whether we are feeling joy or remorse, we experience those emotions in very unselfconscious ways. We are, in those times, being ourselves, feeling emotions in the situation that the honest in heart feel. However, there are other emotions that, when we are beset by them, seem to have a life and a direction of their own. The very having of some emotions is accompanied by feelings of helplessness in having them. Considering how different these emotions seem to be, are we talking about two distinct types, and not just degrees, of feelings?

The scriptures describe people who experience different *qualities* of emotion. When people approach life with a hard heart, they are generally suspicious or defensive. When their view of life is more soft or broken-hearted, their emotions are characterized more by compassion, sorrow, or interest in the welfare of others. They feel to do good continually. In the moments of their broken-heartedness, they do not hold hostile feelings. When people feel hostile, their emotions seem to be beyond their control.

Hostile resentments are also more associated with hard-

heartedness. Thus we can describe two distinct qualities of
emotions. One set is characterized by personal frustrations
and feelings of helplessness; the other set by deep concern
for others. When people are emotionally miserable, it
doesn't matter how the emotion is expressed, in words or in
other ways. The quality of the emotion is of concern.

People with anger, hate, and resentment are miserable.
The very emotions that contribute to their suffering seem in-
escapable to them. Their hostilities seem justified in the face
of what has been done to them by others or by the world or
by their circumstances. To them, their hates are always defensible in light of what has been done to them by hateful
people.

If their view of their being helpless victims of such feelings is correct, then there is little you or I or they can do to
ease their suffering. Perhaps counseling them to wait until
the feelings pass or helping them channel their feelings into
activities that will not harm themselves or others is the best
we can do.

But the gospel of Jesus Christ does not propose that the
solution to emotional problems is simply to grit our teeth
and wait. Evidently, we can actually be free of negative emotions. But this requires living, and not just learning, gospel
principles: "The fruit of the Spirit is love, joy, peace, longsuffering, gentleness, goodness, faith, meekness, temperance."
(Galatians 5:22-23.) Whether or not we are dealt with justly
by others or face pressures and demands, the gospel can be
our salvation if we will but turn to it.

The gospel suggests that the kind of emotional suffering
experienced by those full of hate and hostility can be given
up, and not just coped with. How is such emotional peace
possible?

When we turn our hearts to the Savior and begin to see
one another with his eyes, the very quality of the emotions
we experience changes. These feelings are fundamentally
different from what we experience when we turn our back
on the Savior's invitation. I am not talking here about living
perfectly, but of living in a way that helps free us from irritability, impatience, anger, and resentment.

"Emotional" Problems

What can you do when people share with you their teeth-gritting resentments? Some people have harbored such feelings even across generations. They feel justified in their hostilities, but they are not emotionally at peace.

The Savior offered an invitation for us to come to him. Why? Because, as he said, "My yoke is easy, and my burden is light." (Matthew 11:30.) Hostile and resentful people do feel burdened. They do not feel their yoke is easy. Can the invitation of the Savior bless such people? What does the yoke and the burden described by the Savior mean to people in these circumstances: the man who has been cheated in a business deal; the couple who resent the reprehensible conduct of their daughter's husband; the husband and wife whose time together seems to increase their nervousness or their resentment of one another? How are they to deal with their feelings?

Consider a typical circumstance. A Relief Society teacher has been hurt by the responses of sisters to her lesson. She goes to a leader and tearfully asks to be released, explaining that she is inadequate, that she does not have what it takes, that she has never liked being a teacher anyway; and besides, the people she is trying to teach are being critical of her.

In explaining the challenges and difficulties that this teaching assignment has meant, including being humiliated by her own friends, she breaks down in tears and discloses that from time to time she will sob like this, especially after giving a lesson. Then later she realizes that she doesn't know whether she has done any good, whether she has touched any lives or not.

She also reports that when preparing her lessons, she feels an uncontrollable fear that she will fail. The fear is so strong that she cannot even concentrate on her preparation.

So, not only is her lesson preparation marked by fear, but after the lesson is over she is overwhelmed by feelings of low self-esteem and despair. In fact, only when she is actually delivering the lesson is she free from such feelings. In describing her delivery of the lessons the woman says, "I find that I am so concerned about explaining the ideas, and that I see from my own experience the meaning of the gospel in that lesson, that neither fear nor despair engulf me. But after the lesson is over, and even though some sisters are kind and polite with their compliments, the nagging fears and depression return."

The emotions she feels in her church calling seem detrimental to her well-being. And it seems as if the church calling, or at least the audience she teaches, is responsible for both her fear and despair. Some would suggest it is the sisters' criticism that "causes" her feelings, or that the woman herself, in her insecurity, is the cause. Some might even speculate that, had she not been thrust before her peers as a teacher in the first place, she would not have had to undergo the demeaning comments she later heard in the halls. None of these explanations acknowledge the Savior's promise of comfort.

The Source of Emotional Problems

What should a leader do if he wants to help solve the woman's emotional difficulties, rather than merely treat the symptoms? To release her from her calling as a teacher may not help much. If she is released, she might carry her fears and discouragements with her into her next calling and into other areas of life. The answer lies in recognizing that the problem is primarily in the person, not in the situation. And the solution to the problem may be found in gospel principles that even this troubled woman would give her allegiance to. Yet her troubled feelings seem to be beyond the reach of that very gospel. She may have discounted the meaning of the very principles that could bless her. Now, sometimes changing the situation (releasing the woman) is a positive and necessary step, but it is still treating the current symptom and not addressing the long-term difficulty.

Fortunately, the gospel offers a solution. Unfortunately, a woman with the attitudes we have described may think the gospel solution unrealistic, naive, impossible to act upon. Yet her attitude is not what invalidates the gospel solution; it is her resistance to the gospel solution that produces her attitude. The helplessness she feels seems incompatible with the promises of the Savior. She does not walk by faith, for the kind of despair she feels is a spurning of faith. She lashes out at those who would offer her alternatives. She refuses to yield herself to patience, forgiveness, and love unfeigned. She is experiencing "hardness of heart," and continues to insist on despairing over being wounded in the house of her friends. At the heart of this woman's attitude is her refusal to accept the Savior's promise of peace and rest.

Consider a more extreme example. A young bishop was reporting to his stake president a visit he had with a woman who had attempted suicide. He had listened to her explain how difficult it was for her to manage in her marriage. Even little things like her requests to have family prayer were met by her husband with refusals or ridicule. Finally the only way she saw to escape her difficult circumstances was to take her own life.

The stake president said to the bishop, "What we have here is a refusal to love." The bishop, thinking that his leader was referring to the husband, said, "Yes, President, but as I talk with the husband about that, he seems so resentful and defensive." The president responded, "That he is resentful and defensive may be true, but when I spoke of a refusal to love, I wasn't talking about the husband. I was talking about the wife." The bishop was stunned. "What?" he said. "You criticize a woman who is so driven that she tried to take her own life? You make it sound as if she were responsible for her problem." The president responded, "I am saying that her refusal to love has produced her problem. By insisting that her husband has made her life not worth living, she has run away from gospel truths that would help her. We need to help her understand and live by those principles. If we are to help her, we must focus on her attitudes, on her discouragements. If we can help the husband see his unrighteousness, fine. But the immediate challenge is to help this woman see that the gospel is her rod and her salvation. Until she sees that gospel principles are more powerful than her husband's unrighteousness, she will feel trapped."

Consider the following questions. If perfect love casts out fear, how can trying to take one's own life be considered in any way an expression of love? How does this woman's act represent a positive example of commitment to her husband? Does it represent her forgiveness for his hostile attitude? Does it in any way invite him to turn his heart to God? Has she, through this act, demonstrated the truth of the gospel she claims to believe? Is she demonstrating by her behavior that her yoke is easy and her burden is light?

Such an act is a deep accusation against another human being. And in a certain sense her behavior will be used by her husband to justify his own rejection of her and the gospel. He could say, for example, "*She* is the Christian, she is the one that always wants me to have prayer. A lot of good prayer does her if she is so crazy that she tries to commit suicide. What do you do with a woman like that?"

Now, the man is as wrong in his assessment of his wife as she is in her assessment of him, but this is a perverse collaboration. Both, by refusing to abide by the compassionate light that they could have, instead show how the other is to blame for their difficulties.

It is true that this woman's husband is guilty of wrongs against her. But her response to those wrongs is not innocent. To insist that she cannot go on or that life is not worth living, simply because of the sins against her by someone else, is a denial of the very gospel principles she claims to believe. It may also represent an abandonment of her own moral responsibility, her personal capability. Her attempted suicide and her attitude are powerful ways of placing responsibility on her husband for her inability to meet life. They represent an insistence that her yoke is not easy, that her burden is more than she can bear. (This analysis does not mean that her discouragement is not real, only that it is unnecessary.)

How the Sufferer Discounts Help

This woman has deep feelings about her life and marriage. One can imagine the all-encompassing discouragement that must have engulfed her as she attempted suicide. She expressed her feelings in depressed terms. We might even feel her helplessness as she rehearsed her troubles. If a lay counselor were to say, "You've simply got to pull yourself together and have a better attitude," she might either acknowledge, "Yes, you are right, but you don't know what it is like to try and live with him," or "Yes, I know. I guess I'm just not the kind of person who can buck up under this kind of rejection and pressure." Her first expression blames her husband; her second blames herself. Both assertions eclipse gospel possibilities. Both assertions justify her helplessness.

In other words, she responds to our reminder that a different attitude would be a blessing by showing us in one way or another that she can't help having her attitude. Her feelings are due to what her husband has done to her (and therefore she cannot help how she feels), or there is something about her own personality that makes it impossible to feel other than she does. So, whether she blames her husband or herself, she discounts her own responsibility. In *her* mind, she cannot help the way she feels.

Her view of emotions presupposes that people are acted upon by emotions in a way they cannot help. Seen this way, emotions are simply beyond us; they have a life independent of our will. How is this view to be reconciled with what the scriptures teach about human beings being free, through the atonement, to act for themselves and not to be acted upon? (2 Nephi 2:26-27.)

How to Help

Helping a woman with these kinds of emotions requires our love and compassion. We must teach her through kindness, longsuffering, persuasion, and love unfeigned (D&C 121:41-42) that her capacity to meet life in the face of challenges is real. This may be taught more powerfully through deeds than words, but it is the foundation of any hope we might offer her. If we blame her or her husband, we will be viewing the situation as she does, confirming its hopelessness. We can invite her to see that by her depression and her attitude she denies her own capacity to act. We can help her to acknowledge the gospel principles she claims to believe. By doing so she will acknowledge her agency, her resilience, her dependence on the Lord, and her faith in him to teach her to live by his example.

Similarly, the Relief Society teacher mentioned earlier can be free of her hurt and despair, not by changing the situation, but by changing her heart. Such change is possible.

In Mosiah chapter 3, we learn of people who had hardened their hearts and who were therefore blind to the truth. A hard heart is the result of rejecting the light of the gospel. Emotions such as hostility, resentment, anger, and often even depression can be generated by hardness of heart. It is our own resistance to light that produces such emotions. We cannot blame *other* people for *our* refusal to live by the light, yet that is what hard-hearted people do. They shift responsibility for their feelings onto someone or something else, and they feel both helpless and justified in having such feelings.

It is our task as counselors to invite them to become soft-hearted. We can understand their feelings without accepting those feelings as uncontrollable or inevitable. We can teach them that to be free of their misery requires neither that they control their feelings nor that they express them, but rather that they give them up. The soft-hearted person gives up his insistence that his emotions are externally controlled. Such feelings are given up when the principles of repentance and forgiveness and compassion (love unfeigned) are present in their hearts. When they are willing, in their hearts as well as in their deeds, to do good to those that despitefully use them, they not only will experience the peace the Savior promises regarding yokes and burdens, but they will see what they can do to help solve their problem. Instead of being angry or "sensitive" or hostile or depressed, they will be taking responsibility to do whatever they believe will help.

Giving up a hard heart is no guarantee that other people will change. That is, this discouraged woman, were she to do good to her husband (who she claims has despitefully used her), has no guarantee that he will change his behavior. But by striving for Christlike living, by adopting soft-hearted attitudes, she will issue the most powerful invitation imaginable for him to change. Moreover, she will be free of the kinds of feelings that are associated with suicide attempts.

You can help a couple understand that the world of helpless emotion in which they seem trapped is usually created by their own behavior. Once they establish a negative cycle of behavior, each uses the insensitivities, the wrongs, and the self-righteousness of the other to justify his own resistance or irritability or discouragement. But, in justifying such attitudes, each must insist that his own behavior and attitudes are due to having been a helpless victim of the other. Such insistences are a way of proving they are each being acted upon. Even your reminder to either one of them that they could feel differently might be met with incredulity. They really think they are victims. Until they abandon their self-justifying attitudes, they will not think it possible to feel differently than they do.

The Emotions of the Soft-hearted

When we harbor hostile, resentful, accusatory attitudes, our hearts are not broken, contrite, or guileless. We cannot experience positive and negative feelings simultaneously. Soft-hearted or "authentic" emotions are full, deep, relevant to the situation, and are usually an expression of concern for others. Such feelings, whether of grief or sorrow, joy or ecstacy, are not felt accusingly or helplessly. Such emotions are usually felt unself-consciously, but not uncontrollably. They represent unfeigned love. We not only mourn with those who have cause to mourn, but we mourn with them as the Savior would mourn with us. We share in the joy of the righteous, and we sorrow for those who are emotionally troubled.

Moreover, a person genuinely grieving the loss of a loved one, or a person genuinely joyful at the athletic performance of his child, is not self-consciously patting himself on the back or reflecting on his feelings. A person rarely says, "I'm really grieving right now" when he is authentically grieving. The emotions speak for themselves, and self-consciousness is not usually a part of the attitudes and emotions. These feelings come when faith in the Savior is exercised, when actual, righteous steps are taken to solve problems, to meet challenges, and to be responsible.

The Emotions of the Hard-hearted

The emotions I have described as "hard" represent the feelings of the "natural man" described in Moses as "carnal, sensual, and devilish." (Moses 5:13.) Surely hatred, resentment, hostility, irritability, and impatience are the kinds of feelings we associate with the natural man. They are the feelings we defend and justify by saying "I'm only human." In contrast, feelings of compassion, sorrow, love, patience, commitment, and concern are the emotions the Savior taught and exemplified. They manifest our capacity to put off the natural man and to become as little children, willing to submit to all things we might face in life. (Mosiah 3:19.)

What produces the natural man? Natural man is not an inherent condition within us waiting for the triggers of earthly pressures and injustices to set it off. Rather, it is invited by our repudiation of the atonement. Natural man is the condition we are in when we love Satan, or satanic principles, more than godly ones. (Moses 5:13; 6:49.) We put on natural man as if it were a coat, and the feelings associated with natural man indicate our refusal to yield to the enticings of the Holy Spirit.

When we put off the natural man, we yield to the Spirit, and those feelings that are expressions of our resistance to light and truth disappear. We have "no more disposition to do evil." (Mosiah 5:2.) Whatever our emotions, they are of a different quality than the counterfeit ones we had while in the condition of "natural man." Those feelings do not now need to be constantly controlled or appropriately channeled and expressed. They have been given up, they have been abandoned. They are not a part of the experience of someone who is, in that moment, living correct principles.

Applying Gospel Principles

Is it not unrealistic to believe that a person can be free of negative feelings all the time? Does not this line of reasoning create unrealistic expectations and lay a burden of guilt upon those who experience hostility, resentment, and anger?

The claim is not that we do not experience such feelings; it is that such feelings are manifestations of sins we can repent of. It is not inevitable that we experience hard-heartedness. The Savior's invitations to personal peace require attitudes of meekness and humility; these attitudes strengthen us in the midst of pressures, injustices, or hostilities. To partake of this peace requires faith. The solutions to emotional problems proposed in this chapter are "not as the world giveth."

The question of how to help people with these principles is not so much a question of whether the principles work, but whether people are willing to work. Your example and genuineness with God is your most enticing invitation to emotionally troubled people. But their emotional peace is actually in their hands, not yours. If they reject the gospel promises, you will be limited to helping them just cope with symptoms instead of finding real-life solutions.

Your task with the emotionally troubled is not just to love them. It is not just to understand their feelings. It is to teach them the Savior's invitation to give up those emotions associated with "natural man." You may communicate this invitation more powerfully by actions than by words, for "if ye know these things, happy are ye [and they] if ye do them." (John 13:17.) Anything you do to show the *possibility* that their fears can be cast out by yielding to the enticings of the Spirit is a legitimate attempt to help them find permanent psychological and emotional peace.

SUGGESTED READINGS

Chidester, C. Richard. "A change of heart: Key to harmonious relationships." *Ensign*, February 1984, pp. 6-11.

Kelly, Burton C. "The case against anger." *Ensign*, February 1980, pp. 9-12.

Olson, Terrance D. "The compassionate marriage partner." *Ensign*, August 1982, pp. 14-17.

ABOUT THE AUTHOR

Dr. Terrance D. Olson, professor of family sciences at Brigham Young University, received his bachelor's degree from BYU and his Ph.D. from Florida State University. As a family life educator he has produced materials designed to strengthen families and to promote self-reliance. He has been project director of a multistate project that teaches moral meaning in the public schools.

He has served as a bishop, as bishop's counselor, in district and stake presidencies, and on Church writing committees.

He and his wife, Karen, are rearing six children.

2

Recognizing Mental Disorders

David G. Weight

All societies have been faced with the problem of how to help those with mental disorders. In our society about 15 percent of the population experience serious emotional problems each year. It might seem that these disorders could be easily recognized, but diagnosing a mental disorder is much more complex than it appears. Some symptoms are extreme, as in the case of someone who believes he is commanded by God to kill atheists. But what about the person who believes that recent storm damage shows that God is upset with new laws passed by the city council? Or, consider the person who washes his hands unusually often because he is concerned about shaking hands with others because they might have been recently innoculated against smallpox and be infectious.

What is the difference between those who are eccentric and yet function well in society, and those who are actually a threat to their own or others' well-being? And what about behaviors that are viewed as abnormal in one culture but as reasonable in another?

Consider these observations by Emily Dickinson:

Much madness is divinest sense
To a discerning eye;
Much sense the starkest madness,
'Tis the majority
In this as all, prevails.
Assent, and you are sane:
Demur,—you're straightway dangerous
And handled with a chain.

To complicate matters, we also encounter those who are viewed as normal and successful and yet who feel miserable and confused.

Defining Disorders

A mental disorder is not a disease, but rather a way of thinking or behaving due to a complex set of causes, including heredity, environment, traumatic experiences, and learned reactions to the stresses of life.

The degree of a person's mental health can be judged by his *appearance, behavior, thinking, mood,* and *perception*. If he does not have extreme problems in these areas, he is probably adapting well to life.

Appearance

Although appearance and grooming vary widely among normal people, a person's appearance can give some clue to his mental health. Someone who pays little attention to his appearance may be overly preoccupied with his own thoughts and oblivious to the social needs of others. This may indicate a mental disorder. This is especially true when basic personal hygiene is ignored by a person of normal intelligence. Bizarre dress often indicates unusual thinking patterns as well.

If you are counseling someone you think may have a mental disorder, look for signs of tension and anxiety or depression. Does he seem angry or frightened, or is he demanding and hostile? Pay attention to his eyes. Does he look around nervously or avoid eye contact? Does he stare at you or at something else? Does he seem to look through you rather than at you? Any of these may indicate some mental problem.

Behavior

Perhaps the most dominant symptom in every mental disorder is anxiety. Does the person show constant nervousness? Has he had periods of panic in which he thought he might pass out or go insane? Other symptoms of anxiety are headaches, dry mouth, ringing in the ears, difficulty in swallowing and breathing, sweaty hands, dizziness, numbness and tingling in the extremities, digestive problems, heart palpitations, and strong fears. Still other indicators include strange posturing or very stereotyped movements. For example, the person might sit rigidly for a long time or repeat a certain behavior almost like a ritual, or he might collect items of little value and use or display them in unusual ways.

Any remarkable changes in a person's behavior may suggest a mental disorder. These include a sudden drop in quality of job performance, schoolwork, ability to concentrate, and self-care, and increasing social isolation. Often people who know the person best will report that he is just "not the same."

Repeated abnormal behavior may indicate a mental disorder. If the person keeps coming back for help with the same problem, his behavior may be becoming an obsession. This is particularly true if the person keeps talking about the same concerns without realizing that he has already raised the issue. For example, a man may confess that he has had unacceptable sexual feelings toward a certain girl. Then the next week, he may confess that he had unacceptable sexual feelings toward a different girl.

Thinking

Disturbed thinking is sometimes a sign of a mental disorder. The main symptoms of disturbed thinking are delusions, which are incorrect inferences or false beliefs about reality that are devoutly maintained in spite of obvious evidence to the contrary. Delusions are not merely errors in thinking, as in the case of a person who believes he is completely worthless because he has disappointed his family. Delusions are false psychotic beliefs, such as those held by a man who believes his words are not his own but are being spoken by a supernatural source, a woman who believes that an electronic device has been implanted in her head so that her thoughts can be monitored, or someone who believes he need no longer eat since he has no insides.

A more difficult delusion to evaluate is one where the

person believes he is being attacked, cheated, persecuted, or conspired against. Since such things do occur from time to time, you must evaluate whether the person's fears are justified. If you tell a person that his fears are delusions, he may become angry or feel rejected. Instead, ask the person for the reasoning behind his fears. Try to understand how the person is thinking, and then determine whether he should see a professional counselor.

Some mentally disturbed people have ideas that do not relate logically to scientific views of cause and effect. An example is a person's belief that his environment has particular and unusual significance for him, as when he thinks that the message of a radio broadcast is meant especially for him.

Related to such ideas is *magical thinking.* In this case the person believes that his thoughts, words, or actions might override normal laws of cause and effect. For example, a woman believes that if she has good spiritual feelings all day, her son will not become ill or have an accident. A man believes that if he were around an emotionally ill person it would cause him to become emotionally ill.

There are also other beliefs that may indicate mental disturbances, such as when someone says, "I sometimes have a feeling of gaining or losing energy when certain people touch me," or "I might cause something to happen just by thinking about it," or "I have felt that there are messages for me in the way things are arranged in store windows."

Some disturbed people may overvalue a certain belief. For example, a person may let the principle of good nutrition dominate his life. He may say, "I know mother seemed to get better after her surgery, but if she had just taken the right vitamins every day, she wouldn't have needed surgery in the first place." He may then begin a campaign to challenge the need for any medicine or physicians.

One of the most typical cases of mental illness is the person who believes that his thoughts are known by others and that external forces can control his thinking. Such a person might falsely believe that he has been possessed by evil spirits or that someone is exercising influence by the use of hypnosis, telepathy, or spiritual control. Since there are very few cases of documented possession by evil spirits, we may assume in most of these cases that the person's thinking is disordered. But such delusions can be very frightening to the person, and he may take extreme measures to protect himself—even to the point of killing someone in order to "appease the external forces." Such a person is potentially dangerous, especially if he fears someone is trying to hurt him.

One example is the person who is struggling with impulses to kill himself and who thinks that others want to kill him or are provoking him to attempt suicide by leaving knives on a kitchen table. (In an extreme case a man actually killed his family and himself to protect them against living in a sinful world.)

Some people who claim extreme religious commitment twist religious principles into destructive beliefs. We occasionally hear of such people "sacrificing" family members or ignoring important responsibilities to follow a "holy grail." Such fanaticism is the opposite of authentic religious commitment. Anyone claiming to receive revelation for others should be held suspect, especially when the information is believed to have relevance for the Church or for large groups of people for whom the person has no particular responsibility. In one such instance, a person received a "revelation" that important new documents were about to be found and that he would recognize these documents and point out to his church how policy should be changed. He believed he had been selected for these "revelations" because there was too much corruption in "high places."

Your initial contact with such a person does not require an on-the-spot solution. You can usually schedule another discussion time. Meanwhile, you can consult with a professional as to the next steps you should take.

Disturbed people often think in a confused fashion and use unclear or illogical reasoning. Such thinking includes bizarre associations of words and meanings. These people may create new words, repeat answers that no longer make sense, or use a word for another word that has a similar sound, even though the meaning is totally different. Here are some quotations from people who think in this manner:

"Parents are the people who raise you. Parents can be anything—material, vegetable, or mineral—that has taught you something. A person can look at a rock and learn something from it, so a rock is a parent."

"I'm not trying to make noise. I'm trying to make sense. If you can make sense out of nonsense, well, have fun. Trying to make sense out of sense. I'm not making sense [cents] anymore. I have to make dollars."[1]

In response to the question of why people believe in God a disturbed person responded, "Um, I'm making a do in life. Isn't none of that stuff about evolution guiding isn't true anymore now. It all happened a long time ago. It happened in eons and eons and stuff they wouldn't believe in him. The time that Jesus Christ people believe in their thing people believed in Jehovah, God that they didn't believe in Jesus Christ that much."[2]

Mood

A person's moods may range from manic excitement to the depths of depression. Extremes in mood must be viewed as pathological. The person with borderline manic excitement may be seen merely as very excitable and energetic until the disorder becomes extreme. Symptoms include decreased need for sleep, high levels of energy, and inflated feelings of self-esteem. The person may reduce his food intake, strongly seek out people, demand more sexual activity, talk a lot, and exaggerate past achievements. He may indulge in excessive laughing and joking, buying sprees, or reckless driving.

A severely depressed person may have reduced energy, decreased productivity, sleeping and eating disturbances, reduced sexual interest, and feelings of sadness—even a desire to end his life.

In some cases, the person appears almost devoid of sensation. He seems unable to experience pleasure and does not experience emotions appropriately—he may laugh at the news of a loved one's death, or cry at inappropriate times. If depression lasts for two weeks or more, it is imperative that the person be referred to a professional for treatment—he may be suicidal.

The lay counselor should watch carefully for excessive guilt. Some people have such perfectionistic expectations that they constantly feel guilt where most other people do not. This is of greatest concern when the person responds to guilt through inappropriate behavior or irrational ideas. Examples would be a woman who believes that she has committed an unpardonable sin and that the death of her child is part of her punishment, or a man who feels he is unworthy of his wife and family because he has occasional sexual feelings toward women other than his wife.

Perception

The mentally ill sometimes have disturbed perceptions —they see or hear things that are not really there. Hallucinations are different from illusions, in which the person sees or hears something he perceives to be different than it actually is. A woman who sees a belt lying on the floor and believes she has seen a snake suffers from an illusion. A man who sees snakes wriggling out of someone's mouth is having hallucinations. Hallucinations of sounds most often involve voices but may also include music. An extremely disturbed person might report hearing two or more voices in conversation. Sometimes these voices are frightening. One woman reported hearing a running commentary on her "sins."

The person who has visual hallucinations has a greater probability of having organic causes for his hallucinations than psychological ones.

It is not unusual for people who have undergone open-heart surgery to have a brief period of perceptual changes. They often report visual hallucinations and may even have delusions that nurses and doctors are trying to kill them. This is usually the result of temporary brain changes and usually clears up spontaneously in a few days.

People having hallucinations should definitely be referred to a professional for evaluation.

Although many people are aware of their mental problems, others deny their difficulties and hold to their disordered beliefs. This is an important consideration when making referrals. The person who does not recognize his difficulties can become angry and resist attempts to help him. This is particularly true of those who fear that they will be abused or taken advantage of. You should encourage the person to discuss his own perceptions of his problems. This may help him come to the point where he will ask for help.

Incidentally, the fact that people with severe mental disorders often have extreme religious views does not mean that religion has caused their disorder. When a person begins to have unusual internal experiences, such as seeing things or hearing voices, do not immediately assume that these are supernatural experiences. This does not deny the existence of legitimate religious experience, but it does suggest the importance of making proper diagnosis of the causes of unusual behaviors and then taking appropriate action.

NOTES

1. *Diagnostic and Statistical Manual of Mental Disorders* (Washington, D.C.: American Psychiatric Association, 1980), pp. 361, 355.

2. Ibid., p. 362.

ABOUT THE AUTHOR

Dr. David G. Weight, professor of psychology at Brigham Young University, received his bachelor's and master's degrees from that institution and his Ph.D. from the University of Washington. A clinical psychologist, Dr. Weight has had broad experience in therapeutic work in Washington and Utah. He is a consultant to Utah Valley Regional Medical Center Mental Health Services and a large school district. He supervises a department of the BYU Comprehensive Clinic. Professor Weight has written a number of professional articles. In addition to his professional activities, he has been a member of the board of education of the Provo School District.

In the Church, Dr. Weight has served as a missionary, bishop, high counselor, and Young Men's president.

He and his wife, Shauna, are the parents of five children.

3

Listening and Communicating in Counseling

Richard A. Heaps

The importance of listening and communicating in counseling was illustrated nicely in a classic "Peanuts" cartoon by Charles Schulz. Lucy, with a sour expression on her face, says she really feels crabby. Linus, with an innocent and pleasant expression, says that maybe he can help. He offers to give her his place in front of the television and to fix her a nice snack. "Sometimes we all need a little pampering to help us feel better," he says. After returning with a sandwich, some cookies, and a glass of milk, he asks if there is anything else he hasn't thought of. Lucy, at first quietly and then with great emotion, says, "Yes, there's one thing that you haven't thought of . . . *I don't wanna feel better!*"

An important rule for anyone who would like to help another is to wait until the person has either asked for or agreed to your help before moving ahead. Whatever the reason, quick action, advice giving, or question asking often overlooks the fact that some people want no more than to let their frustrations out to a listening ear. Also, it is less likely to be trusted if offered when a person is resistant to it. And it increases the chance that a person will feel treated like "everyone else" rather than as an individual.

Does this mean that you can't offer to help someone? Certainly not. It is very appropriate to openly express your desire to help. This rule merely reflects the value of being certain you have permission before entering the other's personal world in such a direct manner.

After you have been asked for your help, a second rule is, before you do anything else, *listen*. Be certain what the other person is saying or asking before you move into action. If you don't, you may discover, like Linus, that you have hurried into a solution not appreciated by the person you wish to help.

Once you have started listening, a third rule is, allow the person to express the problem without interruption. Even correct advice, if it interrupts, may not be beneficial. There is little value in being right if your counsel isn't being received. Incidentally, this does not mean that you must listen to elaborate details of a person's "war stories." It means only that *both* of you should be satisfied that you have listened long enough to be accurately aware of what needs your attention.

Once you have listened, without interruption, to a complete statement of the problem, what comes next? Very simply, whatever your understanding suggests. Regardless of what you choose to do, however, the medium for accomplishing your counseling goals is communication. It would be helpful, therefore, to describe some specific types of communication and the counseling needs they are intended to meet.

Understanding

Everyone likes to be understood. The feelings that come from mutual understanding form the basis for trust and rapport in counseling. As you counsel someone, you will often hear the question "Do you know what I mean?" whenever uncertainty is present. Accurate understanding provides the necessary facts for solving the problem. It is extremely difficult to solve problems you do not understand or have misunderstood.

It is important, then, to know how to understand another person and how to communicate that understanding. You have probably had the experience of saying something you felt strongly about and then hearing the other person say, "I know exactly what you mean." If your relationship with the person was not a close one, you may have thought, "How can I be sure you do, since you don't really know me?"

How to Understand

Understanding is often referred to as empathy. Empathy is both an attitude and a skill. The attitude involves a willingness to listen carefully, without judgment. The skill involves accurately perceiving the other person's ideas and feelings.

Scientists have confirmed the commonsense observation that we think much faster than we speak. They have also verified that few of us use that difference to any real advantage. But you can put this principle to work by repeating or summarizing in your mind the other person's words and feelings while he is talking. You can also ask yourself questions about what he is saying. This becomes easy with a little practice, and it will help you focus on what the person is saying. Try it a few times with your family or friends. You will be surprised at how much more aware you will be of what they are saying and feeling.

Communicating Your Understanding

As important as it is to listen and accurately understand the other person, you will be less effective in your counseling if you do not also succeed in communicating your understanding. It is not enough, however, to say, "I understand." Anyone can do that. An effective helper is also able to say clearly what was understood and periodically does just that. This is often referred to as empathic responding.

Probably the best way of communicating your understanding is to say in your own words what you think the other person said and felt.

For example, suppose the person you are trying to help says, "I try to be friendly, but no one talks to me. I need someone to like me, but I don't know what to do anymore. I just want to give up." There are a lot of ways you could respond. If you simply say, "I understand," neither you nor the other person can be quite sure how well you understand.

You will communicate your understanding more clearly if you say something like, "It's a lonely and hopeless feeling not knowing what to do to have people like you."

In the above example, it would be premature to ask what the person had tried or to suggest what he might do to make friends before establishing that you both understand the problem. An empathic response, which places what you understood in your own words, builds trust in your relationship because it shows you care and are trying to understand without judging. Such trust is essential before people will feel good about your questions or advice.

Another benefit to paraphrasing what the person is saying is that almost immediately it can reduce the person's tension or anger. Why? Because it shows you are trying to understand him rather than push your position. This permits more openness and attention to problem solving.

Everyone likes to be understood. When one of my children was only three years old, she squirmed on the floor one day, crying and screaming that she wanted candy. Each time I refused (dinner was about to be served) she became louder and more demanding. When I discovered I was also becoming louder and more demanding, I decided to change things. I turned to her and simply said, "You want candy, don't you?" The result was amazing. The squirming, crying, and screaming stopped instantly, and she said, very softly, "Yes." She didn't get the candy, but I was able to tell her why and she was able to hear me. Although she was disappointed, she did not return to her previous level of behavior.

It's usually better to state a paraphrase as a fact rather than as a question. Too many questions (for example, "Do you feel lonely and hopeless?") suggest uncertainty and lack of confidence or curious interrogation. People usually respond in one of two ways to a straightforward paraphrase. They either say yes and continue explaining themselves, or they say no and restate what they said to correct your misunderstanding. Either response promotes greater understanding and permits the two of you to continue in a positive way.

Clarification

People with problems often find it difficult to speak clearly and specifically about what they are experiencing. They may be embarrassed over something personal or uncertain about the problem or how to discuss it; they may try to avoid unpleasant details. In such circumstances, the person may use generalizations and vague statements such as "He's always bugging me." In this sentence it is not clear what "always" and "bugging" mean. Ambiguous statements must be clarified before you can understand a problem well enough to help solve it.

You can seek clarification directly by pointing out what was unclear in the other person's statement. This can be done with a direct request or an implied question. For example, you might say, "Help me understand what you mean by 'always' and by 'bugging' you." You can also ask, "Always bugging you?" Such statements indicate what is not yet understood and place responsibility on the other person for becoming more specific.

If you would like to become more aware of how often such general statements occur, just pay attention to your own conversations. You will catch yourself frequently using vague or ambiguous terms. Then try to be more specific, and you will communicate better. This exercise will also help you to become aware of the need of others to clarify their vague statements.

A caution: Your requests for clarification can appear too abrupt and demanding if you have not yet won the person's trust. Empathic responses may be more appropriate at first. However, when trust exists, promoting clarity can help you get to the heart of a problem and move more rapidly toward a solution.

Confrontation

It goes without saying that people become emotionally involved in their problems. What is not always so easy to see is that such involvement often prevents people from being aware of contradictions in their reasoning or behavior. The difficulty is that these inconsistencies usually get in the way of their ability to solve their problems. The most helpful response under such circumstances is one that brings the discrepancy to the attention of the person in an appropriate way. This type of response is called confrontation.

Confrontation has two important elements: (1) listening carefully for discrepancies such as those between what the person says and does, says at different times, or perceives compared to what others perceive, and (2) pointing out contradictions in a nonaccusing manner. When people are emotionally caught up in their problems, they are frequently sensitive and defensive about personal accusations, and they may resist your counsel. In other words, how you confront is as important as whether you confront.

The most generally safe and positive approach to confrontation involves clearly stating and contrasting the contradictions you perceive. You can do this by stating its two most contradictory parts and joining these by a phrase such as "on the other hand," "however," or "yet." An example: "You say you have great affection for your wife, yet you spend almost no time with her."

Confrontation helps the other person see contradictions in his thinking or behavior and think about ways to overcome the contradictions.

Feedback and Advice

Once you have the person's trust and understand the problem, you will usually need to make some type of reaction or suggestion. If your response seems too critical or impersonal, the person may become defensive and argue, shift blame, or withdraw. So what do you do?

First, accept *ownership* of your response by using some form of the pronouns *I* or *my*; second, describe your reaction *specifically*. This places responsibility for what you say on yourself and avoids the appearance of relying on outside authorities or of blaming and criticizing the person. Also, it allows the person to know where you stand; this promotes honest, free-flowing communications.

For example, you might say, "I'm getting frustrated. I want to help you, but every time I bring up the real problem, you change the subject." This response shows that you care, that you trust the other person enough to be honest, and that you expect that both of you must work together to solve the problem.

On the other hand, if you were to say, "You are never going to get anywhere if you keep changing the subject every time I mention the problem," you will probably alienate the person. Such responses are often referred to as "You statements." They tend to belittle the other person and create defensiveness even though much of the content is the same as in the more appropriate "I statement."

When giving suggestions to another person, you may find it easy to become detached from your advice by implying or directly quoting authority from some outside source. For example, you might say, "It's well known that once you allow such thoughts, you encourage all the related behaviors." Quoting an outside source can be helpful if the person has asked for such information. When not requested, however, references to outside authority tend to depersonalize and limit the discussion. The implication is that the idea cannot be questioned since it comes from someone with authority.

If you want to promote more thoughtful discussion of an idea or suggestion, you should give it as an "I statement," such as, "I believe that once you allow such thoughts, you encourage all the related behaviors." Since you state the idea as your belief, the person may feel more free to discuss whether or why it is true and how it applies to his problem. Also, if the person considers and accepts your idea, then he becomes responsible for the idea and cannot blame an impersonal, outside authority for his success or failure.

Problem-Solving

A person usually sees his problem as having few reasonable solutions. Although giving advice and suggestions under such circumstances may take less time, you may want the other person to take responsibility for thinking about and deciding what to do to correct a problem. The best type of counseling in such instances is to help the person explore alternative solutions and decide on the steps necessary to put them into practice. You should help the person state his chosen solution as a goal that is specific, measurable, and achievable.

For example, a person may come to you feeling isolated and lonely. You may offer an empathic response that recognizes a need for change, such as, "You really dislike feeling so lonely and would like to do something to change it." The person may agree with you and express a desire to become a more friendly person. You might then help the person clarify his problem and identify solutions by saying, "Help me understand what it means to you to be more friendly. What would I notice you doing that you aren't doing now?" After listening to the explanation, you may help the person set a specific goal by saying, "Now that you've decided you'd like to become more friendly by introducing yourself and talking casually with a few people at church, let's discuss how to begin."

This communication process gives the person hope by opening new ways to solve his concerns.

SUGGESTED READINGS

D'Augelli, Anthony R.; D'Augelli, Judith Frankel; and Danish, Steven J. *Helping Others.* Monterey, California: Brooks/Cole, 1981.

Egan, Gerard. *The Skilled Helper,* 2nd ed. Monterey, California: Brooks/Cole, 1982.

Heaps, Richard A., and Rhode, Norma. *Interpersonal Communications: A Skill Development Workbook.* Provo, Utah: Brigham Young University, 1974.

Jensen, Vern H.; Heaps, Richard A.; Nelson, Bruce D.; and Shingleton, Richard N. *Interviewing Skills Workbook.* Provo, Utah: Brigham Young University, 1981.

ABOUT THE AUTHOR

Dr. Richard A. Heaps, professor of educational psychology at Brigham Young University, received his bachelor's degree from Brigham Young University and his master's and Ph.D. degrees in psychology from the University of Utah.

A counseling psychologist in Counseling and Personal Services at BYU, he is a member of several professional societies and associations and is a licensed psychologist and marriage and family therapist. He has been a member and president of the board of education for the Alpine School District.

He has served the Church as a missionary, an Aaronic Priesthood adviser, a high councilor, and a bishop.

He and his wife, Joyce Ann, are the parents of four children.

4

Addictive Behavior

Brent Q. Hafen and Kathryn J. Frandsen

Addiction. It's an emotionally charged word that brings visions of darkened alleys, empty whiskey bottles strewn in a gutter, a desperate soul with his fingers wrapped tightly around a bundle of fine white powder. It brings to mind the alcoholic, the junkie—those who have lost control, surrendered to chemicals.

Strictly speaking, scientific authorities haven't arrived at a concrete definition of *addiction.* As a word, it stems from the Latin *addicere,* meaning to bind a person over to one thing or another. One thing we do know for a certainty: it is not limited to the craving of alcohol or drugs. There are many kinds of addictions, and they manifest themselves in many kinds of behavior.

Some people are addicted to food—or, more correctly, to eating. They eat to relieve boredom, frustration, anger, unhappiness, loneliness, jealousy, and hatred—or to reward themselves for some special achievement. They eat to console themselves in times of grief. They eat to inspire themselves. They reward themselves emotionally by eating.

Other people are addicted to watching television. Instead of talking or reading or participating in athletics, they watch television. Television, in fact, becomes a way of escaping into a life they deem more pleasurable. It's easy to forget their worries and frustrations by identifying with a fleeting character who appears every Thursday or Friday night. Deprived of the experience, they become distracted, jittery, or hypnotic—unable, really, to function normally in the world around them.

Still others are addicted to gambling—not to winning money, but to the thrill associated with the roll of the dice, the spin of the wheel, or the horses pounding down the home stretch, all the while knowing that their lives (or fortunes) are on the line. Gambling—taking a risk—becomes an exciting prospect that, much like eating or watching television, relieves boredom, soothes unhappiness, and allows an escape into another, more desirable world. The addiction to gambling, one of the fastest growing addictions in the nation, has recently been defined as a disease by a chain of self-help groups called "Gamblers Anonymous," fashioned after the popular Alcoholics Anonymous.

A closely related addiction is the addiction to risk: not only gambling, but literally placing one's life in danger. A "risk addict" gains actual arousal or excitement from placing himself in danger—scaling a sheer rock cliff with a small pick hammer, catapulting from an airplane and waiting until the last second to release the parachute, heading into a hairpin curve at seventy miles an hour.

Some become addicted to crime or violence, gaining arousal from the violation of other people or the destruction of other people's property. Some become addicted to sex, suffering an overwhelming obsession with pornography, sexual fantasizing, sexual paraphernalia, or promiscuous behavior. Still others become addicted to people: while they have difficulty with one-on-one relationships, they thrive on group socialization. Scarcely a night goes by without a visit to a bar, private club, or party.

Some addictions don't appear to be harmful on the surface, but they are actually good habits gone awry. Consider exercise, for example—a person may take the good habit of exercising three times a week to excess until it becomes a twice-daily ritual during which he avoids dealing with his problems. Deprived of his exercise for even a brief time, he becomes hostile and angry; he gradually but steadily loses the ability to view things in perspective.

Similar is the "workaholic," the person who drives himself nearly to the point of extinction with his hard work. He may spend fifteen hours a day at the office, bring work home, stay up until the wee hours agonizing over a problem, and even creep into the office on weekends. He scarcely admits he has a family, or that his family may have problems that need his attention. He neglects home, friends, and personal life—but who can fault him? He's usually a success in business and is rewarded profusely for his dedication and loyalty to his job.

Because addiction can take any of these—and many other—forms, it is critical to separate it from the most common manifestation of alcohol or drug abuse. It is essential to understand how addiction (regardless of its manifestation) occurs. It is critical that we be able to determine when addiction exists. And it is helpful to list the characteristics of addiction and of those who are addicted or who are most prone to become addicted. If we are to succeed in making a difference, we need to understand how to help people change addictions into healthy habits—and how to prevent addiction from occurring in the first place.

Factors Leading to Addiction

Why does addiction occur? There are almost as many theories about what leads to addiction as there are theorists —almost everything has been blamed, from the overbearing mother to the arrangement of chemical transmissions in the brain. Many of them make sense, while others seem less rational.

Some of the major thoughts on how or why addiction occurs include the following:

The behavior is reinforced. Before an addiction can occur, the behavior must be reinforced in some way—usually by creating pleasure. The workaholic is reinforced because he gains honor and recognition from his superiors at the office. The person addicted to chocolate enjoys the taste. The Russian roulette player thrills to the arousal associated with the risk.

The addiction is an attempt to meet basic needs. Human

growth and developmental psychologist Abraham Maslow described human needs as a pyramid. At its base are the most basic needs—the need for food and water in order to survive, for example. At its pinnacle is the highest level of human need, the need to become the best you possibly can (termed *self-actualization* by Maslow). Called "the hierarchy of human needs," Maslow's model describes five levels of need that must be met:

1. Basic physical needs—the need to survive, which includes the need for food, shelter, and water. Because these needs are the most basic, when they are not met, other needs become inconsequential. A person deprived of food or water will worry about little else: his primary efforts will center around getting what he needs to survive.

2. Safety needs. A person must feel secure. His life must have some sort of predictability. He must feel safe from outside forces that might destroy him. A person who does not feel safe or secure might retreat into a world where he *does* feel safe, even if that security is false. He may gain emotional comfort and a facade of safety from eating, sleeping, drinking, using drugs, or watching movies, for example.

3. Belonging needs—the need for love, affection, and a sense of being important to other people. A person who feels he doesn't belong, who feels he can't deal with the stress of developing close interpersonal relationships, may retreat into an addiction.

4. Esteem needs. Every person needs to feel important, to achieve something great, to feel worthwhile. Again, addictive behavior may seem to fill the emotional void for those who feel inadequate or unappreciated. Addictive behavior may also provide escape to those who feel unable to cope with the pressure to achieve.

5. Self-actualization needs. Even when all other four need levels are being filled, there is still the fifth, the need to be the best person we can possibly be. We all want to achieve our potential, develop our talents, and reach our goals. The woman who married and abandoned her plans for a career in medical technology during her sophomore year may feel

resentful and imprisoned by her decision, especially when she contemplates a sinkful of crusted dishes, an overflowing diaper pail, or the demands of small children. She tries to escape these feelings of frustration and anger by retreating into the world of daytime soap operas. Suddenly she worries about whether Jenny will ever discover that Brad has been unfaithful; that consuming preoccupation saves her from worrying about whether she should have struggled to finish college.

The addiction relieves stress. Life without some kind of stress would be worthless, but when stress becomes overwhelming, it can be destructive. Some people are successful in dealing with stress; others try to escape by denying the problem or somehow running away from it. Addictive behavior is often a way to run from problems, to hide from problems, or to deny that problems exist. The workaholic whose teenage son is failing in school can blissfully escape the grueling problem of having to work with his son: after all, he's so busy at the office that he doesn't have time for family problems.

The addiction results from peer pressure. At various stages in our lives, particularly during adolescence, we are especially vulnerable to peer pressure—the subtle or overt influences exerted by people our own age, in similar circumstances, or simply close to us physically or emotionally. Peer pressure can not only influence the addiction to begin with, but it can help determine its extent.

The addiction can exist within our value system. Our own value system, including the behaviors we consider acceptable, are typical sources of many addictions. We have beliefs about what is right or wrong. If our socioeconomic position, religious beliefs, education, traditions, and role expectations do not allow shooting heroin, then we will probably not develop such an addiction. However, we may become addicted to otherwise acceptable behaviors. Overeating, oversleeping, compulsive gambling, or obsessive television watching may become an addiction.

Serious physical illness is present. Serious physical illness—especially chronic or terminal illness—can create for an individual a situation much like a steel trap: he envisions that he is going to be held prisoner forever, with no rational way out. To escape from the stress of the situation, he may turn to addiction. In some cases, the addiction may provide an escape from pain or disfigurement.

There is pressure to perform or succeed. One of the most powerful factors leading to addiction may be the pressure to perform or succeed; the person who feels he just can't measure up might try to escape into an addiction. Within his own value system, he now has an excuse for his failure, which somehow makes it more acceptable.

The person hates himself. A person who actually comes to hate himself may seek an addiction as a subconscious way of punishing himself. The addiction may seriously hamper his ability to cope with life, but he reasons that he doesn't deserve any better anyway. With that rationalization, the addiction seems defensible.

There may be a genetic link. At least a few prominent researchers believe there may be genetic determination of those who are susceptible to addiction, just as some believe that susceptibility to cancer may be genetically determined. This genetic makeup does not guarantee addiction, they say, but does determine whether a person will become addicted as a result of repeated reinforced behavior. Some even say that a true addict must have an abnormal chromosome— and without it, the person will never be truly addicted.

Addiction may be due to varying brain activity. Closely related to the genetic theory is one that says a person is highly susceptible to an addiction if messages are transmitted in his brain with varying intensity. When nerve transmissions occur with unusual speed in certain parts of the brain, researchers say, the feeling linked to an addictive behavior may be much more intense than usual, leading to the important reinforcement required to establish addiction.

Society allows addiction. While peers may pressure a person into addictive behavior, society contributes by allowing it—in other words, we have evolved into a society that has become much more lenient. Gone are the strictures that bound us even half a century ago; the byword is "do your own thing," and few people are persecuted for addictive behavior until it becomes clearly destructive (such as severe alcoholism). Medicine and psychiatry have become much more accepting; the media views addictions of all kinds as part of life.

Determining When Addiction Exists

Taking into consideration the many factors that can lead to addiction, it is extremely difficult to always determine exactly when addiction exists. When does a person cross the fragile line between habit and addiction? When does an activity go from being considered normal to being considered too much?

The distinctions are difficult to draw, but some signs can help:

1. The addictive behavior dominates the person's life; he begins to neglect other facets of his life (even basic ones, such as cleanliness).

2. The person's usual behavioral patterns or day-to-day patterns of living become seriously disrupted.

3. The abrupt discontinuation of the addictive behavior after continued or prolonged involvement results in a state of extreme anxiety, a hypnotic trance, or, in some cases, an actual physical "withdrawal" illness (such as that seen among drug or alcohol addicts).

4. The person cannot seem to get enough of the addictive behavior or substance—or, after getting "enough," he still can't stop.

5. The person shows no sign of the ability to make choices about the addictive behavior—he can't rationally determine whether it is an appropriate time or setting for the behavior. He does not act appropriately. In simple terms, he feels compelled into the behavior, regardless of his own feelings or circumstances at the time.

6. The person continues the addictive behavior even after it has lost some of its excitement or appeal to him; even

though it isn't as pleasant as it once was, he continues regularly. A person who once got a real thrill out of betting on horses may continue to do so even when he is ridiculed or nagged, loses continually, or no longer feels the same thrill.

7. The person no longer does something because he wants to progress and improve; he does it because he wants to be left alone, because he fears he can't progress, or because he wishes to escape a stressful situation. He may not find any joy or pleasure in the addictive behavior, but it may be a way of erasing other things in his life that he dreads.

The Characteristics of Addiction

Using the criteria listed above, it is possible for a lay counselor to determine when an addiction exists. Another important consideration is to determine what distinguishes a healthy habit from an addictive behavior.

Some of the signs of a healthy habit include:

1. The person is readily satisfied by the behavior, and when that level of satisfaction is reached, the person can then stop and go on to something else.

2. The person derives pleasure from the behavior. That pleasure lasts not only while the behavior is taking place, but becomes part of a general sense of well-being and satisfaction that endures long past the behavior.

3. The behavior is spontaneous instead of being predictable. The person may seize the opportunity to watch television because something exceptionally interesting is on that evening—not simply because it is part of his routine to watch television every night.

4. The person welcomes the chance to do something else. A woman might have established a routine (or habit) of running two miles before she goes to work each morning. When a friend calls and suggests a tennis match instead, she eagerly accepts the tennis match as an equally good way of getting some exercise.

5. The person genuinely feels better about himself as a result of the behavior; over the long run, it contributes to his feelings of self-esteem and worth.

6. The person genuinely enjoys the activity or behavior—and when he stops enjoying it, he stops doing it.

7. The person feels exhilarated and expanded because of
his behavior and uses it to build his confidence in himself.
He eagerly looks for new challenges and behaviors that can
take him a step further and readily abandons the old for
something more challenging or rewarding.

8. The person becomes more aware, more educated, or
more enlightened as a result of the behavior.

Some of the signs of addictive behavior include:

1. The person can't seem to achieve satisfaction from
the behavior; no matter how much he gets, it just isn't
enough. He is constantly frustrated by the need to do more
or get more. This frustration is negative, and it is much different from the motivation to do more out of challenge and
determination.

2. The behavior is not pleasurable or does not contribute
to an overall sense of well-being.

3. The behavior becomes predictable. A man knows
that *every* morning he will arrive at work an hour early and
that he will stay two hours after everyone else in the office
goes home; the pattern never changes. A woman knows that
no matter what, she will eat three chocolate bars before
lunch.

4. The person becomes inflexible about the behavior. A
woman who has established the pattern of running two
miles before work each morning will balk at a friend's invitation to play tennis instead; if the friend won't join her in
running, she'll run anyway—either before the tennis match
or in place of it.

5. The person feels a lowered sense of self-worth or self-
esteem because of the addictive behavior but feels unable to
change.

6. The person does not necessarily enjoy the behavior
but feels driven to do it anyway. A man may feel disgusted
by his obsession to look at pornographic magazines and
may feel that his is a "dirty" habit, but he can't seem to stop,
regardless of those feelings. The behavior may even sicken

the person, but still he feels incapable of changing it.

7. The person remains locked in the behavior as a means of escaping demands or stresses, not because the behavior is seen as an exhilarating challenge.

8. The behavior serves to dull the senses, provide an escape, or otherwise help the person get away from stress, unhappiness, boredom, or frustration. When the person gets the opportunity for challenge or reward, he resorts to the addictive behavior instead of abandoning it and accepting the challenges of some other behavior.

By stubbornly clinging to addictive behavior, the person creates all kinds of problems for himself. His health may be compromised, as in an addiction to alcohol, drugs, or eating. He may no longer be able to function properly, and other aspects of his life fall into neglect, sometimes seriously compromising his status within the family or the community. His relationships with his spouse, other family members, and friends may be compromised. He may even experience serious social problems, such as involvement in criminal activity or problems with creditors.

Healthy habits, on the other hand, enhance life. They increase the ability to function normally, and they usually promote health. As a result of healthy habits, a person is better able to communicate and relate to friends and members of his family; a person whose habits are healthy is not likely to experience serious social problems, because his awareness is acute and his priorities are not with the habit to the detriment of other things.

Characteristics of Addicted People

In any case of addiction, the real factor is not the substance or the behavior, but the person himself. Pulling the handle on the slot machine may be a passing fancy for one person and an overwhelming compulsion for another. Eating sugary sweets may be an occasional treat for one person and an almost hourly ritual for another.

Regardless of the addiction, an addicted person shares certain traits and characteristics with other addicted people.

One of the most common and overwhelming of these traits is the fact that the addicted person does not have the confidence to face life without the addictive behavior. He may simply feel as though he can't go on without the addictive behavior, or he may actually feel that life wouldn't be worth living if he were denied the chance to indulge himself with the addiction. A woman who was addicted to drinking cola drinks was told she had become diabetic and that she would need to severely limit her consumption of soft drinks. She literally decided that life was not worth living if she could not have the cola—and died at the age of twenty-five from complications of diabetes, still drinking twelve to fourteen cola drinks a day. Clearly, she may not have consciously wished to be dead, but her addictive behavior led to her death.

The addicted person is generally negative. Instead of anticipating joy and pleasure, he fears pain, failure, and disappointment. A nonaddicted person looks forward to life's experiences for the joy and fulfillment they bring; an addicted person has convinced himself that life holds plenty to be anxious and unhappy about and little to look forward to.

The addicted person suffers from all kinds of fear—fear of interaction with others, fear he may not perform well on the job, fear he may fail at school, fear he may not be a suitable husband or father. By constant fears and worries, he escapes into the addictive behavior, however falsely, to gain some reassurance that is never forthcoming.

Some addicted persons believe they have no control over what happens to them. They think that their addictive behavior and the substances associated with it are more powerful than they are, and that they are mere victims with no ability to refuse or overcome.

The addicted person regards life itself as a burden—something he can't cope with or handle. The nonaddicted person regards life as a pleasurable, fulfilling challenge and regards life's problems as temporary hurdles that can be overcome with work and effort. The only way the addicted person sees to overcome life's problems is to escape them.

The addicted person feels extremely dependent—either

on other people or on addictive substances or behaviors. He feels incapable of making an acceptable life-style for himself free of the addictive behavior. He views the addictive behavior as inevitable—something he can't (or won't) give up or escape.

The addicted person often feels emotionally detached from other people, and, when other people stand in the way of the addictive behavior, he may view them as mere objects to be manipulated or exploited. He may even be able to relate somewhat normally to others until it comes to the addictive behavior, and then he may lose the ability to view others with rationality. He may even seek out others who share his addiction.

Finally, the addicted person welcomes the control that the addiction places over him; he feels some kind of safety and reassurance in submitting himself to it. If he is deprived of that chance to submit, he feels fearful and incapable of going on.

Characteristics of Addiction-Prone People

Because we have been able to identify common characteristics of addicted people, we have been able to a large degree to identify those who are *prone* to becoming addicted. Consider the following list. It is only suggestive of traits people may have developed that allow them to be more addiction-prone than fully healthy people.

Addiction-prone people:
1. refuse to tackle life's problems head-on;
2. view success as a magic solution to life's ills;
3. don't set realistic, reasonable goals;
4. turn appropriate diversionary activities into obsessive activities;
5. worry about their own capabilities and express low self-esteem;
6. are often dependent, conforming, and compliant;
7. are frequently fearful of others and detached;
8. see problems as overwhelming burdens or obstacles that must be escaped;

9. often lack problem-solving skills;

10. don't cope well with stress;

11. often lack the spontaneity, creativity, and eagerness for life that others possess. Addiction-prone people are often bored with life.

Latter-day Saint lay counselors should remember that all people have their agency to choose what they will do and be. That certain people have personality traits that match those listed above in no way *determines* their future behavior. The role of the lay counselor is to help an addicted person recognize that he has the freedom and the power to change his thoughts and his behavior.

How to Help Addicted People Change

Addicted people *can* be helped to change. Some people are able to cure themselves of addictions. You've probably heard stories of or know someone who just decided to stop smoking and did it; who decided to stop overeating and did it; who decided to stop gambling and just walked away. For the vast majority of addicted people, however, self-help just isn't enough. Usually, the problems that led to the addiction to begin with are overwhelming, and until they are gone or the person feels strong enough to confront them, the addictive behavior will persist. In many cases, a person may simply trade one addictive behavior for another—escaping into the fantasy world of television instead of the fantasy world of drugs, for example. Before you make any attempts to help another person, you need to recognize certain realities that accompany addictive behavior:

1. The problem centers on the *person*, not the substance or the behavior that the person is addicted to. If you want to help someone stop smoking, it isn't sufficient to just take cigarettes away; if you want to help a child who is obsessed with watching television, you can't just remove the television set. The person has problems that led to the addiction in the first place, and that's where help needs to be centered.

2. Many addicted people want help in overcoming their addictions, but many do not. For them, the addictive be-

havior represents safety, security, warmth, escape, and help in facing the stresses and problems of life. If you try to remove that addictive behavior, you are seen as a hostile, threatening intruder, not as a caring person who wants to help. Before a person can be helped, he must want that help and must recognize that life without the addictive behavior will be more pleasant and rewarding than life with it.

3. The addictive behavior may be (and probably is) a self-destructive way of pursuing important needs in the person's life—the need to feel more worthwhile, to feel capable, to escape problems, to relieve pain, to escape boredom. Before you help the person conquer the addictive behavior, you need to help him collect an arsenal of workable alternatives, including gospel principles, as ways to promote positive fulfillments.

4. Determine the person's needs and help him discover authentic ways of meeting them. A woman who becomes addicted to her work may have done so because she feels incapable of caring for her new baby; she is afraid of making mistakes, and she fears that she will hurt the baby in some way. The longer she stays at work, the greater share of the burden falls on the babysitter, who is an experienced mother who lives in the neighborhood. The woman doesn't really enjoy her job that much, but she feels a certain sense of relief and safety when her baby is with the sitter—and she feels terrified and inadequate when the baby is with her instead. You can offer help by recognizing this young mother's need to build competence and confidence in her motherhood. She may not realize that everyone shares her feelings at first—that few women have a wealth of experience to bring to a first baby. Bring her books and magazines on parenting and possibly include her in a group where she has a chance to support others. Share your experiences with her. Fulfill her need to have expert care for her baby by helping *her* become the expert.

5. For the addicted person, his addictive behavior may be the "best thing" he has yet discovered in his life (as if the personal and family consequences were irrelevant) so he may be understandably reluctant to give it up. You must

offer him the opportunity to discover appropriate alternative approaches to the tasks of life.

6. Help the person discover genuine ways of gaining rewards—help him realize, for instance, that he can conquer stress by getting enough rest, exercising, eating properly, and doing other things rather than drinking alcohol. Encourage him to outline his own alternatives, and help him to have some solid successes at first. As he improves, he will begin to experience his own successes and can wean himself from the addiction.

7. Help the person investigate his family life to determine where changes can be made; a great deal of stress and unhappiness that lead to addictive behavior begin in the family unit. Professional help will probably be needed in many cases, but you can get the ball rolling by helping the person realize that problems exist.

8. If a person was led to his addictive behavior through peer pressure, you may need to help him change his friends. Often it is not simple to make a switch in peer groups; it will probably be a gradual change. Help the person meet new people, have new experiences, and discover new activities. The addicted person may stubbornly resist this at first, so be patient.

9. If the person is addicted to a substance, encourage him to get rid of that substance; if the person is addicted to a behavior, help him avoid the patterns that lead to that behavior. A man who is trying to overcome an addiction to coffee shouldn't keep a can of it in the cupboard; a woman who is trying to overcome an addiction to gambling should go to the movies instead of playing cards on Friday night.

Those who are trying to break the habits of smoking, chewing tobacco, drinking alcoholic beverages, drinking coffee or tea, or abusing drugs should be encouraged to stay close to the Lord through prayer and regular Church activity. Probably they will feel unworthy, but they must learn to rely on the powers of heaven. Help them to remember the great blessings that can come from overcoming their addiction.

10. Help the addicted person realistically and vividly

imagine the rewards that will come once the addictive behavior is conquered. Stress improvements in appearance,
health, behavior, acceptance, or other areas that apply to
the situation.

11. Help the person set realistic goals and map out a
method of achieving them. A person needs commitment to
a goal in order to reach it; help him identify goals that he can
form a commitment to so that he can experience success
and the confidence that come with responsible action.

12. Help the person develop new interests. They could be
something as simple as needlepoint or gardening—but they
should be things that the person is genuinely interested in.
Help in the initial stages: if you decide to encourage her to
start gardening, loan her a few books on gardening, go with
her to buy seeds, visit another friend whose beautiful garden
you've both admired, and get down on your knees in the
warm soil with her. Watch her progress; praise her efforts.
Take photographs of her garden and consider asking her to
donate a basket of vegetables to an elderly neighbor or
friend.

13. Help the person be realistic in his expectations. A person who decides to stop overeating because of the desire to
be thin may hope to lose fifty pounds in a few months. When
the weight does not come off quickly enough, he may become discouraged and return to his addictive behavior. Help
him set realistic goals that anticipate what can reasonably
be expected, and remember to acknowledge the progress he
does make. You may need to help him consult a professional
to determine what he can reasonably expect as he stops the
addictive behavior and changes to new behavior patterns.

14. Examine your own relationship with the addicted
person. To be of help, you should be warm, concerned, caring, and respectful; you should allow the person to examine
his own alternatives, and you should provide support. If you
do not acknowledge his importance to you, you may be
withholding a basic truth that can invite his success. If he is
under stress, do what you can to relieve it; if he is fearful or
anxious, do what you can to relieve his fears. Help him make

positive changes that will help him discover new ways he can meet his needs and free himself from his addiction.

15. Finally—and this is a difficult reality to accept—the person may have deep, destructive feelings associated with the addictive behavior. If this is the case, the person will require professional care by those qualified to help him resolve his destructive feelings.

ABOUT THE AUTHORS

Dr. Brent Q. Hafen, professor of health sciences at Brigham Young University, received his bachelor's and master's degrees from the University of Utah and his Ph.D. degree in health sciences from Southern Illinois University. A member of numerous professional associations, he has been a member of the advisory board of the Utah State Division of Alcoholism and Drugs.

A regular speaker at professional training seminars and workshops, Dr. Hafen is also the author, coauthor, or editor of many books and manuals and as many articles and workbooks.

Dr. Hafen has served as a counselor in the Provo North Stake presidency. His previous Church callings include bishop, bishop's counselor, member of branch presidencies, member of a stake mission presidency, and high councilor.

He and his wife, Sylvia, are the parents of seven children.

Kathryn J. Frandsen, press secretary for Congressman Howard C. Nielson and writing colleague of Dr. Hafen, has studied at Brigham Young University. She has worked as an editor and editorial writer for four publications, including the *Ensign* and *BYU Today,* and she has coauthored a number of books. She is an active Church worker.

She and her husband, Cullen, are the parents of two children.

5

Drug Behavior

Brent Q. Hafen and Kathryn J. Frandsen

Seventeen-year-old Greg is exhausted. The school year is drawing to a close, and he feels a frantic pressure to perform well on exams—after all, he wants desperately to get the highest grade-point average possible so he can get into the college of his choice. His dream is to become a lawyer, and he needs all the help he can get. He thrusts his hand into his pocket; the small capsules he fingers are his key to mustering the energy to get through the next three weeks.

Robin was functioning on less than three hours of sleep. The twins had spent a fretful night, and throughout the long hours of the day they had been fussy and demanding. Between changing diapers and spooning baby food into their mouths, she has tried to keep the main floor clean and get a good start on dinner. The guests would be arriving in two hours, and she was hopelessly behind. Robin headed for the medicine cabinet; she needed something to calm herself down.

Everything at the office seemed to be caving in, and Bill didn't know which way to turn. Two of the employees he supervised were causing problems and demanding too much of his time. With a busy period drawing near, the work was piling up, and there didn't seem to be enough hours in the day. Right at the worst time, the boss demanded that he take a few trips—and he knew he'd fall even further behind. He knew he shouldn't stop in at the club for those drinks after work each night, but it became so difficult for him to relax at home that he felt he really needed them.

Greg, Robin, and Bill have something in common—they all have a drug problem. A person who enjoys an occasional drink with friends doesn't necessarily have a drug problem; a woman who uses a sleeping aid very infrequently doesn't have a drug problem. But people who come to depend on drugs (including alcohol) to help them "get through the day" have a drug problem.

And it's a problem that's growing rapidly in the United States today.

The Extent of the Drug Problem

Falling under the category of "drug" is a variety of substances that can sometimes be used legally and that can be obtained with a doctor's prescription in a pharmacy. Some "drugs of abuse" can even be purchased over the counter by anyone with the money to do it. Drug abuse doesn't always involve substances that are bought from a street seller or obtained in some other illicit way.

In order to understand the extent of the drug problem, it's important to understand the wide variety of drugs that can be involved.

Depressants

As the name implies, depressants are drugs that depress the central nervous system—in other words, they slow down circulation, slow down breathing, and make you sleepy. Common depressants include tranquilizers, like Valium; barbiturates, like Seconal; alcohol; and methaqualone (Quaalude).

Tranquilizers—such as Valium and Librium—are the most commonly prescribed drugs in the United States; at one point, Valium was used more frequently than aspirin by women in this country. Doctors prescribe them to help relax muscles or to help relieve tension and anxiety. But because they are safe under controlled conditions, people tend to misuse them—to take them more often or to take more than prescribed. That's when people get into trouble: they decide they need the tranquilizer just to cope with the stresses of everyday life.

Barbiturates are much less safe than tranquilizers; doctors use them to sedate patients in hospitals and to treat insomnia, tension, or anxiety. The potential for overdose is high: barbiturates can cause loss of memory, confusion, drowsiness, and even coma. The potential for abuse is also high: barbiturates cause physical dependence, which means that you have to increase the dose to get the same effect.

One of the greatest problems with depressant drugs is that people aren't aware of the danger of mixing them with alcohol. Alcohol is a depressant too, and when you mix it with another depressant, you can get much more sedation than you had intended. A frequent cause of overdose is taking Valium and then having a drink or two.

Stimulants

A second classification of legal drugs is stimulants. The stimulants (such as nicotine, caffeine, and amphetamines) stimulate the nervous system, making you nervous, alert, and more active. Some people use them to disguise the effects of fatigue; others use them to relieve drowsiness.

Some stimulants—such as the caffeine in tea, coffee, and cola drinks or the nicotine in cigarettes—are available without a prescription. Others, such as amphetamines, usually do require a prescription.

Amphetamines, usually prescribed as diet pills, are also used medically to treat people with chronic fatigue or to help people overcome mild depression. Unfortunately, the same thing occurs as with depressants: people who get stimulants by prescription end up abusing them by taking them more often or in greater quantities than prescribed. The result is tolerance, psychological dependence, and exaggerated drug effects—the person can become extremely alert and active, or he can become angry, suspicious, and irritable.

One stimulant—cocaine—is obtained most often illicitly and is the subject of growing abuse throughout the country.

Narcotics

Used medically to suppress coughs or to relieve intense pain (generally following surgery), narcotics—such as Demerol, morphine, and codeine—can produce a feeling of euphoria and are highly addictive. Narcotics are safe when used under strict medical supervision, but much narcotic use is illicit and dangerous.

Marijuana

A drug surrounded by controversy, marijuana causes different effects on each person who uses it; some become relaxed or euphoric, while others become anxious or panic-stricken. Most often, a user loses a keen perception of time and loses some short-term memory. Use and sale of marijuana is illegal in all fifty states, while a few states have decriminalized the possession of a small amount of marijuana.

Much of the controversy surrounding marijuana is due to the fact that little is known for sure about its long-term effects; while some argue that marijuana is harmless, others have made claims about devastating long-term consequences.

Inhalants

Inhalants—substances that are sniffed or inhaled—are generally not illegal themselves, but the practice is. A number of common household items (such as gasoline, aerosol sprays, cleaning products, or glue) are used as inhalants, mostly by children. This cuts oxygen off from the brain, resulting in an extreme "high."

Inhalant use is extremely dangerous; lung and kidney damage is common, and death can result.

Hallucinogens

None of the hallucinogens (such as LSD or PCP) currently have recognized medical uses; they are obtained illicitly and have been the subject of intensive law-enforcement efforts. Hallucinogens affect perceptions—users have a warped feeling of what is seen, heard, felt, and understood. Some hallucinogens occur naturally and are derived from plants; some mushrooms are hallucinogenic, as is peyote (which comes from the peyote cactus). Other hallucinogens, such as "angel dust" and LSD, are produced in the laboratory.

At the beginning of this decade, the government identified seven drugs that give particular cause for public concern because of their potential for serious health problems, the extent to which they are used, or the way in which they are used.

1. *Heroin* is of highest concern for two reasons: first, it has an obvious relationship to crime, and second, it is extremely addictive.

2. *Cocaine* is of concern because it has come to be associated with status—it is the drug of the rich and famous. In addition, it is the most powerfully reinforcing of the illicit drugs, usually creating a strong addiction.

3. *Marijuana* has become a major concern because of its rising incidence of use; while some other drugs are tapering off or even declining in use, marijuana use continues to increase sharply, especially among the young, and long-term effects have not yet been established.

4. *Inhalants* are a cause for serious concern because of their considerable danger: because they cut off oxygen to the brain, they can cause sudden death. Another source of concern is the fact that inhalants are so readily accessible (many are just under the kitchen counter) and are used by young children.

5. *PCP* (Phencyclidine), commonly called angel dust, is a cause of concern for many reasons. First, it is easily manufactured in home laboratories, so it has the potential of being available in huge quantities; and because it can be manufactured by relative amateurs, it is also susceptible to dangerous contamination. More serious, however, is its association with a sizable number of violent and bizarre deaths, especially among the young.

6. *Amphetamines* have been of concern since they were first introduced more than fifty years ago because of their potential for tolerance and phychological dependence.

7. *Barbiturates* share the number-one spotlight with

heroin because they are so highly addictive and because they are linked to about 20 percent of accidental drug deaths.

Today some of the most alarming drug use occurs among high school students—once not heavily involved in drug use, they now use marijuana, cocaine, amphetamines, barbiturates, hallucinogens, opiates, and alcohol in growing numbers. Still another source of concern is among women: the number of women alcoholics has doubled since the close of World War II, and the rate of women using all kinds of drugs (legal and illicit) has grown tremendously in the last twenty years.

American society is drug-oriented. We spend more than $30 billion each year for legal drugs, including over-the-counter medications, chocolate, coffee, tea, cola drinks, tobacco, and alcohol. One study estimates that you could easily find at least thirty such substances in any American home—but most Americans take their legal drug behavior for granted. What's more, most of us would defend it—we simply don't consider it to be addiction or abuse.

Perhaps it's time to rethink our definitions of those words. By *addiction* we don't mean the skid-row bum who slurps cheap wine in a bleary trance or the high-school dropout who hovers in a dark room with a heroin needle in hand. Addiction can refer to anyone who relies on any substance to gain a sense of well-being: the joint after class, the cup of coffee in the morning, the mild sleeping pills at the end of a hard day.

Nor does the word *abuse* apply only to extreme cases. Abuse means using any substance that is illegal, but it also means using a legal substance in a situation where it is illegal, using a drug or other substance without medical approval, or using a substance in excess of the accepted standards for self-medication.

You are abusing a substance when you can no longer control your behavior or when you can no longer control your desire for more. You are also abusing a substance if you use it *only* to alter your state of mind or to impair your consciousness.

To put things in a nutshell, there are certain realities

about drug use and abuse that we need to face. People use drugs because they want to feel better; they keep taking drugs because they derive certain pleasures or rewards from the drug use. A person won't stop taking a drug until he finds something better—some more effective way to feel good.

Personality: Who Uses Drugs?

Obviously, not all drug users are alike; they can be as different as the sixty-eight-year-old woman who abuses the aspirin her physician advised her to take sporadically and the sixteen-year-old boy who gathers with his friends to smoke marijuana during lunch hour. But researchers *have* been able to identify certain personality traits or characteristics that may make a person more likely to get involved in drug abuse.

Just because a person possesses some of the identified personality traits does *not* mean that he will begin abusing drugs; it *does* mean that he has traits that may lead to drug abuse.

What does that mean to you? It doesn't mean that you should become alarmed if your teenage daughter or some teenager you are working with has some of the traits. It doesn't mean you should jump to conclusions if the woman next door fits the picture. Nor does it mean that you should panic and resign yourself to eventual addiction if you recognize them in yourself. What it does mean is that we can all be more informed about the things that make us act as we do. If you recognize that your teenage daughter has a number of the traits, for example, you can begin early to help her learn to change those traits, and, when possible, you can help her examine alternatives that can fill her needs.

The personality traits that have been identified among drug-addicted people are almost identical to those shared by others who have addictive problems. This subject may be reviewed by turning to page 40 in the previous chapter.

Apart from specific personality traits, the U.S. Department of Health and Human Services identified four major groups who appear to be at extremely high risk for drug abuse. Those groups include the following: youth, women, ethnic and racial minorities, and the elderly.

The Role of the Home and Family

People who come from happy homes and who grow up in well-adjusted families have much less tendency to use drugs than do people who come from troubled surroundings.

Adolescence is usually the time when drug behavior begins; the impact of the home and family is great, and certain home and family situations have been identified as leading to drug abuse.

The following situations have a tendency to precipitate drug use among family members:

1. Family relationships as a whole are troubled.

2. One or more family members feel alienated from the others.

3. One family member is strikingly different from the others in appearance, physical ability, mental aptitude, interests, or behavior.

4. Parents are not involved with and concerned about the children.

5. Parents are overly strict, imposing unrealistic or impossible limits on children.

6. Parents are domineering, attempting to maintain control over all aspects of their children's lives.

7. Parents are too permissive, and children are not subject to conventional rules and guidelines, such as curfew, check-in, and regular hours at home.

8. The family is under an unusual amount of stress, such as the stress that comes from divorce, terminal illness, death in the family, severe financial problems, or problems with the law.

9. The parents have an extremely different value system than do the children, prompting the children to reject the parents' values and to look for an appropriately dramatic way to express their rebellion.

10. Children have not been provided with an adequate environment to learn how to develop relationships and share intimacies with other people.

11. A parent constantly tries to render the child helpless and emotionally dependent in a conscious or subconscious effort to maintain control over him.

12. The parents are unable to accept the fact that the children are growing up; they continue to treat the children in ways that impede their emotional development instead of treating them like adults.

13. The family is generally devoid of joy.

14. One or both parents lack the skills to deal with their own problems or disappointments, and one or more children become scapegoats for the parents' problems.

15. One or both parents use drugs or alcohol heavily, conveying a message to the children that drugs or alcohol are to be relied on to help cope with problems.

16. Someone in the home is suffering from deep depression or from a depressive disorder.

17. Family members, though obviously part of a group, are lonely; they do not turn to each other for companionship or emotional satisfaction.

18. The parents do not claim responsibility for the major development of the children but instead shift responsibility to schools, agencies, the Church, or social services.

19. Parents isolate children from their peer group, discouraging them from having friends.

20. The family has no religious beliefs and no church affiliation, leading the children to seek for a set of values and a form of worship (which can become drug centered).

21. There is no extended family; children are not privileged to know and associate with grandparents, aunts, uncles, cousins, and in-laws.

22. The parents are experiencing serious marital problems; they are in a cycle of divorce and remarriage.

23. Trust is missing from the family.

Why People Turn to Drugs

In general, people turn to drugs to fill a felt need—a need

to relieve anxiety, to grow, to experience adventure, to relieve boredom, to cope with stress, to escape from problems. When drugs begin to satisfy those needs—or when a person is simply convinced that they do—the drug behavior is reinforced. A teenager who turns to drugs to escape his chaotic family atmosphere finds solace and escape while he is high; the behavior is reinforcing, and he goes back for more. Before long, he is dependent on the drug to remove him from his family situation. He is addicted.

As a society, we are taught to turn to drugs and alcohol. According to critics, television is a major offender—situation comedies portray drug and alcohol use, advertisements for beer proliferate during prime time, and movies give the subtle message that drugs are a great solution for what ails you.

What Signs Indicate Drug Involvement?

While occasional drug use may escape detection, there are many signs that enable you to determine whether someone is using drugs regularly. Some of the signs are physical (such as needle marks on the arms), while others are changes in behavior. Here are some of these signs:

1. A child who has been content to follow parental guidelines and rules around the house suddenly becomes unwilling to do so.

2. A child who has been reliable and dependable at home changes; he starts coming home past curfew, is absent without explanation, or cannot justify other unusual behavior.

3. A child who has been a good student suddenly starts having trouble in school, and you can discover no reasonable explanation. You should be particularly concerned if the trouble involves frequent tardiness, unexplained absences, inappropriate classroom behavior, or the inability to concentrate in class.

4. A child who has not needed much money in the past suddenly seems to need an almost endless supply; traditional allowance is no longer sufficient. You should pay close attention if your child keeps coming to you for money but

you can't readily see how it is being spent. Some children re-
sort to shoplifting or theft to finance a drug habit, but many
fabricate stories for their parents about why they need
money.

5. You discover evidence of drug use, such as empty liquor bottles, empty beer cans, syringes, or papers used to
roll marijuana. You may even discover the drug itself.

6. Watch out for a person who suddenly undergoes ter-
rific changes in interpersonal relationships; anyone can
acquire a new friend now and then, but you should be concerned if your child suddenly seems to abandon most of his
old friends for the sake of a new group of friends.

7. A child, teenager, or adult dresses in a way that is inappropriate for the weather conditions. A person who wears
a long-sleeved shirt consistently throughout sweltering summer weather may be trying to hide needle marks on his
arms or other evidence of drug use. A person who wears
sunglasses indoors or during periods of darkness may be trying to hide dilated pupils.

8. A person who is generally calm and able to relate well
to other people suddenly becomes aggressive and hostile.

9. A person who was once active in community affairs,
civic organizations, church groups, or in pursuit of a hobby
suddenly loses interest and stops participating.

10. A person who has been responsible and reliable suddenly becomes less so. A child stops mowing the lawn on
Saturdays, stops doing his homework, or stops cleaning his
room or doing the other tasks that are assigned him at
home; an adult fails to complete assignments at work,
forgets important family occasions (such as birthdays), and
doesn't follow through on commitments.

11. A person who has been warm and open suddenly
shuts down the channels of communication.

12. A person undergoes fairly rapid physical deterioration: he loses weight, becomes slovenly in appearance, fails
to groom himself well, or starts to suffer some of the physical symptoms of drug use—trembling, slurred speech,
drooling, a fixed stare, dilated pupils, redness around the
eyes, and so on.

13. A person undergoes fairly rapid mental deterioration: he can't think as quickly, doesn't seem oriented to time or place, loses motivation to achieve, or seems confused.

14. A person undergoes fairly rapid and extensive personality changes. You should be concerned about a person who seems to go through extensive personality changes in a period shorter than one year—especially if the person becomes moody, angry, hostile, sullen, secretive, apathetic, withdrawn, depressed, or uncooperative. As a general rule, any sudden and unexplained change in appearance, personality, behavior, or performance should be watched.

It is difficult to face up to the fact that someone you care about may be abusing drugs, but you should watch for the signs and face the problem if you confirm it. A child who was once well behaved and advanced at school may become a completely different person as a result of drug use: she may lie, shoplift, steal, stop doing homework, get involved with prostitution, drop out of school altogether, abandon her old friends, demand more privileges at home, demand complete privacy, or even attempt suicide. Watch for dramatic changes that you can't explain.

If you think that you might have a problem with drug abuse yourself, it's just as important that you confront your own problems. You might think that drug abuse is a clearcut situation, but it isn't always that way: drug abuse can creep up insidiously. The National Institute on Drug Abuse has outlined ten questions you can ask yourself to determine whether your drug behavior is a problem:

1. Do you think you might have a drug problem? If you do, chances are that you are right.

2. Do people who are close to you mention your drug behavior? You might be abusing drugs if you notice that your mother, wife, or child has begun asking you questions about how many tranquilizers you are taking or how many drinks you're having during the day.

3. Do you have to take a pill or have a drink in order to get going in the morning?

4. When a relative or friend mentions your drug use to you, do you find yourself getting defensive?

5. Do you find that you really need a few drinks or a couple of pills in order to fall asleep at night?

6. Have you experienced occasions when you are frightened about the way you act or the things you do when you are under the influence of drugs or alcohol? Or, worse yet, do you find that you often can't remember what you did after having a few drinks or taking a drug?

7. Do you mix alcohol and drugs?

8. Have you ever gone to see a new physician because your regular doctor refused to give you a prescription for the drugs you wanted?

9. When you get a prescription drug from your doctor or buy an over-the-counter drug on your doctor's advice, do you take more than he recommended, or do you take the drug for purposes other than that which your doctor outlined?

10. When you begin feeling anxious or start getting under pressure, do you automatically turn to drugs or alcohol? At the first sign of tension or anxiety, do you take a tranquilizer or have a drink?

What Can Be Done to Help

Researchers generally agree that drug use stems from unmet needs (real or imagined), and that a person will continue using a drug as long as it helps fulfill an important need for him. Drug use is not always pleasant or enjoyable in itself, but it almost always works to reinforce something, or the drug use would not continue.

In order to help someone get away from drug use, you as a lay counselor have to help him discover alternative ways of meeting his need. This involves the difficult first step of *identifying* the need that has precipitated the drug behavior in the first place.

Two words of caution are necessary here. First, a person must *want* to change his drug behavior before you can help him. You can't simply force an unwilling person to give up something that has been a source of relief or pleasure.

Second, you may be able to help a person who has inappropriate drug behavior, who is experimenting, or who is

ical exercise, which can help in many ways. Many people balk at the idea of touching toes and doing pushups; point out that there are plenty of enjoyable activities, such as swimming, bicycling, walking, or dancing. Follow through by making participation feasible—find out if the person needs equipment, transportation, someone to care for her children, and so on.

5. Encourage the person to seek help from Heavenly Father through prayer, faith, and hope. Also help the troubled person to attend Church. Service and association in the Church can do much to overcome drug abuse.

In general, be available to help provide alternatives. Encourage constantly; drug use and its associated entrapments are discouraging, and a person who is trying to steer away from drugs needs constant help, love, and reinforcement.

Preventing Drug Use and Abuse

While the suggestions for helping someone get away from drugs are by necessity limited, there are almost a limitless number of things you can do to prevent those around you from falling into the trap of drug use to begin with.

The family is the key to preventing drug use and abuse; the home environment and the family unit are central to the drug use and abuse pattern. Try the following in your own home as you relate with family members, and encourage other parents to do the same:

1. Develop a nurturing atmosphere in the home.
2. Show respect to each family member, whether three years old or twenty-five.
3. Take time to be aware of your family's lives.
4. Build friendships with your children.
5. Spend time with your family.
6. Encourage family members to communicate clearly and honestly.
7. Carefully define reasonable limits within the family, and let family members know that they are trusted and expected to comply.
8. Set aside time that your family can use for fun activities together.

9. Help your children build their skills and expand their abilities by providing opportunities for them.

10. When problems arise in the family, take a rational, problem-solving approach.

11. Set up a regular time for a family conference or meeting where each family member can discuss concerns and help set goals for the family.

12. Help your children learn how to make choices when they are very young.

13. Help your children learn how to be good friends— with each other and with others outside the family.

14. Help your children develop appropriate values.

15. Help your children feel valuable to the family by giving each one something significant to do.

16. Recognize the need for adolescents to become independent; independence is not an attack on you, but should be an exciting experience for them.

17. Allow your children to have different opinions than you do.

18. When you impose limits on your children, be willing to discuss the reasons why.

19. If you don't understand what's going on with your adolescent, don't be afraid to ask questions.

20. Allow your children to have privacy.

21. If you suspect that your child might be using drugs, resist the temptation to go on a search-and-destroy mission in his room. Instead, confront him privately.

22. Examine your own drug behavior.

23. If you do discover that your child is using drugs, confront the child openly and be honest about your feelings. Emphasize the child's worth, and separate your disappointment about the behavior from your disappointment in him as a person.

In conclusion, build an atmosphere of love, respect, and trust in the home. Set limits for your chidren, but be flexible and reasonable. Respect their growing need for independence, but help them understand that you still care about them and want them to be happy.

Parents must spend time with their children and make

them feel a valuable and worthwhile part of the family. By helping children establish a firm value system and a good sense of self-worth, you are helping them gain the skills they need to make responsible decisions about drug use in the future.

6

Alcohol Addiction
James R. Goodrich

Our family recently attended church in a nearby community. We enjoyed the meetings, but during the children's activities in Primary, something happened that was interesting yet disturbing to me.

During singing time, the chorister innocently passed out a piece of candy to each child and said, "These are singing pills I'm passing out. After you finish eating them, you will be able to sing extra loud and pretty."

Sure enough, it worked: singing time was a great success. But I worry about the subtle, unintentional lesson taught.

We live in a drug-oriented culture that has produced a host of commonly used and abused drugs—aspirin, remedies for colds and acid indigestion, nicotine, marijuana, alcohol, heroin—pills to pick us up, bring us back down, and solve all our problems. People in such cultures have come to believe that no one should suffer any pain or discomfort and that every problem in life, even learning to sing, can be solved with a few grains of powder, a drink of something, or a pill.

Let's look at some statistics for the United States that give us an idea of the dimensions of the problem for other nations.

Aspirin is consumed in enormous quantities. In 1978,

Americans spent approximately $600 million for 17,000 tons of aspirin. That's more than 25,000 tablets a minute. Like aspirin, most drugs have a useful and intended purpose, but when misused, they can lead to serious negative consequences.

Illegal drugs and the abuse of prescription and over-the-counter drugs are a serious health threat. But the greatest drug problem of all lies in alcohol consumption.

In 1979, Americans spent $83,000 a minute on alcoholic beverages. That same year, approximately $61 billion, or $116,000 per minute, was spent to pay for the damages or losses created by those who drink. These costs reflect such things as lost production, vehicle accidents, health and medical costs, crime, social programs, and fire losses.

Also in 1979, 25,000 automobile fatalities, a third of all self-inflicted deaths, and half of all homicides were alcohol-related. Public drunkenness accounted for about one million arrests, and 60 percent of the people in county jails were in for alcohol-related offenses. What's more, of the estimated 10 to 12 million American alcoholics, nearly half a million are teenagers.

These statistics only partially reflect the cost of alcohol in heartache, broken homes, and destroyed souls. Elder Milton R. Hunter summed it up well when he said, "The devil has never found a better tool in the history of the world to destroy the happiness in human beings than liquor." (*Vital Quotations*, comp. Emerson Roy West [Salt Lake City: Bookcraft, 1968], p. 10.)

What does any of this have to do with members of the Church, all of whom are counseled to avoid alcohol?

Although the percentage of Church members who drink is smaller than the percentage among the general population, some Church members do act contrary to the Word of Wisdom and choose to drink, often to the serious detriment of themselves and their families.

In my work, I have encountered many Church members in the saddest of circumstances. One man who had a serious alcohol problem said to me, "I've lost my wife. After pleading with me to no avail to stop drinking, she has divorced me, and now I'm alone. No one can depend on me any-more—my business associates, my family. I've lost respect for myself. I've lost everything."

Another said, "Even after wrecking two cars and sub-mitting my family to extreme financial burdens because of my drinking, I wouldn't admit that I was drinking too much, and I refused to go for help."

One sister in tears reported, "I'm afraid to go home. Re-peatedly my husband has come home drunk and severely beaten me or one of the children. How much longer can we live like this? I love him and want him to get better. Please help me."

What is the solution? Can friends, family members, or anyone else do anything helpful when a loved one's drinking begins to destroy important relationships?

Although there is no single answer for every situation, understanding the following principles and guidelines may help.

People Drink for a Reason

At first a person might try alcohol for any of a dozen dif-ferent reasons—curiosity, rebellion, peer pressure, or media influence, to mention just a few. However, the process that leads to habitual drinking usually includes the following steps:

1. *A person discovers the short-term pleasure of alcohol use.* The initial effect of alcohol on the body is usually a feel-ing of well-being or euphoria. It helps one to relax, to be more spontaneous, uninhibited, and friendly (as perceived by the drinker). It's a change from the routine. In this stage of addiction, the drinker might be heard to say, "How can anything so good be wrong?" or "Why didn't someone tell me about this a long time ago?" or "Look! I made it home. No harm done. Even the headache is worth it." Unfortu-nately, many of the ill effects of drinking don't develop for some time—and therein lies the cruel deception of alcohol.

2. *The person seeks the continued short-term pleasure of*

drinking. Alcohol is effective in creating short-term pleasure time and again; therefore, opportunities to drink are sought out. As drinking continues, the person may also discover that such emotional pains as loneliness, rejection, fear, inadequacy, or failure are temporarily lost. Since these painful feelings return with soberness, the need to drink again is reinforced.

3. *The drinker's body develops a tolerance for alcohol.* Eventually, one finds that one must drink more and more to create the same effect. At this stage, a person may openly boast about how much he can consume and how well he can hold his liquor.

4. *The drinker develops a dependency on alcohol.* The person moves to the point where he or she can't function without alcohol; activities can't be completed unless alcohol has been consumed.

5. *The drinker begins to suffer negative effects.* Because of the frequency and amounts of alcohol being consumed, the inevitable negative consequences begin to be quite noticeable. Productivity at work may decrease. Family relationships begin to seriously suffer. Perhaps a car is wrecked, something foolish is said or done during intoxication, a jail sentence or fine is levied, or a spouse or child is abused.

6. *The drinker suffers emotional or psychological pain.* Because of the impact from the problems caused by drinking, the person's self-esteem is lost, his feelings of remorse and guilt become common, and he begins to suffer intense emotional pain.

7. *The person now drinks to escape the pain caused by drinking.* Sadly, past drinking experiences have effectively taught the person that the way to alleviate pain is to drink again, and so the pattern continues. The victim finds himself caught in a vicious cycle spiraling downward. What began as a sense of euphoria is now a nightmare of psychological pain coupled with severe physical reactions when alcohol is not consumed. The person is frequently depressed, may think of suicide, and may feel total despair—yet, ironically, he or she continues to think of alcohol, the very cause of the problem, as the only means of escape.

Although the drinker does not readily accept help from anyone, it's almost impossible for him to break out of this cycle by himself. He needs help from friends, family members, and the Lord.

Some Attempts to Help
Can Make the Problem Worse

Unfortunately, the well-intentioned behavior of concerned family members, friends, employers, and others frequently contributes to the problem.

Consider, for example, the case of one Latter-day Saint couple I worked with, John and Susan. Several years after they were married, John began to drink. Susan, because of her love for him, tried everything she could think of to make him stop. She would hide his liquor or his wallet and try to keep him away from drinking friends. Repeatedly when he came home drunk she explained away his unusual behavior to others. She would call his boss and make excuses: "John has a touch of the flu. I'm afraid he can't come to work today." She also began lying to the children, saying, "Dad's just having trouble at work and is under a lot of pressure." When John was finally jailed for drunken driving, Susan immediately ran to his aid and bailed him out, only to find that on the way home John had to stop for a drink to calm down.

The children soon realized what was going on. Because of the pressure at home they stopped bringing friends over, and they protected their father by covering up or making excuses for his behavior.

Susan was also ashamed to go to the bishop. How could she possibly tell him that John was drinking?

This story, or one similar to it, is reenacted over and over. And a surprising number of people may get involved. The bishop may step in to provide meals and clothing when family resources are depleted. Friends at work may cover up or assume extra responsibilities so that men like John won't lose their jobs. Employers may ignore shoddy performance or give the person repeated chances because they feel it would be unchristian to fire him: "What would happen to his family if I did?"

These behaviors usually prove to be destructive. They shield a person from the consequences of his behavior and make it convenient for him to continue drinking. After all, as John put it, "Someone will come to my rescue. Besides, if they had my problems they would drink too."

One of the first steps in helping families like John and Susan's is to help Susan and the others involved to eliminate their supportive behavior that makes the problem worse. They have to learn how to exercise "tough love," which I define as doing what has to be done even though it hurts, or not doing something for others that they should do for themselves.

"Tough love" isn't always easy. It isn't easy to break the silence and confront a loved one in a firm spirit of love and helpfulness. It can be extremely painful for a woman to leave her husband all night in the chair where he passed out, and to make him clean up after himself in the morning. It's hard for children to say to their friends, "Mom's drunk," instead of covering up for her.

And it's hard to always be sure of yourself when you're dealing with someone who has become expert at shifting responsibility to others. As a matter of survival, drinkers become expert manipulators. John, for example, manipulated Susan into believing that it was her fault that he drank. "If only I'd married someone who wasn't such a nag," he said. "All you do is spend money. Why can't you ever clean up the house or have dinner on time? It's no wonder I have to drink."

Susan began to believe this and would go out of her way to cook the meals on time, keep the children quiet, clean the house, and be frugal so that John wouldn't be upset. She was hurt inwardly and became more and more resentful—until she learned what he was actually doing. When it was impressed upon her that one person can't *make* another become a problem drinker, she began to take control of her feelings and was thus able to avoid manipulation and the bitterness that sometimes follows such manipulation.

One way or another, a drinker must suffer the consequences of his negative behavior before he can be motivated to change.

Negative Attitudes about Those Who Drink Contribute to the Problem

Unfortunately, our negative feelings about alcohol may include bad feelings toward those who drink. Harsh opinions, injudicious labeling of the drinker, and misunderstandings about alcohol and what it does to people commonly interfere with our ability to help.

Consider the rejection John felt when he attended a Church activity and a couple nearby got up and moved because they could smell liquor on his breath. This doesn't always happen, of course; but when it does happen, the pain felt by a person like John can be intense. He needs to be helped, not ignored.

We can better help a drinker when we view him as a child of God with the same eternal worth as any other person, but as one who needs appropriate help. This is a time when love, concern, and acceptance are needed more than at any other time.

Let's compare John's experiences with those of a Latter-day Saint teenager named David.

In open defiance and rebellion against his father, David stole the family car. Succumbing to the excitement of high speed, he failed to negotiate a turn, rolled the car several times, and was critically injured. Fortunately, those who were riding with him received only minor injuries.

The family and ward members fasted and prayed for David's recovery. He was given a special blessing by his home teachers and was visited often in the hospital. Even the other young men in the accident and their parents visitedand expressed hope for his recovery. Although David was left somewhat crippled and scarred, he recovered, and everyone thanked the Lord for preserving his life.

David had made a serious mistake, but he received the support he needed at a critical time in his life. John's experience was much different, however. When John finally acknowledged that he needed help and was admitted to a local drug and alcohol treatment center, only his wife visited him. Ward members did not fast and pray for his recovery. He was not given a special priesthood blessing. And when he returned from the center, he was met with apprehension, uncertainty, and doubt that he could stay sober.

I have learned that pure love, personal fellowship, and increased understanding can bless the lives of those suffering from the effects of alcohol as much as they can bless the lives of those suffering from other problems.

Never Give Up

Perhaps the hardest part of supporting a problem drinker in his struggle to overcome alcoholism is learning to take his relapses in stride. Recovery takes time, and usually there are setbacks and disappointments. Often there is a great temptation to simply give up—to feel that all your hopes have been wasted and that all progress has been for nothing.

The difficult thing is to maintain your perspective—to be able to stand back mentally and view the problem from a position of faith instead of feeling mentally trapped with nowhere to turn. Family members can learn to relax and to accept small improvements, always maintaining hope that this family problem can be overcome, and sharing that hope with one another. Of course, they must continually seek divine help. The Lord can bless us with insight far beyond our own, and an increased testimony of the gospel can give us strength to endure.

Patience and perseverance will help the family to continue in love and encouragement after a relapse instead of being demeaning and discouraging.

This does not mean that we will always be successful in influencing a loved one to stop drinking. The principles still apply, though. And if the problem drinker is unable to solve his problem, at least our own lives will be improved.

Seeking Help Early Is
the Best Chance for Cure

A great deal of heartache can be avoided if nondrinking family members will get early help. It is important that everyone involved take the initiative to learn all they can about alcohol, addiction, and the ways in which family members and others unintentionally contribute to continued drinking.

For nondrinking family members there are (in the United States) Alanon and Alateen groups, counseling centers (both public and private), special drug and alcohol centers, and, of course, the resources of the Church. Potential resources include home teachers, quorum leaders, the bishop, and other concerned priesthood and Relief Society leaders, as well as LDS Social Services and members who are recovered drinkers.

For the drinker, in addition to the above resources, there are Alcoholics Anonymous groups, hospital programs, special drug and alcohol rehabilitation centers, detoxification centers, and other similar resources. In many cases recovery without professionally conducted detoxification is virtually impossible. Help for alcohol-related problems is available in most communities.

Application of the above guidelines, although challenging, has given many families a meaningful course to follow and has led to some beautiful experiences. Seeing a person overcome an alcohol problem and watching a family unite once again is a wonderful thing, as the following experience demonstrates.

Sam, to be part of a group, began drinking relatively early in life. As he put it, "Once alcohol got hold of me, I just couldn't control my drinking, and yet I was unwilling to admit I had a problem. After several years of rapidly deteriorating health, a couple of wrecked cars, and near financial ruin, my wife decided she had to get help. Prayer and personal discussion with others finally convinced her to help me take responsibility for my behavior and enroll in a rehabilitation program.

"Even though I took a drink to get the courage to go, I finally reported to a local drug and alcohol rehabilitation clinic. My wife faithfully attended counseling and group meetings with me. Slowly I began to realize I wasn't the only one with problems and that maybe I could lick this one. I had a couple of relapses, but now I've been sober for nearly fifteen years.

"I thank the Lord for a wife who had the courage to do what had to be done to make me realize the seriousness of my problem and accept help. It is special to me that she was willing to stand beside me as I struggled. We're progressing in the gospel, and our family has been to the temple at last. I thank the Lord that I came to my senses before it was too late."

The Lord's declaration that "the worth of souls is great" and that "great shall be [our] joy" if we bring "save it be one soul" to him (D&C 18:10, 15) is certainly true of our labors with those who have alcohol addiction. With the help of the Lord, we *can* bless the lives of those who are affected by alcohol, offering them real hope for recovery.

SUGGESTED READINGS

Hafen, Brent Q. *Alcohol and Alcoholism,* 2nd edition. New York: West Publishing Company, 1983.

Kellerman, Joseph. "Alcoholism, the Merry-go-Round of Denial." Pamphlet available from Cottage Program, Inc., 736 South 500 East, Salt Lake City, Utah 84102.

Resource Manual for Helping Families with Alcohol Problems. Salt Lake City: The Church of Jesus Christ of Latter-day Saints, 1984.

ABOUT THE AUTHOR

James R. Goodrich, assistant manager of health services for LDS Social Services, received his bachelor's and master's degrees from Brigham Young University. A specialist in health education, he taught at Central State University at Edmond, Oklahoma.

He has served the Church in three different stake presidencies, on a high council, as branch president, and in many other teaching and administrative assignments.

He and his wife, Beth, are the parents of five children.

7

Eating Disorders:
Anorexia Nervosa and Bulimia

Della Mae Rasmussen

Billions of dollars are spent by millions of Americans each year in an unending quest for one thing: slimness. There is a national obsession with dieting, calorie counting, and beautiful thin models in books and magazines and on television and billboards. The message bombarding us from every direction seems to be: if you are thin you will be happy, you will have wonderful relationships, be admired, and have a fine career, and all your problems will be solved. Nearly everyone has been on a weight loss diet at one time or another, and millions of people go from one diet to the next, always hoping for the magic wand that will produce a beautiful, lean body without too much effort. Even though we see a great emphasis upon exercising and proper nutrition today, the most important thing seems to be getting slim rather than maintaining good health. A person's weight, measurements, and appearance have become too much a measure of a person's worth.

Most people can go on a diet, go off a diet, overeat one day, and cut down the next day, managing to stay somewhere within their normal weight range. They become rather philosophical about never being really thin. With certain people, however, the desire for thinness eventually takes first place in their lives. These people suffer from an eating disorder, either anorexia nervosa or bulimia. They have the distorted belief that the thinner they are, the happier they will be. In their efforts to achieve happiness and thinness they become involved in the dangerous behaviors of an eating disorder. These behaviors become a way of coping with the demands of life. Kim Lampson, one of the most experienced therapists in the field, states that "the behaviors are like a life preserver, simultaneously a means of survival and a signal of distress."

Anorexia Nervosa

Anorexia nervosa has sometimes been called the "starving disease." Historically, a number of cases of anorexia nervosa have been reported, but until recently it was thought to be rare. In the last fifteen to twenty years there has been a great increase in diagnosed cases. People are becoming more aware of the name and the extent of the problem. Perhaps one in every one hundred or two hundred white females between the ages of twelve and eighteen may suffer from anorexia. Between 90 and 95 percent of those who have the disorder are female. This may be the result of the greater cultural emphasis on the physical attractiveness expected of females.

The age of onset is usually early to late adolescence. Medically, the diagnosis is made for anorexia nervosa when the following conditions are present:

1. *An intense fear of becoming obese that does not diminish as weight loss progresses.* Severe weight loss is the obvious symptom of anorexia nervosa. The person often suffers from dangerous physical and psychological symptoms, yet she is terrified of gaining weight and would seemingly rather die than get fat. Typically, the victim of anorexia nervosa rigidly controls her food intake to the point of self-starvation.

2. *Distortion of body image—the person claims to "feel fat," even when emaciated.* On a recent television talk show an anorexic girl was being interviewed. She wore a bikini, and, standing about 5 feet 8 inches tall and weighing around

85 pounds, was almost skeletal in appearance. The show's host looked at her and said, "Surely you cannot think of yourself as fat." She picked at a tiny fold of skin on her abdomen and replied, "Oh, yes, I am. Look at this!" She was totally unable to see her emaciated body for what it was.

3. *Weight loss of at least 25 percent of normal body weight for age and height.* Anorexic weight loss is generally achieved by self-starvation, but the anorexic may also use self-induced vomiting, drastic curtailing of fat and carbohydrate intake, incessant exercise, laxatives and diuretics, diet pills, or a combination of any of these.

4. *Refusal to maintain body weight over a minimal normal weight for age and height.* No amount of coaxing by family and friends can get the anorexic to eat normally. Even during hospitalization medical personnel often find it difficult to get an anorexic person to gain weight. During hospitalization one anorexic would cover herself completely with her stuffed animals at night, hoping to perspire enough to lose weight.

5. *No known physical illness would account for the weight loss.* Amazingly, the anorexic may be highly resistant to physical illness and exhibit a high energy level in an exercise program. For example, one anorexic girl regularly ran fifteen miles a day while consuming around 300 calories.

Some Characteristics of Anorexic Girls

A common evidence of anorexia nervosa is amenorrhea (the absence or cessation of menstruation) in females. It occurs in almost every case.

Anorexics fear loss of control, and by rigidly controlling their food intake they feel they can at least control one area of their lives. An anorexic girl may spend a great deal of time thinking about and preparing food, and she may watch her family eat an elaborate meal she has prepared while she eats a piece of celery, some lettuce, and a glass of water. One anorexic reported that one apple made her feel as if her stomach would literally burst.

Most people with this disorder steadfastly deny their illness and resist getting help. They like the feeling of losing weight and resent any interference from family, friends, or professionals. People who do not know of the problem will often compliment the person on her weight loss, thus reinforcing the anorexic behavior, since the motivation behind the refusal of food is the obsessive fear of weight gain and the accompanying pleasure of weight loss. The thinner she becomes, the more "special" she feels. Anorexics appear to be frightened of the demands of adulthood, preferring to remain in their childhood with an undeveloped body. They show little if any interest in dating and boyfriends.

Typically, one who develops anorexia will be characterized as a "model child," one who never gave her family any problems. The girls tend to be "people pleasers," perfectionistics, overachievers, compulsive, and self-disciplined. As weight loss continues, a girl's thinking tends to become more irrational and distorted, caused in great measure by the starvation state and the malnourishment of the brain.

Physical Abnormalities from Anorexia Nervosa

Some of the physical abnormalities resulting from anorexia nervosa include the following:

1. Emaciation
2. Amenorrhea (cessation of menstruation)
3. Fine body hair called "lanugo"
4. Stomach distress and intestinal cramps
5. Dry skin
6. Hair loss
7. Yellowish tinge to the skin
8. Low blood pressure
9. Lowered body temperature (the person feels cold all the time)
10. Slowed heart rate
11. Fluid and electrolyte imbalance

Fluid and electrolyte imbalance causes dehydration and potassium deficiency and is the most serious symptom, resulting in muscle weakness, apathy, mental confusion, and irregular heartbeat. Death from kidney or heart failure may result.

Recovery

It is estimated that 50 percent of anorexia sufferers will completely recover normal weight and eating patterns, and 25 percent will improve but retain significant eating or weight problems. Mortality rates are estimated to be as high as 15 to 21 percent. Of those who return to normal weight, from 3 to 50 percent remain amenorrheic. As anorexics recover, most of the abnormalities are reversed; however, some remain permanent.

It must be remembered that despite the characteristics of anorexia, each individual is unique. Every case must be treated on an individual basis.

Factors in the Development of Anorexia

Some factors in the development of anorexia nervosa include the following:

1. *Stressful life situations.* Life's demands may appear to be overwhelming to the anorexic. For example, concern for school achievement, personal attractiveness, acceptance by friends, or family conflict may be more than she can bear. She does not feel adequate to cope with these demands.

2. *Perfectionism.* The person's need to be perfect is strong. Nothing is ever good enough. Her initial goal for weight loss may be reached, but she will think, "I should lose five pounds more, just to be safe." She thinks in terms of "all or nothing." One slip and all is lost.

3. *Ineffective interpersonal relations.* The person avoids true closeness with others because she fears rejection. She does not assert herself and express her own needs, feelings, and ideas in open communication. She typically has few close friends.

4. *Biological predisposition.* There may be a biological predisposition to anorexia that is related to the functioning of the hypothalamus gland, but it is still uncertain whether the starvation damages the hypothalamus or a malfunction of the hypothalamus promotes the development of anorexia nervosa.

5. *Family disturbance.* There is no typical family from which anorexics emerge, although they tend to come from

families where food and weight have been focal issues. Excess attention is paid to what people are eating, or perhaps parents have tried to force people to eat, or not to eat, as the case may be. One young anorexic told how as a small child she followed her older sister and her friends around as they constantly discussed how fat they were and what their newest diet would be.

Families of the anorexic appear most often to be "enmeshed." They value "rightness" and not being different. They have a high degree of concern and involvement with each other. They want everyone to think and act in the same way, and, to avoid conflict, they do not discuss personal needs and feelings openly. The anorexic child is often involved in parental conflict in some way and may feel responsible for such conflict because she is not a perfect daughter. She will often feel guilty and unworthy and attempt to find acceptance through her achievements and being attractive.

Families of children with eating disorders are not bad families; they are most often simply families doing the best they know how. They feel great pain over a daughter's problem. One mother wrote to me as follows:

> What It's Like to Be the Mother of an Anorexic Child
>
> While the key word to an anorexic is *control*, the word that expresses the feelings of most parents of anorexics is *helpless*—helplessness, frustration, anxiety, fear, guilt, and lots of pain. In just a short span of time, you watch your beautiful, happy, well-adjusted, and successful daughter go through a frightening metamorphosis. Overnight you seem to be the mother of a frighteningly thin, unhappy, spiteful, angry, noncommunicative, and very manipulative individual whom you barely know or recognize.
>
> You feel totally unequipped to deal with, let alone help, this new person in your home. All of the normal motherly feelings of love, nurturing, and caring are still there, but where they were welcome before, now they are rejected suspiciously and angrily. After all, "*You* are what caused this problem!" Then come the feelings of guilt, failure, and self-recrimination. It is not a case of "What did I do to deserve this?" Rather, you start wondering "What did I do wrong? Why couldn't I be a better mother?"
>
> Where communication had been pleasant, it now becomes loud and tense on both sides, if it occurs at all. Then there are the tears. Gallons of tears. In front of her, in the privacy of your room, in re-

sponse to a query from a friend about your daughter. You read all you can find about this illness that previously had been an unknown word to you. But what you read is of little comfort. In fact, it can easily have the opposite effect.

You start to feel a real strain in your relationship with your husband as you invariably disagree on how to relate to your daughter or on what direction to go to help her get professional help. You turn to what seems to be one of the few sources of reassurance, friends who have already been through this hell and know just what you are feeling and just what to say. Through it all, you are scared to death! And you pray a lot.

Rapid recovery is not to be expected, and, in severe cases, hospitalization is necessary to prevent death by starvation or one of the other severe symptoms. The victims cling tenaciously to their distorted beliefs, and I strongly suggest professional help for the sufferer and her family. Those professionals involved should be a medical doctor for a thorough physical evaluation, a nutritionist for help with healthy food intake and eating patterns, and a counselor or psychotherapist to help with emotional needs. These professionals should be chosen from those who thoroughly understand eating disorders and can offer continuing assistance. The victim is not helped by the admonition "Now you just go home and put on some weight, my dear."

Signs to Watch For

If you suspect that someone is beginning to suffer from anorexia, you should watch for these signs:

1. Dieting excessively; refusing to eat, to the point of self-starvation.

2. Claiming to "feel fat" when the person is actually normal weight or underweight.

3. Paying excessive attention to food, calories, nutrition, and cooking.

4. Refusing to eat but often watching others eat.

5. Excessive exercising, overactivity.

6. Loss of menstrual period.

7. Spending much time in the bathroom, perhaps vomiting in secret.

8. Obsessive or unusual eating behavior, such as cutting up food into tiny bits and arranging them on the plate in ritualistic patterns.

9. Complaining of a "bloated feeling" after eating small or normal amounts of food.

10. Eating in binges (possibly in the middle of the night), followed by purging, overexercising, or fasting.

11. Use of laxatives, vomiting, or diuretics to control weight.

12. Constantly weighing herself.

Some few anorexics are not starvers but bingers. This group appears to have several characteristics more like the eating disorder of bulimia than the anorexic who controls her weight in ways other than purging.

Bulimia

Bulimia is an eating disorder in which the person binges on huge quantities of food, usually high-calorie foods and sweets, and then purges the food through self-induced vomiting or the use of large amounts of laxatives and diuretics. The word *bulimia* is derived from the Greek and literally means "ox hunger." Like anorexia, bulimia often begins as the result of dieting. The person tries to lose weight but still eats large quantities of food. She panics over her overeating and uses purging to prevent weight gain. Eventually the behavior becomes compulsive. It is difficult for people who have never experienced this horrible, out-of-control feeling to understand it. Since the person feels guilty and embarrassed, she is usually secretive about her behavior and may suffer from bulimia for several years before seeking help. Bulimics are usually of normal weight or perhaps slightly overweight, although one bulimic of record weighed almost three hundred pounds!

Bulimia usually starts in the late teens or early twenties, but it varies from early teens to much later ages. The incidence is growing and is of almost epidemic proportions. According to some experts, between 20 and 30 percent of college-age students are involved in bulimic behaviors. The incidence is growing and is of near-epidemic proportions. As with anorexia, probably over 90 percent of the victims are female. Recently, however, reports show that the number of males appears to be increasing.

A bulimic is usually similar in many ways to an anorexic in her behavior and attitudes, but she may differ in the following ways:

1. Food becomes an obsession and an addiction.

2. She wants to be attractive to men and to please them, and she is interested in having boyfriends.

3. She may have spent her life trying to please her father through her accomplishments and her beauty.

4. She is more socially skilled.

5. She will not lose a great deal of weight.

6. She may or may not lose her menstrual periods, but she may have irregularities.

7. Her body image is probably not distorted.

8. She recognizes that her eating behavior is abnormal.

9. Her eating is more impulsive, and thus less controlled.

10. She may use drugs and alcohol more often.

11. She eats huge amounts of food and then purges the food through self-induced vomiting or taking large amounts of laxatives or diuretics.

12. She may feel guilty and depressed when she falls short of expectations.

Many bulimics report that as their binge-purge behavior becomes a compulsion, they spend almost every waking hour thinking about food—how to get it, how to eat it without being detected, and how to get rid of it once it is consumed. Some bulimics binge and vomit many times a day, some once or twice a week. The practice becomes bulimic when it can no longer be controlled. Although generally bulimics have high moral principles, they sometimes lie, hide, and even steal to support their food habits. Expenditures of $100 a week are fairly common, with one bulimic telling of a habit amounting to $100 a day. One young woman reported that she spent every noon hour driving from one fast-food place to another, gorging as she drove, and then using up to seventy-five laxative tablets to purge. A person would die from this dosage if her tolerance had not been built up over time. Ironically, it has been estimated that only about 12 percent of the calories consumed are purged by the use of laxatives. It is also clear that no method of purging rids the body of all the calories taken in binges, since bulimics seldom achieve thinness with their purging methods. The binge-purge behaviors themselves are reinforcing, however, because they relieve the anxiety suffered by the victim.

Physical Abnormalities Resulting from Bulimia

Bulimia is a serious disorder and may result in lasting physical effects and even death. There may be extensive erosion of tooth enamel from the stomach acid. The habitual use of vomiting or laxatives can cause permanent kidney damage. Losing large amounts of body fluids may result in kidney failure. The salivary glands often become swollen, giving the chipmunk-like look of some bulimics. Sometimes the stomach will rupture or develop ulcers, and the esophagus may be punctured. As with anorexia, the electrolyte balance is thrown off, and the potassium level may be severely depleted, causing heart difficulties.

Binging and purging rewards the sufferer because it fills up her time so that she can avoid facing the demands of life. The behavior, therefore, becomes relaxing and reinforcing.

A bulimic has difficulty expressing her true feelings, which become so distorted that she does not recognize them for what they are but feels them as hunger. Her attention and energy are taken up with the binge-purge activities.

As with anorexia nervosa, there is no quick fix for curing bulimia. The bulimic, being caught up in her "all or nothing at all" thinking, may declare, "I am going to recover quickly and completely. Fast is best." But eating disorders are among the most difficult problems to deal with for the individual, for the family, for school and church leaders, and for professional counselors.

using drugs to meet unfilled needs. You probably will *not* be successful in helping someone who has developed a strong addiction to a drug; he will almost certainly require professional help. You should also be aware that some drug addiction carries with it physical dependence, and that sudden cessation of drug use can result in severe withdrawal symptoms. In some cases withdrawal can threaten life, and physicians try to hospitalize a person so he can be closely monitored and the withdrawal can be gradually accomplished with safety.

Following are suggestions as to how you can help a person who wants to change by helping him discover his alternatives:

1. If the drug use appears to be an attempt to relieve stress, try to find out what the source of stress is. For example, if a young mother feels trapped at home by her three preschoolers, offer to take her children one or two mornings a week so she can get out of the house or so she can just have some private time to herself.

2. If a person feels trapped in a low-paying job or does not feel rewarded at work, help him explore ways of expanding his skills so he can get a new job.

3. If drug use seems related to boredom, help the person develop some new interests. You'll probably have to work hard: a person who has suffered long-term boredom is genuinely convinced that life doesn't have much to offer.

4. If you determine that the drug is being taken to relieve chronic tension, help the person learn how to perform physical relaxation exercises that can help relieve physical tension. There are many of them—massaging tension spots in the neck, massaging the scalp, kneading the feet, and assuming various yoga postures. Remember, it is much easier just to pop a few pills in your mouth and swig some water than it is to spend half an hour doing exercises, so it will take some work to convince a person that the exercises are better. You are also battling reinforcement: with drugs, gratification is almost instant—with exercise, it may take longer. Be encouraging, and keep with it.

You might also encourage the person to get more phys-

Treatment for Eating Disorders

Kim Lampson, a recovered anorexic-bulimic who has worked with hundreds of victims, says, "Before 'curing', a foundation must be laid for personal growth, self-esteem, quality relationships, and the ability to live each day. It is essential for all involved to realize that the disorders are not a food problem, but a self-esteem problem."

Recovery requires personal choice and perseverance. The person must decide to get well. But much support is needed once the person wants to stop her destructive behavior. The cooperation of the individual, the family, school and church leaders, counselors, or psychotherapists is needed. Those affected by the person and her behavior also need support in dealing with the problem. They should remember that pressure to change immediately is premature and will only force the sufferer deeper into her behavior.

In order to recover, the person suffering from anorexia nervosa or bulimia needs the following:

1. Education about nutritional requirements of the body and the adverse physical effects of starving, binging, vomiting, and the use of laxatives and diuretics.

2. Knowledge about her disorder. She needs to be able to discuss her fears and anxieties without fear of rejection or ridicule. If there are therapy groups nearby it may be beneficial for her to join one. This is true particularly of bulimics. Anorexics often do better in individual therapy.

3. To be able to recognize her distorted thinking. She may use all-or-nothing thinking: "If I can't do it perfectly, I'm a total failure." She may keep up a constant stream of negative self-talk: "I am stupid." "I always blow it." "I'm worthless." Perhaps she believes that she knows what other people are thinking about her: "They think I'm a loser." She may live by her feelings, acting according to her feelings without thinking things out. Or she may fill her life with "shoulds" and "oughts," expecting perfect compliance with her unrealistic ideals and then feeling guilty because she can't measure up.

4. Unconditional love with no pressure to change im-

mediately. She must be convinced that she has worth; then she can listen to the truth about herself and her relationships with other people and with food. She needs help from people who *understand* her disorder. Also, she may feel so guilty and unworthy that she won't look to God for help. Care and acceptance from those around her will help her pray again.

5. To deal with her perfectionism. She wants to recover quickly and perfectly. But she must learn to accept two steps forward and one step back. Part of recovery is to realize she can't do things perfectly. She must give herself permission to fail and be imperfect. Kim Lampson puts it this way: "Anything worth doing is worth doing poorly, and with practice it gets better!"

Patience is essential. She can practice saying, "It is okay to fail. It is an opportunity to learn rather than an opportunity to punish myself." A setback then becomes a learning experience, not a disaster.

6. To learn and use assertiveness and communication skills. She can practice the honest expression of her feelings. She should be encouraged to tell others her needs and feelings *directly* in a loving way. Most victims of eating disorders are afraid to do this because they believe they will say the wrong thing, cause conflict, and lose approval and love. One recovered bulimic said, "I could never express myself. Everything was all closed up inside of me. If I stood up for my rights, I thought others would be unhappy with me, and I couldn't stand anyone being displeased with what I said or did. Obsession with food helped me survive. It was a way to escape from the world. By focusing on eating and purging I didn't have to think about my poor relationships or anything else."

The sufferer must understand her right to be treated with respect, to have and express personal feelings and opinions, to be listened to and taken seriously, to say no without feeling guilty, to ask for what she wants, to make mistakes, and to make choices based on rational thinking.

She must realize that she is not responsible for the feelings of others. They have their own rights and the power to make choices just as she does. She can be direct and honest and behave appropriately. She can show a genuine concern for the rights of others and their feelings as well as her own. Her assertiveness will not drive people away but will enrich her relationships with others. She can express her love and care for others without fear. She can disagree with someone and be close at the same time. This knowledge is crucial. There is no cure, according to Lampson, until a person can honestly express feelings in ways that bring about closeness rather than distance.

7. A feeling of self-worth. A feeling of self-worth is enhanced by people around the sufferer who give her unconditional love without expecting perfection or superior achievement or anything more than allowing her to be herself. She has intrinsic worth as a human being, regardless of her accomplishments. What she *is* is more important than what she does or how she looks. Is it more important to be remembered for clothes, grade-point average, thin body, musical or sports ability, and a pretty face, or for listening ability, compassion, cheerfulness, kindness, and a love for others? She can practice identifying qualities that make her special. She might ask someone, "What do you really appreciate about me?" She can also realize that qualities not so desirable are also lovable. She does not have to be perfect for people to love her; often a person's weaknesses and mistakes make them easier to relate to and thus more lovable. As she shifts from a worldly to a godly perspective, she will look at the heart instead of the appearance. She can learn to encourage herself in all her righteous endeavors and to take pride in her character.

8. To give others permission to be imperfect. She should practice loving others unconditionally in spite of their weaknesses and mistakes. She needs to listen to their feelings and try to understand them. Especially, she can give her family permission to be imperfect. They have made mistakes in the past, and they will again, but they need acceptance too. She can forgive others for their trespasses against her.

9. The ability to make wise decisions. She can practice developing solutions for herself. She can be confronted with choices, alternatives, options, and the consequences of her decisions. Knowledge and practice of problem-solving skills will help her feel "in charge" in her life.

10. To learn effective strategies for dealing with stress and anxiety. Ways to reduce stress and anxiety include practicing relaxation techniques, talking out frustrations with a close friend or family member, participating in hobbies and in sports, helping others, refusing to criticize others or herself, and trying to be a good friend.

11. To develop normal eating patterns. The person needs to establish eating habits that are flexible, meet nutritional needs, and maintain a healthy body weight. She should do away with her list of "forbidden foods." She should force herself to eat a little of everything without guilt in the presence of others.

12. To choose her own goals separate from expectations of family and friends. It's okay if these are different, and it's also okay if they are the same.

13. Accept her body and stop criticizing her own body and the bodies of others.

14. To think of her struggles as *change* taking place. She should learn from the pain and use it to motivate herself rather than trying to avoid it.

Family Issues

Those who attempt to help the child and her family should follow certain guidelines: Families do not need more guilt and blame. They do need acceptance and the reassurance that they have probably done the best they could. All family members could heal hurts by recognizing that no one is perfect. They need to forgive each other for their real or imagined weaknesses. Families are usually tired and frightened from the stress of living with a child with an eating disorder. Family therapy can be helpful if members are available to meet together. Families can help the sufferer in important ways:

1. Let go. The family should not seek to meet all the social and emotional needs of the child.

2. Do not try to force a child to eat, or to not eat. Don't watch her eat or discuss her weight.

3. Never compare the child to anyone else. Help build her sense of self-worth. Accept her for what she is at this moment in time. Love her unconditionally, even when she is depressed, irritable, and moody.

4. Don't treat her as if she were "sick" or crazy. Instead, encourage her independence and her initiative, and let her make decisions for herself.

5. Insist that she be responsible for her behavior. For example, she should be required to replace family food supplies or family money she has secretly used to buy food.

6. Do not center your whole life around the child. She must understand that the lives of others in the family are not more or less important than her own. Everyone needs love and attention.

7. Be patient. There is no quick road to recovery. It may take months and even years of treatment and anxiety.

8. She must do the work for her own recovery. Everyone involved should think in terms of *progress*, not perfection.

Fortunately, most anorexics and bulimics do recover, in time. While there are no "pat answers" in treatment and recovery, skilled counselors are available and research is going forward. There is hope.

SUGGESTED READINGS AND RESOURCES

Anorexia Nervosa and Related Eating Disorders, Inc. P.O. Box 5102, Eugene, Oregon 97405, phone (503) 344-1144.

Bruch, Hilde. *The Golden Cage: The Enigma of Anorexia Nervosa.* Harvard: Harvard University Press, 1978.

Chernin, Kim. *The Obsession: Reflections on the Tyranny of Slenderness.* New York: Harper and Row, 1982.

Lampson, K. Kim, M.Ed. Lecture given at Brigham Young University, November 1983. For additional information write to: K. Kim Lampson, M.Ed., Providence Professional Building, Suite 301, 550 16th Avenue, Seattle, Washington 98122.

National Anorexic Aid Society, Inc. P.O. Box 29461, Columbus, Ohio 43229.

Neuman, Patricia A., Ed.S., and Patricia A. Halvorsen, Ph.D. *Anorexia Nervosa and Bulimia: A Handbook for Counselors and Therapists*. New York: Van Nostrand Reinhold Company, 1983.

Vincent, L.M. *Competing with the Sylph: The Pursuit of the Ideal Body Form*. New York: Berkeley Books, 1979.

ABOUT THE AUTHOR

Dr. Della Mae Rasmussen, a counselor at BYU Counseling and Personal Services for almost two decades, received her bachelor's degree from the University of Utah and her doctorate in counseling psychology from BYU. She has published in professional journals as well as in children's literature.

In the Church she has served on the Primary General Board, on the Church Teacher Development Committee, on a Church writing committee for parent education, and in many ward and stake callings.

She and her husband, Paul, are the parents of six children.

8

Guidelines for Weight Control
A. Garth Fisher and Dennis W. Remington

Many common problems seen by counselors relate in some way to being overweight, and no other problem has been so poorly treated. The traditional idea has been that people who are overweight obviously overeat. Logically, based on this idea, the treatment involves decreasing food intake to solve the problem.

However, recent research questions the "overeating" hypothesis of obesity. Several studies have reported that overweight people simply do not eat more than their normal weight peers. In fact, one researcher worked with two women who weighed more than 260 pounds and maintained their weight on only 1,000 calories per day.

The question, then, is what causes obesity if not overeating. The evidence is mounting that body weight is controlled by a center in the brain called the "weight regulating mechanism (WRM)" and that this center choses a "setpoint" weight for each person and then does all in its power to maintain that weight.

The WRM apparently acts like a thermostat in a house that turns on the heater or air conditioner to maintain the "setpoint" temperature of the house. In a similar manner, the "fat thermostat" in the body turns certain systems on or off to maintain the "setpoint" body weight (the weight it thinks is proper for that person). For example, when a person goes on a restricted intake diet, several important adjustments take place to keep that person from losing too much weight. First, after a week or so of the restricted intake, the body begins to decrease its metabolic rate to compensate for the decreased intake. The metabolic rate may decrease by a third of its original level. This means that a decrease in intake from 1,500 calories a day to 1,000 calories a day (a one-third decrease in intake) would be completely compensated for by a decrease in metabolic rate. Second, when the weight begins to decrease, the fat thermostat feeds information to the hunger centers in an attempt to increase the intake of calories. This accounts for the hunger experienced by most dieters. A third change occurs in the fat cells of the body. An enzyme, lipoprotein lipase (LPL), whose job is to help fat into the fat cells for storage, is increased dramatically until there is from three to ten times more available. This means that any food eaten during the diet can be more easily stored in the fat cells. This is why it is so easy to regain lost weight after a few weeks or months after going off a diet. The fourth change causes the dieter to feel fatigue, malaise, and headaches in an attempt to slow down activity. It's as if the body realizes that activity will use calories, so it causes the person to feel bad so that energy is conserved.

Some scientists think that these changes are part of an "anti-starvation defense system" designed to protect the organism from losing too much weight. Obviously, a person who tries every diet that comes out actually programs his body to be an efficient fat storer; and, the more he diets, the worse the problem becomes.

So how does a counselor help a person who wants to lose weight? The first step is to help them stop dieting. Remember, dieting just makes the problem worse because the body feels threatened and makes changes to conserve and store fat. The second step involves lowering the fat thermostat. If the fat thermostat is set lower, the body can actually learn to *waste* energy to help get the body weight to the new setting, just as it conserved energy to keep the weight up during restricted intakes.

How do you lower the setpoint? Scientists have found certain foods that raise the thermostat and other foods that lower it. For instance, rats fed a "supermarket" diet (corn chips, bologna, marshmallows, bananas, and so on) got extremely fat; when put back on the less rich rat chow they lost the excess weight. This and other similar studies suggest that the diet for lowering the setpoint must be low in fats and sugars and must increase the complex carbohydrates such as vegetables, beans, grain, and fruit. Eating a low-fat, low-sugar diet high in complex carbohydrates not only allows the thermostat to go down, but it also decreases the caloric density of food so that fewer calories are ingested when a person eats to his own satisfaction. A recent study showed that subjects on a low-fat, low-sugar diet needed only 1,570 calories a day to feel completely satisfied compared to 3,000 calories a day for those eating the typical high-fat, high-sugar American diet.

Decreasing fat and sugar intake

Since fats are common in so many favorite foods, a few simple guidelines for decreasing fat intake may be helpful:

1. Decrease the fatty dressings, spreads, and sauces that are so often added to foods.

2. Use only nonfat or low-fat dairy products. These generally are limited to skim or 1 percent milk, skim or low-fat cottage cheese, and skim or low-fat yogurt. All regular cheese should be avoided.

3. Eat only low-fat meats such as chicken, turkey, and fish, and eat only three or four ounces of these a day. Certain lean cuts of beef such as rump, round, and flank may be added from time to time. Avoid pork and fatty beef cuts.

4. Learn to cook without adding fat. Use nonstick pans, broiling, steaming, and microwaving. Use defatted chicken broth or bouillon for moisture—cut down the oil added to recipes.

5. Learn to read labels. Avoid foods high in fat. A gram of fat contains 9 calories. If a label shows 4 grams of fat, that food contains 36 calories from fat. If the total calories per serving is 100, it would be 36 percent fat and should be avoided.

6. Learn to order low-fat meals at restaurants. For instance, order baked halibut with a baked potato instead of prime rib with fries; order baked chicken instead of ribeye.

Avoid the typical bacon-and-egg breakfast in favor of oat-meal or other cooked cereals.

To decrease sugar intake, avoid desserts, sweet snacks, and sweetened breakfast cereals. For example, a dish of grapenuts with skim milk and a few raisins could substitute for ice cream as an evening dessert, and whole-wheat bread (without butter) or fruit could be substituted for candy or cookies as a snack.

Exercise

In addition to eating the proper foods, a person must exercise regularly to lower the fat thermostat. And the exercise must be aerobic to be effective. There are some basic rules for exercise. First, choose large-muscle, rhythmic activity such as walking, jogging, riding an exercise cycle, jumping on a mini-trampoline, or aerobic dance. Then be content to work at a moderate intensity. High intensity work is not effective for lowering the fat thermostat and should be avoided, especially during the initial stages. Work at an intensity that causes heavy breathing, but not so heavy that you cannot carry on a conversation. The following heart rate table can be used to determine the approximate ten-second heart rate for any age. Simply exercise for a few minutes and then stop and count your pulse for ten seconds. Then speed up or slow down your exercise as needed.

Ten-Second Heart-Rate Guideline

Age	(for people who have not exercised much— 70% of maximum)	(for people who have exercised for a while— 80% of maximum)
20	23	27
30	22	25
40	21	24
50	20	23
60	19	21
70	17	20

Exercise for about twenty minutes a day the first week or so and then increase the duration until the exercise period lasts from forty-five to sixty minutes a day.

Having established the pattern, continue to exercise daily. Research shows that daily exercise is much more effective than exercise every other day, even if the total exercise time is the same. During the first few weeks or so, you can exercise twice daily but not for more than twenty to twenty-five minutes each time. Too much exercise often results in injury during the early stages.

The value of aerobic exercise is much greater than previously thought. In addition to lowering the fat thermostat, aerobic exercise also helps make all of the weight loss fat. Dieters often lose as much muscle as they do fat. Loss of muscle decreases their ability to burn fat, lowers their metabolic rate, and can cause weakness. Also, aerobic exercise actually increases the body's ability to burn fat by causing an increase in the enzymes needed to burn fat effectively. In other words, exercise not only conserves muscle but makes that muscle better able to burn fat. Therefore, long-distance running or similar aerobic exercise is ideal for anyone trying to lose weight.

In addition, exercise helps modify abnormal insulin responses (which helps the body store less fat) and causes a release of chemicals called endorphines that make a person feel better. Finally, aerobic exercise burns a significant amount of energy. Walking only one mile a day could theoretically account for ten pounds of fat loss a year, and an hour a day would lead to a forty-pound loss each year.

To summarize, successful weight control requires adherance to three basic rules: (1) stop dieting, (2) decrease fats and sugars and increase complex carbohydrates in the diet, and (3) exercise daily for forty-five minutes to an hour at a moderate pace using some large-muscle rhythmic activity.

Counseling and Weight Control

The major problems a counselor will encounter with these guidelines may include the fact that it will be difficult for people who have been on hundreds of diets to eat enough to avoid the starvation defenses. These people will have a hard time feeling right about eating until they are satisfied, even though the low-fat, low-sugar, high complex-carbohydrate diet has a very low caloric density. They must be encouraged to eat enough and regularly. Often, it will be difficult for most people to change the way they prepare and eat food. Eating habits are often difficult to break, especially if the new food doesn't taste as good as the old. Tastes take two or three weeks to change. If you can get them to try the new approach for this period of time, they will begin to enjoy the new tastes and will often discover these tastes are even better than the ones they are giving up.

Of course, exercise has often been difficult for people with weight problems because they try to do it while dieting. Since dieting triggers a need to decrease activity (to save calories), exercise for most dieters has been unpleasant. When eating properly, exercise becomes a pleasant experience and will result in a new feeling of energy and excitement. Be sure to encourage moderate exercise so that fatigue doesn't begin too early.

Setting Realistic Goals

It is critical to realize that this program may take more time for success than the traditional dietary restriction program. However, if followed it will yield lifelong success. Be positive during the first four weeks or so even if weight loss does not occur. Measuring circumferences or skinfold thicknesses may be helpful until metabolic changes are made that allow weight loss to occur.

Some people have unrealistic goals about how much they think they should weigh. Remember that as a racehorse differs from a workhorse, so people also differ from each other in basic body build. It is unrealistic for a muscular girl to expect to weigh the same as a more naturally slender roommate.

You must be aware of these differences in basic body build and help people accept themselves as they are. If this program is followed carefully, most people will lose weight until they reach their best and most naturally healthy weight.

SUGGESTED READING

Remington, Dennis W.; Garth A. Fisher; and Edward A. Parent. *How to Lower Your Fat Thermostat.* Provo: Vitality House International, Inc., 1983.

ABOUT THE AUTHORS

Dr. A. Garth Fisher, professor of physical education and director of the Human Performance Research Center at Brigham Young University, received his bachelor's degree from BYU, his master's degree from Sacramento State College, and his Ph.D. from the University of New Mexico. An exercise physiologist, Dr. Fisher is a fellow of the American College of Sports Medicine. He is the author of many articles and books.

An active Church worker, he has served as a stake president, a bishop, an Aaronic Priesthood quorum adviser, a gospel doctrine teacher, and in other callings.

He and his wife, Geraldine, are the parents of nine children.

Dr. Dennis W. Remington, M.D., is a family physician and a specialist in Bariatric medicine (treating obesity and related disorders). He is the director of the Eating Disorder Clinic at the BYU Student Health Clinic and is an eating disorder consultant for the Utah Valley Regional Medical Center Mental Health Services.

In the Church he has served as elders quorum president, in a bishopric, and as a high councilor.

He and his wife, Jolayne, are the parents of three children.

9

Premenstrual Syndrome
Robert N. Gray, M.D.

Premenstrual syndrome, or as many refer to it, PMS, has become a household term over the past few years. It has been discussed widely by the press, on television news and information programs, and to some degree in nearly every type of magazine. PMS has become a major concern if not a problem for many people.

What Is PMS?

Although recognized by clinicians for centuries, PMS was first described in medical literature in 1931 by R.T. Frank, who called it "premenstrual tension" and described it as "a feeling of indescribable tension," "a desire to find relief by foolish and ill-considered acts."[1] Even though women have long experienced the symptoms of PMS, it has been poorly understood by both the public and the medical profession. Until recent years few women with PMS reported their complaints, and those who did seek medical attention were often thought to be irrational or emotionally unstable. Since Frank's work and observations in 1931, considerable effort has been directed toward the clinical characterization of the syndrome and toward delineation of the physiology of PMS.

It has long been known that many women become tense, irritable, and anxious or depressed during the seven to ten days before menstruation. This state frequently leads to a deterioration in their relationships with family, friends, and co-workers. These emotional changes have been responsible or at least implicated in marital problems, child abuse, and even criminal behavior (any of which may be totally out of character for the person except during that time in her cycle). In two recent court cases in Great Britain involving women who committed murder, PMS was recognized as a mitigating factor, resulting in the court finding the women to have been in a state of "diminished responsibility." However, in 1982 an attempt to use this plea in the United States was unsuccessful.[2]

With women playing an increasingly prominent role in business and industry, attention has been focused on the effect of PMS on absenteeism and inefficiency. It has been observed that 36 percent of 1,500 women in one plant sought sedation in the premenstrual week, and estimates suggest that absenteeism due to PMS caused a loss of $5 billion in 1969 alone.[3] Although the association between PMS and intellectual impairment has not been clearly established, there are an increased number of psychiatric hospital admissions, accidents, and suicide attempts in women during the premenstrual phase of their cycle.

Due to the tremendous exposure of society to the term PMS, the sensationalism PMS has been afforded by the media over the past few years, and the frequently non-specific symptoms it causes, PMS has become the female hypochondriac's favorite diagnosis. Many women who feel they have PMS simply do not fit the diagnostic criteria and are most likely experiencing anxiety or depression due to other causes.

Symptoms of PMS

PMS encompasses emotional, behavioral, and physical symptoms. The symptoms occur cyclically beginning seven to ten days before onset of menstrual bleeding and regressing or disappearing at the onset of the menstrual period or within one or two days thereafter. In most women with PMS, the symptoms are most severe two to five days before their period, with rapid relief with the onset of bleeding.

Pain after menstrual flow has started (dysmenorrhea) is an entirely different problem. Dysmenorrhea and its treatment will be discussed later in this chapter. Though PMS and dysmenorrhea are separate problems, some women experience both.

The symptoms most frequently associated with PMS are abdominal bloating, swelling of the extremities, fullness and tenderness of the breasts, and mood changes, including irritability, depression, and anxiety. Additional symptoms include fatigue, headache, constipation, acne, and an increased thirst or appetite, which may include a craving for sweets or salty foods.[4] In some women, the premenstrual symptoms are consistent from cycle to cycle; in others, however, they vary in type and severity from month to month. Transient weight gain may occur during the premenstrual period but is not a criterion or symptom of PMS.

The most frequently reported emotional states associated with PMS are tension, anxiety, depression, and hostility. Some women also report feelings of loneliness or guilt. Some quite abruptly feel incompetent or worthless and, consequently, become unwilling to take any risks for fear of being rejected.

Behavioral changes may include feelings of lethargy and inability to cope with normal day-to-day activities. Some women cannot face going to work, engaging in social activities, or interacting with people in any way. They may also have erratically alternating spells of lethargy and bursts of energy. Some report sudden flurries of compulsive activity, such as housecleaning or desk organization. In more severe cases of PMS, there may be abrupt outbursts of anger and aggression, particularly toward family members. Another area of behavioral change is fluctuation in sexual desires, which can increase or decrease, depending on the individual.

The Incidence of PMS

In an effort to assess or establish the incidence of PMS in the general population, several large studies have been done in the United States and in Great Britain. These studies indicate that 80 to 95 percent of women have at least one of the symptoms of PMS, and that 30 to 40 percent have symptoms severe enough to temporarily disrupt their life-style through mental or physical incapacitation. The diagnosis or classification of PMS is applied to this latter group of 30 to 40 percent. The studies indicate that the onset of the symptoms of PMS can occur at any time between the onset and the end of a woman's menstrual life. In addition, some women may experience symptoms during the first several months of pregnancy, usually at the same time a period would be due. Women who have had a hysterectomy or other surgery on the reproductive system may continue to have PMS or may develop PMS unless both ovaries were removed at the time of surgery. Women who have had both ovaries removed, for whatever reason, will no longer experience PMS, but will commonly have the hot flashes and sweating that go along with a surgical menopause.

Painful Periods

Dysmenorrhea, or painful periods, needs to be differentiated from PMS. Media coverage, particularly in women's magazines and on television talk shows, has tended to lump PMS and dysmenorrhea together, suggesting that both are medical disorders with a known cause and physiological basis and with accepted specific medical treatments.[5] This is not the case; the two problems are related only by the fact that they both affect the reproductive system. The cause of dysmenorrhea seems to be an excessive production of hormones called prostaglandins. Prostaglandins appear to cause us to sense pain, particularly visceral or deep pain. Since the discovery of the prostaglandins, control of prostaglandin pain has changed radically through the development of drugs known as anti-prostaglandins. These medications function by preventing the synthesis or production of prostaglandins or by preventing binding of the prostaglandin at the receptor sites. Some of the more common drugs in this group are Ponstel, Motrin, Naprosyn, and Meclomen (trade names).

What Causes PMS?

The cause of PMS is not nearly as clearly defined as that of dysmenorrhea. Since it was first described a variety of causes have been proposed.

In 1931, R. T. Frank was the first to propose that PMS was caused by an excess of female sex hormone in the blood, and he recommended cathartics or strong laxatives to try to eliminate excessive sex hormones. Similar studies presented much discussion and deliberation about the two major female sex hormones, estrogen and progesterone. Every woman with intact ovaries and pituitary gland produces these hormones in a cycle each month of her menstrual life, except during pregnancy. (See figure 1.) In figure 1, day one is the first day of menstrual bleeding or flow. By following the lines you can see that during the first six days of the cycle the hormone levels remain constant in relation to each other. Between days six and eight the estrogen level begins to rise and rapidly peaks out at day twelve, then falls just as rapidly to just above baseline levels by day fifteen. Then it starts another slower rise to peak at day twenty or twenty-one and then drops gradually to baseline levels by day twenty-eight. Progesterone begins to rise at day twelve and continues to rise, peaking at day twenty-two; then it makes a long, steady drop, reaching the baseline level by day twenty-eight. During this time ovulation occurs about day fifteen, interestingly enough, shortly after the hormone levels cross on the graph, and menses begin again on day one of the next cycle. PMS occurs during the last week or so of the cycle when both hormones have peaked and are in a downward course.

Several proposals as to the cause of PMS involve the relationship of these hormones during the premenstrual period of time. One proposes that women with PMS have an estrogen excess; another proposes that they have a progesterone deficiency in the premenstrual period. Another speculates that unopposed estrogen causes fluid retention, swelling of the breasts, abnormal metabolism of sugars, and accumulation of estrogen in the brain, thus causing the an-

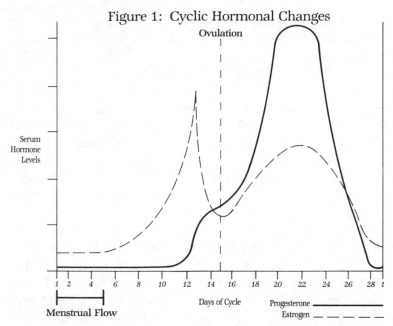

Figure 1: Cyclic Hormonal Changes

Ovulation

Serum
Hormone
Levels

1 2   4   6   8   10   12   14   16   18   20   22   24   26   28   1

Days of Cycle

Menstrual Flow

Progesterone _____
Estrogen _ _ _ _ _ _

xiety and depression. However, in contrast, some women with normal estrogen levels still had PMS. These researchers concluded that PMS must be due to progesterone deficiency because of the rapid drop in progesterone in this phase of the cycle. However, no large doubleblind studies have been conducted that unequivocally substantiate this fact, and trial therapy with progesterone has not been completely successful in the treatment of PMS.

Vitamin-B therapy for PMS was popular in the 1940s and is used in some areas today. Some physicians feel that vitamin B_6 in large doses can correct defective estrogen metabolism in women with PMS.

In 1947 Simkins proposed vitamin-A deficiency as a cause of PMS, although little success was found in using vitamin A for therapy in PMS. It is doubtful that a cyclic vitamin deficiency could exist, due to the composition of the average diet in the United States and the amount of supplemental vitamins present in our foods and taken as dietary supplements.

Some researchers have proposed hypoglycemia as a

cause for PMS, but it seems unlikely that hypoglycemic episodes could occur exactly when the symptoms of PMS are present, nor does the ingestion of food seem to help PMS, whereas it does relieve hypoglycemic symptoms.

Allergy to progesterone has been proposed as a possible cause of PMS. Some interesting though not completely successful treatment has been carried out using allergy management principles and small doses of progesterone.

Psychosomatic causes have been examined carefully, but there is no proof of a psychological origin for PMS. Rather, the symptoms of PMS tend to cause psychosomatic illnesses in the afflicted person.

Some researchers have cited water retention as the cause of PMS; however, some rather involved studies regarding fluid retention show quite contradictory results. Some women gained from one to three pounds at the time of ovulation and again in the premenstrual period, but others actually lost weight during the same times. Premenstrual breast swelling and pain does not correlate with an increase in total body water. During the normal menstrual cycle, breast volume gradually increases by 100 milliliters starting just before ovulation and reaching a maximum on the first day of menstruation. Hence, again, there is no correlation with the onset of PMS.

Numerous other causes have been and are under investigation, including many so-called minor hormones such as renin, aldosterone, angiotensin, vasopressin, prolactin, epinephrine, norepinephrine, dopamine, and most recently alpha-melanocyte stimulating hormone and the endorphins. The latter two theories seem to present some strong hopes for an answer to the real cause of PMS.

Treatment of PMS

Treatment of PMS has run the gamut from witchcraft and laxatives to sophisticated hormone blocking agents. Presently experts begin treatment with nondrug therapies, including insight into the problem, relaxation techniques, biofeedback, exercise, weight reduction, and nonprescription medications such as vitamin B_6. If not successful, they progress to drug therapy with a variety of agents including spironolactone (a diuretic and aldosterone antagonist), bromocriptine (particularly effective for breast engorgement and irritability), and natural progesterone (cannot be taken orally).

Specialists or clinics may or may not be effective in treating the average woman with PMS. The success of treatment frequently depends as much on the woman's relationship with her doctor as it does on the method of treatment. Frequently the family doctor or the woman's own gynecologist will be much more effective in her long-term care than the less personalized but perhaps more scientifically oriented clinic.

Both lay counselors and professional counselors should not only be aware of the existence of PMS but should have at least a rudimentary understanding of the physiology involved and the variable symptoms. PMS should be considered whenever a woman complains of cyclic disturbances of any kind. A counselor's knowledge of PMS should be extensive enough that he or she may discuss the problem with the woman and her family in at least enough depth to give them an overview of the problem. The counselor should be able to suggest further care available to the woman.

SUGGESTED READING

The most complete and most recent article on PMS is titled "Premenstrual Syndrome," by Robert L. Reid and S.S.C. Yen. It was published in the *American Journal of Obstetrics and Gynecology*, vol. 139, pp. 85-104. This paper contains an extensive bibliography of 305 references relating to PMS. It is well written and is relatively easy reading. It should be available through most hospital medical libraries and will definitely be found in all medical-school libraries.

NOTES

1. R. T. Frank, "The Hormonal Causes of Premenstrual Tension," *Archives of Neurology and Psychiatry*, 26 (1931): 1053.

2. M. Laughlin and R. E. Johnson, "Premenstrual Syndrome," *American Family Physician*, 29 (3), (March 1984): 265-69.

3. Robert L. Reid and S. S. C. Yen, "Premenstrual Syndrome," *American Journal of Obstetrics and Gynecology*, 139 (1981): 85-104.

4. H. Sutherland and I. Stuart, "A Critical Analysis of the Premenstrual Syndrome," *Lancet*, 1 (1965): 1180.

5. R. M. Rose and J. M. Abplanalp, "The Premenstrual Syndrome," *Hospital Practice,* 18 (6), (June 1983): 129-41.

ABOUT THE AUTHOR

Dr. Robert N. Gray, an emergency-room physician at Utah Valley Regional Medical Center, received his undergraduate education at Adams State College in Alamosa, Colorado, and his M.D. at Northwestern University Medical School. He was a family practitioner for ten years before becoming an emergency-room physician in 1978.

In the Church he has served as a seventies president, a bishop's counselor, a bishop, a high councilor, and in a stake presidency.

Dr. Gray and his wife, Nancy, are the parents of five children.

10

Counseling Singles
Rita M. Edmonds

Even though many singles feel they are part of a small minority in a "married church," in reality single life is a common experience among Church members. Approximately 30 percent of the adults in the Church are single. This number includes all types of singles—not-yet-married young adults, divorced, separated, over-thirty-never-marrieds, and widowed persons.

But for all people, married or never-married, life's basic struggles are pretty much the same. Most of us wrestle with desires to be purposeful, emotional and sexual needs, economic problems, emotional dependencies and loneliness, physical well-being, and obedience to gospel commandments.

The unique task of the single person is to recognize that being single can be a gift, not a problem. Being single is neither good nor bad. Some singles, as is the case among marrieds, are depressed and unhappy. But there are many single people who are happy and productive. Being single just is. It is a temporary state in the eons of a person's eternities of experiencing, learning, and developing. The challenge lies in how the single person mentally deals with the single state while in mortality. Accepting the situation and making the best of it can mean fulfillment, but using singleness as a stamp of divine or human disapproval breeds unhappiness. That kind of thinking blocks progress. People who use their singleness as a license to avoid responsibility help create their own limits for effective living.

Who Are the Singles?

Because marriage is considered by most people to be a preferred status in society, singles are sometimes marked as "left-overs" and are lumped into a category classified by what they are not—that is, not married. But negative stereotyping of singles inhibits understanding of who they are and what their lives are like. However, it is possible to define how singles regard their singleness and how that affects the way they deal with the challenges of their lives.

According to sociologist Peter Stein,[1] there are four ways that singles evaluate their singleness. These four types are based on perceived choice about their marital status and perceived permanence (stability) of their situation:

Type 1: Voluntary Temporary Singles

Voluntary temporary singles are open to the possibility of marriage but are not actively seeking a mate. They have set aside the search for a marriage partner indefinitely to allow time for other activities such as education, work, career, politics, self-development, a mission, and so on. Typically the singles in this group are the younger never-marrieds and the divorced who need some time to heal and readjust before they remarry. This group is postponing marriage, not making a decision never to marry. Some will marry about when they expect to. Some will marry at a later time than they wished. And some will not find appropriate mates and will move into one of the other groups.

Type 2: Voluntary Stable Singles

Voluntary stable singles have chosen to remain single permanently. The motivation may be positive, as in the case of priests, nuns, and others who want to give a life of service. Or, there may be a degree of negative motivation, such as fear of pain associated with close relationships in the past. Other reasons may be somewhat neutral, as in the case of widows who still feel married, or single parents raising their children alone who do not seek mates because of the disruption it would bring to the family system. Some of these people feel unsettled.

Type 3: Involuntary Temporary Singles

Involuntary temporary singles would like to marry. They do not want to be single and are actively seeking partners. These people may be younger never-marrieds, people whose marriages ended through death or divorce, or older never-marrieds who may or may not have wanted to marry previously.

Type 4: Involuntary Stable Singles

Involuntary stable singles believe in marriage and would like to be married. However, they have adjusted emotionally to the probability that marriage is not a realistic expectation for them. Included in this type are older divorced, never-married, and widowed men and women. It might also include those who do not marry because of physical, mental, or emotional impairments.

Of course, people change the categories in which they place themselves. How singles feel about being single may vary with interpersonal circumstances. For example, nuns and priests who would type themselves as voluntary stable singles may change their minds about getting married if they have a serious opportunity. Types 1, 3, and 4 may even represent stages experienced by never-marrieds. Or a person who is a voluntary temporary single as a college student may move into an involuntary temporary classification as his schooling is completed and he wants to get married. Other voluntary temporary singles may enjoy their single status and, if the possibility to marry does not occur, adjust more or less comfortably into the voluntary stable type.

Where Do the Problems Occur?

Voluntary temporary singles are genuinely concentrating on purposeful, rewarding tasks in life, such as serving missions and completing college degrees. They view their singleness as temporary and feel confident that they will eventually get married. Though aware of their singleness and their lack of fitting the cultural mold, they have little anxiety about postponing marriage. They are receptive to family, social, and institutional (church) support for the task they are centering on.

The problems for the younger voluntary temporary singles tend to be related more to finances, employment, housing, breaking away from their family and becoming an adult, and making friends.[2]

Many involuntary temporary singles, however, face the same challenges without the advantage of feeling that they are in control of their lives and their future happiness. Involuntary temporary singles want to be married. Much of how they feel and what they do is influenced by this desire. Many of them enjoy life and are happy meeting people, dating, and courting. But anxiety about not being married is much more likely to occur among the involuntary temporary singles than among the voluntary temporary singles. Many involuntary temporary singles will marry because they are prepared to love and take responsibility for a family. But if the desire to marry is based on a need to conform to cultural, parental, and peer pressure, marriage may be a source of frustration, loneliness, and diminishing self-esteem. Such desires are not grounded in a faith in gospel principles but in worldly concerns. Even if such a person had the chance to marry, his happiness would not come automatically. But some singles will marry to escape the anxiety of wondering if they are normal and acceptable, because they fear loneliness, or because they dislike the emptiness of celibacy. In such cases, marriage will often be a disappointment.

Women between the ages of twenty-six and thirty-four are most likely to experience this turmoil.[3] They may feel helpless to achieve their goal of marriage and may simultaneously worry about being ostracized because of their perceived defeat. Their feelings of inadequacy can overflow into their employment and careers, where they question the purposefulness of their work, which is a major part of their lives. Because they see themselves as lacking the validation that marriage supposedly gives, they may experience confusion in many aspects of their lives.

Anonymously authored articles in *Exponent II* (Fall 1982) reveal that a number of single women believe—rightly or wrongly—that the Church institution has made unrealistic promises that chaste and righteous women will be rewarded with returned missionary husbands who will marry them in the temple for time and eternity. These writers are now in their late twenties and early thirties. They feel that "the promise" has not been fulfilled though they have kept their part of the bargain. Other Church blessings promise husbands and children. Yet these do not come for everyone. Therefore, they question the validity of other gospel promises and wonder why they should continue to conform to gospel standards.

Each case is different. Perhaps the foregoing reactions are more extreme than usual; but whether the disappointment is lack of marriage, lack of good health, or lack of economic opportunity, the sorrow of these singles need not be borne without faith and hope. All Church members face the challenge to "submit to all things the Lord seeth fit to inflict upon us." (Mosiah 3:19.) Yet continued pressure to marry often influences people to feel inadequate or a failure and is often associated with depression and anger. People who suffer this kind of pain sometimes want to escape from or to tear down the system. Seeking relief, some singles explore other value systems by turning to drugs, alcohol, masturbation, heterosexual promiscuity, and homosexuality. They wander farther into the desert instead of drawing from the well of living water. Feeling deserted, they draw sterile thoughts from empty wells. They think they cannot "play the game" outlined by their parents and society and win. As long as they are losers anyway, they rationalize, why not enjoy temporary pleasure? Some, considering themselves to be deviant because they are not married when their peers are, take license to behave deviantly in other ways.

Involuntary stable singles believe they will not marry

and are not actively seeking marriage. Some of their challenges include: (1) keeping their hearts open in spite of the uncertainties of relationships; (2) keeping peace of mind even when their marital status appears to be out of step with their personal goals, with society, and with their religious culture; (3) fostering emotional intimacy through friendship; (4) developing meaningful employment; (5) managing finances and other resources; (6) encouraging intellectual and spiritual growth and development; (7) finding purposeful community service opportunities; (8) taking responsibility for personal well-being through good nutrition and exercise; and (9) finding a place in a "couples culture." Lay counselors can help by focusing on one or another of these challenges.

Voluntary stable singles may or may not be comfortable with their singleness. Their peace of mind depends largely on their motive for choosing singleness. A decision not to marry because of fear of failure, avoidance of responsibility, selfish desire to live life for oneself, hostility toward the opposite sex, choosing to cope with life by simply not coping, misdirected sexual affection, or dependencies usually bring unproductive or unhappy consequences. On the other hand, some singles choose not to marry because they feel satisfied with their personal growth and the contributions they make to society, science, or the arts. Some singles feel an inner confirmation that their direction is appropriate for their circumstances.

Some voluntary stable singles worry about the challenges of living with their own turmoil and the constant reminders of their self-perceived inadequacy and its emotionally demoralizing energy drain. Caught between the desire for marriage and the despair of helplessness, singles find that this dilemma affects spiritual and intellectual growth, career development, ability to manage financial and other resources, motivation to care about physical well-being, desire to prepare for the future, and social relationships.

In contrast, other voluntary stable singles feel fulfilled in their work. They are free to establish friendships that take care of their intimacy needs. They view interaction in the community as an opportunity to give of themselves. Therefore, they are more able to give attention to the positive messages from society and to overcome the insensitivities of a married society. Their being positive and giving provides them inner strength to reach out to others in service and friendship, the courage to take charge of financial matters, and the energy to control their own environment so they can be productive.

Voluntary stable singles who have accepted their singleness view it as a gift. They reject the myth that to be single is to be selfish. They say that selfishness is in the mind, not in a particular marital situation. Adults in this group give through community and church service, careers, and networks of human relationships. Singles have the opportunity to deliver proportionally more community service than marrieds.

Why Singles Don't Marry

In a society where adulthood and emotional maturity are synonymous with marriage and parenthood, and where "the righteous life" is the married life, many people wonder why someone would not marry. The norm is to get married; any behavior outside the norm is considered by many to be deviant. Assumptions about why singles are not married include: (1) they have not found the "right person"; (2) they have emotional handicaps from their families of origin; (3) they have physical defects; (4) they are recovering from divorce.[4]

But there are further reasons. Among these reasons are: (1) there are more women than men eligible for marriage;[5] (2) certain careers and graduate-level education reduce marriage opportunities for many women;[6] (3) some people have high need for autonomy and function better as singles; (4) some singles are living out parental wishes that they not marry; and (5) some people simply lack a desire to marry.

The most common reason reported by singles is that they have not had the opportunity to marry. "Opportunity" can be defined in many ways, of course. Elements of "opportunity for marriage" include perceived equality about each partner, presence of genuine love and desire to be together, inner confirmation about the decision, and opportunity for personal development through relationship and shared responsibility. Today more people are deciding that an "opportunity" without all of those elements is no opportunity at all. There is an emerging group of single adults who feel that they have not found a relationship that offers more opportunity for growth than they can achieve singly.

Counseling Guidelines

If, then, many singles are choosing to remain single, how can you, as a counselor, help them? How can you guide singles so that they can develop their full potentials? The counseling goals of Church counselors and leaders need to include the following: (1) help singles talk about their situation in an effort to overcome emotional immobilization; (2) help singles develop support strategies appropriate for different stages of singleness; and (3) help singles focus on positive principles as a way of gaining control of their lives.

How to Help Singles Talk about Their Situation

As a married person you may fear rejection by singles because you are not familiar with their life-styles and experiences. But you can overcome this disadvantage by wanting to know about their lives and by asking questions. The lay counselors who listen to learn and to understand another's views of life, and then who communicate love and acceptance, will not be rejected. Ask questions and listen to singles' answers. Really listen until you feel what they feel. Listen until you see the world as they see it. You do not have to agree with their views, but you can understand their world. Listen—even if they are critical of you or your leadership. Ask for clarifications if necessary.

You want to be trustworthy so the singles will feel comfortable to explore with you the misconceptions, attitudes, and beliefs that cause them pain. To build this trust, it is important that you communicate your understanding. Try saying back to them in your own words what they have just shared with you. You can appropriately communicate your concern for their feelings and help open the conversation by using such phrases as:

"There's a lot of frustration with being single when you want so much to be married."

"It's easy to feel like there's something wrong with you because you're not married."

"I'll bet you're sometimes afraid you'll spend the rest of your life alone."

"I wonder if it feels unfair."

"It must be difficult to get on with your life when marriage is an unknown for you."

When a person feels you truly understand him, he may share deep feelings with you. If this happens, you should listen and let yourself feel what is being shared. It is not always the leader's responsibility to solve the problem or to make the pain go away. You cannot be responsible for another person's life. But you can provide an atmosphere of love and safety where he can talk about his problems and discover solutions so that he can make decisions and get on with his life.

Develop Support Strategies
for Different Stages of Singleness

The kind of support and teaching that singles need is related to how they feel about themselves and their singleness. Their needs are varied. Dances, firesides, and admonitions to fast and pray are helpful to many, but not for all. For example, voluntary temporary singles are still full of hope. They may be frustrated with feeling socially inadequate and financially inexperienced. They may need extra encouragement to stay close to the Lord and to look for ways to give service. But their goals are usually set on purposeful tasks, and they experience relatively little anxiety about their singleness.

Voluntary stable singles are already involved in the

Church, with service, and with being self-sufficient. These people are probably strong resource people for others. Other voluntary stable singles probably need to work with a professional counselor to discover the role family interaction patterns have played in their rejection of marriage. They may need professional help to examine and modify beliefs and behaviors that block their progress.

Older involuntary temporary singles who are still dating—courting and full of hope—need encouragement from time to time when their hope wanes. Furthermore, they need to be taught to accept the idea that they may always be single.

Older singles who feel cheated and denied may need to be taught to look for the positive aspects of their situation and to take responsibility for their own happiness.

Single women from ages twenty-six to thirty-four most often fit in the involuntary temporary singles group. The "alarm clock" syndrome is most likely to affect singles in this stage—they panic when they realize that the normal marriage years are slipping by and they have not found a partner. Initial reaction is either social withdrawal or frenzied reaching out and indiscriminate dating. Unfortunately, because of the cultural pressure to marry, a big wedding rather than a true marriage becomes the goal.

If there is a critical period for singles, it is probably this period. Toward the end of the stage, sometimes when they are in their late thirties, single women actually go through the emotional stages of grief—mourning the loss of hope never realized. There is a last flurry of denial that they will face life single; then they have angry feelings about having to live life without companionship, sex, children, and the affirmation of marriage. They may bargain with the Lord. Finally, they accept life as a single. These stages may present themselves in part, all at once, or in any order before final acceptance is achieved.

Involuntary stable singles are older singles who have accepted singleness as a permanent life-style. If they also are assertively self-reliant, they need to be encouraged with opportunities for top-line executive leadership and teaching positions in the Church. They need to be recognized as whole, complete individuals. However, some involuntary stable singles have resigned themselves to singleness without really taking charge of their lives and their happiness. If they are in quest of additional peace and freedom to fulfill their potential, they should be taught to be positive and to make decisions that can bring them fulfillment.

Response to the needs of such a heterogeneous group should include the following three elements: (1) referrals to professionals; (2) being available to listen; and (3) teaching helpful principles.

Referrals to professionals may be the most helpful response in cases where a person has come from a family with unhealthy interaction patterns. Extreme resentments of the opposite sex and rejection of the marriage and family lifestyle indicate a need for professional help in examining and working through those issues.

In normal situations, however, the most important support to give is the message that you care, that you see singles as important, valuable human beings who are worth your gift of a reasonable amount of time. They will care what you say when they know that you care. Their needs differ. Some will not be ready to receive any more than your gift of time and nonjudgmental listening. Some will not need any more than periodic opportunities to have you show that you value them enough to listen to them so they can see more clearly how to organize and carry out their lives. You will be able to judge what they need by listening to them.

How to Help Singles Focus on Positive Principles

Because feelings and behaviors are based on what we think and believe, singles who struggle with accepting their singleness need additional information. With added information they can develop a new, more productive way of seeing their situations and can be open to more productive ways of living. The following principles are guidelines for counseling singles. However, the singles' success in accept-

ing and applying these principles depends on their willingness to make their lives happier.

1. As they accept responsibility for their happiness, they
will find personal power and increased self-esteem. Teach
them that choosing self-fulfilling thoughts and behavior is
the ultimate personal freedom. In order to have charge of
their lives, they may need to break emotional or financial dependencies on others. Taking this step is frightening because
it requires responsibility, energy, and risk of failure. Yet it is
encouraged by Church leaders as the only way to work out
personal salvation. Elder James E. Faust said, "This life is
not a passive life. The word of God constantly sets before us
images of vigor and power, all of which images and actions
under his benign guidance can be directed and controlled."[7]

2. As singles turn to God through prayer and repentance, they will find new vision. Without vision we perish.
They will experience a new perspective on life and the ad-
vantages of being single.

3. As singles choose to love themselves, they will be able
to love others.[8] Self-esteem is their choice. It cannot be given
by others. If they look for it outside themselves, it will be
"other-worth" rather than "self-worth." Patricia Russell and
Karen Jensen wrote in the February 1974 *Ensign*, "A woman
can and must have an identity, be useful, and feel important
and needed whether she is single or married. She must feel
that she has something to offer."[9]

4. As singles put marriage in its proper eternal perspective, they will be free from worldly expectations that marriage must happen in this life. Life begins with discipleship,
not at the altar. Discipleship is a reaching toward second
birth and a reawakening followed by an eternal searching
for what is noble and good.

Elder Faust said, "Too many women think that marriage
is the most important thing in the world. . . . The Lord tells
us our first responsibility is to love him and seek his will."[10]

At a women's conference at New York City in April 1978,
Sister Barbara B. Smith taught that the purpose of this life is
to follow Christ and become like him. Some people need the

challenges of marriage to do this, while for other people different trials are given to help them become like him. The important message is that we should put first things first—spiritual rebirth before marriage.

5. As singles give service to others, they are fruitful and multiply and replenish the earth with good will and good works. A multitude of discouragements are overcome through service. Isolation and turning inward lead to depression and a failure to reach out to others. Companionship, self-respect, happiness, and life itself are gained through giving up our time, talent, and energy to others. Elder Faust's advice to singles is, "I wish to affirm that the principal benefit which will come to the adult singles of the Church . . . is service . . . the Christlike quality of service on a one-to-one basis. Cultural and social activities are very important, but the primary emphasis should be on service. A daily selfless service to another should be on the agenda of our activities."[11]

NOTES

1. Peter J. Stein, *Understanding Single Adulthood,* paper presented at the annual meeting of the National Council on Family Relations (Boston: 1979), p. 3.

2. Ibid., p. 3.

3. Cynthia S. Burnley, *Identities and Life-Style Adaptations of Never-Married Women,* paper presented at the annual meeting of the Society for the Study of Social Problems (Boston: August 1979), p. 4.

4. Peter J. Stein, *Single* (New York: Spectrum Books, 1976), pp. 63-64.

5. Ida Smith, "Demographic, Social, and Personal Dimensions of Singleness," *Family Perspectives* (Winter 1983), p. 3.

6. Charles W. Mueller, "Female Occupational Achievement and Marital Status," *Journal of Marriage and the Family* (August 1977), p. 587.

7. James E. Faust, "Married or Single: Look beyond Yourself," *Ensign* (March 1980), p. 36.

8. Ibid., p. 37.

9. Patricia Russell and Karen Jensen, "Put First Things First: A Single Woman's Perspective," *Ensign* (February 1974), p. 37.

10. James E. Faust, "Married or Single: Look beyond Yourself," *Ensign* (March 1980), p. 36.

11. Ibid., p. 37.

SUGGESTED READINGS

Anonymous essays, *Exponent II,* Fall 1982.

Avant, Gerry. "Singles Urged to Aid Others." *Church News,* July 12, 1975, p. 4.

Burnley, Cynthia S. "Identities and Life-Style Adaptations of Never-Married Women." Paper presented at the annual meeting of the Society for the Study of Social Problems, Boston, August 24-27, 1979.

Cargan, Leonard. *Singles: Myths and Realities.* Los Angeles: Sage Publications, 1982.

Dyer, Wayne. *Your Erroneous Zones.* New York: Avon Books, 1976.

Faust, James E. "Married or Single: Look beyond Yourself." *Ensign,* March 1980, pp. 35-37.

Hoopes, Margaret H. "Alone through Divorce." *Ensign,* November 1972, pp. 52-55.

Kearney, Kathryn. "Home Evening, Singles Style." *Ensign,* March 1981, pp. 30-31.

Lubeck, Kathleen. "I Love My Work: Enjoying This Stage of My Life." *Ensign,* July 1980, pp. 66-67.

Mueller, Charles W. "Female Occupational Achievement and Marital Status." *Journal of Marriage and the Family,* August 1977, pp. 587-93.

Osborn, Anne G. "The Ecstasy of the Agony: How to Be Single and Sane at the Same Time." *Ensign,* March 1977, pp. 47-49.

Porter, Blaine R. "Alone through Death." *Ensign,* October 1972, pp. 74-78.

Russell, Patricia, and Karen Jensen, "Put First Things First: A Single Woman's Perspective." *Ensign,* February 1974, pp. 36-37.

Silver, Cherry. "When a Woman Is Alone." *Ensign,* June 1978, pp. 40-43.

"Single Woman Improves Her Self-Image." *Church News,* February 28, 1981, p. 11.

Smith, Ida. "Demographic, Social, and Personal Dimensions of Singleness." *Family Perspectives,* Winter 1983, pp. 3-18.

Stein, Peter J. *Single.* New York: Spectrum Books, 1976.

————. "Understanding Single Adulthood." Paper presented at the annual meeting of the National Council of Family Relations, Boston, August 14-16, 1979.

Underwood, Jan. "Seeing Beyond the Category: Reflections on a Single Life." *Ensign,* March 1984, pp. 24-29.

Ward, Russell A. "The Never-Married Later in Life." *Journal of Gerontology* 1979, vol. 34, no. 6, pp. 861-69.

ABOUT THE AUTHOR

Dr. Rita M. Edmonds, core faculty member at the Brigham Young University Comprehensive Clinic, received her bachelor's and master's degrees from that same university and her Ed.D. in family and community education from Columbia University. Prior to joining the BYU faculty, she taught and worked as an administrator at several institutions of higher education. Since joining the BYU faculty she has developed a course on singles in family and society.

Dr. Edmonds has been a speaker at numerous women's conferences in the United States and Canada. Because she organized the LDS Indochinese refugee program in

Thailand (under the direction of Elder Marion D. Hanks), she has since organized conferences on, published a book about, and served on the Utah State Refugee Advisory Council.

Dr. Edmonds has served in many Church callings, including institute instructor, ward Relief Society president, Relief Society teacher, and stake Relief Society board member.

11
Intercultural Marriage
R. Lanier Britsch

A great amount of social progress has been made in the United States during the past twenty years in civil rights. Attitudes toward intercultural, interracial, international, or interethnic marriages (I will use the word "intermarriage" as a generic term hereinafter) have become more liberal and the number of intermarriages has increased. Intermarriage has gradually become more acceptable, particularly among overseas service personnel and on college and university campuses. (Intermarriage in Hawaii is fairly common.) Even though there are growing numbers of intermarriages, the matter is not one of civil rights alone. Traditionally intermarriage has not been well accepted in America and is frequently more harshly viewed in many other countries. Today, intermarriage remains an emotional issue for many people, both inside and outside the Church.

Intermarriage is not new among Latter-day Saints. One of the first two LDS missionaries to the South Pacific married a Polynesian woman and, upon her death, yet another. His reasons for intermarrying were no doubt similar to those of thousands of other returned missionaries since that time. Familiarity with people of other cultures generally brings understanding for them; understanding brings appreciation; and appreciation often leads to love. One of the greatest by-products of the LDS missionary system is the enhanced level of international concern and understanding felt by vast numbers of the Mormon people.

It is not surprising that many returned missionaries meet people from the lands where they served, appreciate them for their fine qualities, and fall in love with them. Through the mission experience, most cultural barriers are torn down, and people are seen simply as people—children of God—rather than as representatives of some other race or culture.

But there are both positive and negative results of this situation. For various reasons, even in marriages in which there is considerable cultural appreciation and the shared foundation of the restored gospel, some intermarriages run afoul.

Counseling about intermarriage is a very sensitive process. The lay counselor who seeks to help people who are considering such marriages, or those who are already married, must be aware of the pitfalls that lay before him. It is difficult to be neutral in the eyes of both parties. The cultural, ethnic, or racial background of the counselor can be used by a counselee as justification for not considering or acting on the counsel given. This issue, the supposed prejudice of the counselor, should be brought into the open and clarified at the beginning. The lay counselor might suggest that if either party feels that he is giving biased counsel, they should all pause to examine the prejudice or bias. (The word prejudice means to pre-judge someone or something. Its implication is that a person judges someone or a situation without enough facts to do so fairly.) The result of this examination should be even clearer communication of your ideas, or, if you are prejudiced, your admission of this fact may suggest that the counselees seek help from someone who can be more fair.

As a lay counselor, you can check your own prejudice level by asking yourself if you would be as willing to take counsel from a counselor of another race, ethnic group, or culture as from your own. If not, you are prejudiced and need to carefully consider your ability to counsel others.

You, as a lay counselor, must be honest with yourself. It is very important not to try to "play it" Black, Polynesian, or Asian if you are not. You must be yourself. And, fortunately, there is a second way to check your potential as a counselor to those in intermarriage. Are your suggestions going to be based on defensible principles, or just on personal preferences?

Some counselors try to give advice based on their beliefs about what the world and society should be. That is, they are committed to the idea of racial and cultural equality and therefore give advice based on their hopes for some future time rather than on society as it is today. This is not realistic. Such counselors are prone to argue that all the difficulties of intermarriage are the result of problems, doubts, and complications that have resulted from attitudes of the past— attitudes that are surely temporary. Such an argument is moot. No one knows when there will be a total change to toleration and equality. Meanwhile, a not-too-sturdy relationship might crumble if sound counsel is not given.

General Considerations

The first thing to remember when counseling couples on intermarriage is that most of their concerns and problems are probably much like every other couple's. In a sense, every marriage is a mixed marriage—it consists of a man and a woman. Experience has shown that the two sexes think somewhat differently and bring different expectations to the marriage altar. Also, in a sense, every couple is an intercultural marriage. No two families are alike. Customs and traditions differ considerably from home to home. The nature of communication varies from family to family and from person to person. One father will be warm and give physical affection to his wife and children; another won't. Such differences do not necessarily relate to race or national origins. People are different, and their differences must be recognized apart from culture, sex, or nationality. In short, be careful about crediting attributes to culture that should be credited to individuality.

Premarital Counseling

Basically two kinds of people will come to you for counsel: those who are considering an intermarriage but are having doubts or questions; and those whose parents have persuaded them to ask for advice. You can discuss the same issues with both types of people. Your role is to discuss marriage and its many dimensions realistically. It would not be wise to tell a couple that their prospective intermarriage has no chance for success. There are too many happily intermarried couples to make such an assertion. It is wiser to deal with factors that predict—not predestine—success or failure in marriage.

Counselors need to realize that some intermarriages are composed of people who are far more similar and suited for each other than are couples who have been reared in the same neighborhood by extremely different parents. Predicting success among intermarried couples is much like predicting success among other couples: if they share the same values, if they come from the same economic level, if they share similar aspirations for themselves and their prospective children, and so on, their differences in nationality and race can make almost no difference to the success of their marriage. The key lies in the rationality of their decision to marry and their personal strength in facing problems that might arise because of their intermarriage.

Generally, but not always, it is wise to make a clear distinction between culture and race. Marriages have the greatest chance for success when the couple comes from the same culture. Here I am talking about national culture, subculture (such as a distinctive set of societal patterns within a country or ethnic group), and microculture (such as a distinct community or family tradition).

John Taneguchi was a brilliant engineer who had been reared in eastern Wyoming. He filled a mission in Japan and learned to speak Japanese. Later, while at Brigham Young University, he met and married Kiyoko Moriyama, a lovely Japanese girl reared in Japan. But although they looked alike, they did not think alike. Each had certain expectations that the other did not fill. Kiyoko had more problems adjusting to John than he had adjusting to her. He looked Japanese, but he did not act Japanese. He was as American as he could be. She expected him to behave like her father. He did not.

On the other hand, John had some disappointments too. Through his American upbringing he had picked up the idea that Japanese women are more submissive, subordinate, and serene than American women. He expected her to behave like an "Oriental doll." Both partners had some significant adjustments to make.

Several important points are evident in this marriage. Race is clearly not the most important factor. Culture, the established patterns of belief and behavior, is more important. As you talk with prospective intermarriage couples, you should make this clear. They need to find cultural similarities if they hope to have success.

This marriage illustrates two other points about expectations and stereotyping. Kiyoko had watched her father for years. He regularly stayed out late in the evening with his office associates. Kiyoko's mother did not complain because this was the Japanese way. When he did come home immediately after work, he usually put on his comfortable clothes and settled in front of the television until dinnertime. He seldom lifted a finger around the house. Everyone waited on him. He was king of the home. But John saw things differently. Although he hoped Kiyoko would wait on him hand and foot, and thus fulfill his stereotype of how "Oriental" women behave, he also wanted her to be just like his mother, and he expected to behave as his father had. He expected to help around the house. He liked to cook. He thought he had just as much responsibility to make domestic decisions as Kiyoko did. Actually, it did not take long for John to find out that his Oriental bride had strong opinions of her own. Part of her desire to marry an American came from her belief that American husbands are more kind, understanding, and egalitarian than Japanese men. Clearly, both partners had mixed perceptions, expectations, and stereotypes. They both wanted the best of both worlds, but they were also bound to the traditions and expectations of their own past. "Each partner," writes Richard Markoff, "may view the other not as an individual but as the representative of his or her culture or ethnic group."[1] This places the partner in a role or function that he or she is not willing to discharge. Stereotypes and unexpressed expectations constitute hidden terms in the marriage contract that the other partner may not be willing to keep.

Motivations for Intermarriage

As a lay counselor, you have the opportunity to help couples evaluate their motivations for marrying each other. Marrying for the wrong reasons is a drastic mistake. Some people marry out of their own race or culture because they want to make a statement about social equality or some shared cause. Others marry the first person available in the hope that they can escape from preexisting problems—unhappy homes, feelings of insecurity and loneliness, revenge, repudiation, and so on. People in this category should be convinced to take their time before marrying, and they generally should be referred to a professional counselor who can help them reassess the meaning of marriage as well as explore what could be neurotic attitudes. A neurotic marriage can only bring grief to all parties involved.

Some people intermarry because they have been separated from their own culture or group and no longer share the traditions and values of family and friends back home. Often such motivations are tied to the desire for new experiences, for excitement, or for the need to be different. Although stereotypes sometimes play a role in these motivations, it is possible for such motivations to prove rational and valid. Among college students, in particular, couples find themselves in a setting where both parties develop new values, similar goals, and new tastes. It is safe to assume that this group would be more likely to have better adjustment in intermarriage. However, people in university and college environments are more liberal and accepting of most social anomalies than is society in general. College life can be a safe haven before a life of storms.

Some people actually marry out of their own culture in order to remain in America (or some other desirable country). Others have different but equally base or unrighteous reasons for marrying a person from a preferred nation or culture area.

Love is probably the most frequently cited motivation for intermarriage. That true love exists must not be denied. But it is well to remember that most couples who are in love seek privacy and isolation. In their somewhat isolated state, they sometimes forget that life must be lived within society, not alone. Marriage is not an isolated state. The feelings of family and friends seep into the lives of married people much more than into the lives of those who are falling in love. A dating couple will either ignore the cultural differences or remain blind to them, but the rest of society generally refuses to allow such blindness. Such couples should be encouraged to get to know as much as possible about each other's cultures. They can do this through reading; by associating with the other's family, friends, and relatives; and, when possible, by visiting and living in the other culture for a time. The idea is to get both parties into the open where they can view their future life more realistically. Women especially should evaluate themselves to see if they are willing to adapt to family life in the countries from which their prospective husbands come. Often—perhaps usually—life as we know it in the United States cannot be duplicated abroad. A prospective bride should evaluate just how tough and adaptable she really is.

The process of evaluating oneself in relation to another culture is extremely important. For example, young American women who are contemplating marriage with a Polynesian or Fijian need to realize that the role of women in the islands is much different than in the United States. In the U.S. women are steadily gaining fuller equality with men and are becoming more assertive, but such is generally not the case in the islands. In Tonga, for instance, men usually control the money and usually feel a greater responsibility to their parents and brothers and sisters than to their wife and children. Tongan men spend most evenings with other men, away from their wives and families. Most American women have trouble adjusting to these "island ways." Such cultural traits must be understood and considered before marriage. Prospective marriage partners should evaluate whether they can live with the limitations intermarriage will impose.

Counselors should assign both partners to talk to at least five couples who are intermarried. They should do this separately. In their discussions they should ask about social acceptance, customs that are strange or obnoxious, use of money, children and their adjustment to being neither of one race nor another, and so on.

A lay counselor might also suggest that the couple separate for at least four or five months—maybe with no strings attached—to see their relationship more clearly. If they are mature, such a suggestion should seem reasonable. After all, life is usually long, and marriage should not be entered into quickly, particularly a marriage with an extra adjustment problem.

If the woman is planning to leave America and live in the land and culture of her husband, she should be willing to learn the language of her husband's people before going there to live. In an effort to find out if she can live comfortably within that culture, she should also be encouraged to go alone (that is, without her prospective marriage partner) to the new culture to experiment with it. This may sound expensive, and it may also have an appearance of prejudice, but it is better than creating a miserable marriage that will cause grief to the couple and possibly their children too.

Predicting Success in Intermarriage

Regardless of their motivation to marry, a couple should evaluate their relationship on the criteria of barriers. Does their relationship create or remove barriers? The surrounding society may not accept a particular intermarriage. Barriers may arise in housing, employment, and other areas. By marrying, will they reduce their number of friends and supporters, or will they enlarge their circle of loved ones? A realistic look at the implications and consequences of their intermarriage is advisable.

The couple should consider their relationship with both

sets of parents. Do both sets of in-laws accept their child's prospective marriage partner? If not, can the hostile parents be won over? Counsel that the effort to win them over should be made before the marriage. Patience must be employed in developing love where prejudice or disappointment exist. Because support from the whole family is essential to the success of any marriage, it is worth the time it takes to win everyone's support.

Cultural similarity is an important factor in predicting intermarriage success. American marriages to Western Europeans do not hold the same degree of culture conflict that American-Asian or American-Polynesian marriages do. The degree of difference between any two cultures is significant.

Another important predictor is the emotional and rational maturity of the people involved. This is true of all marriages, but it is especially true of intermarriages. Do both partners have a clear, rational idea of what marriage is and is not? In different countries and cultures marriage serves different purposes. Do both parties understand the expectations regarding marriage in the other culture? In Japan marriages are generally motivated and arranged on political, social, and economic grounds rather than on the basis of romance and personal fulfillment, as is true in America. Each marriage partner should seek to understand the traditional basis for marriage in his partner's society. A counselor may wish to assign each partner to research the role of marriage in the other's society.

"All the personal qualities and attitudes that militate toward success in marriage," writes Richard Markoff, "such as tolerance for diversity, a positive orientation toward change, and flexibility, may be tested to their utmost in the intercultural marriage." It is important for the lay counselor to assess as far as possible the individual strength of each partner. Does he or she have a solid record in school, at work, in interpersonal relationships? Does he or she cope well with life's problems? Does the couple handle differences well? Or does one member always give in, but with resentment? Do they argue a great deal? Does their arguing lead to compromises and growth or to dead ends that are no longer discussed? Do they respect each other as human beings?

These and other similar questions apply as well to non-intermarriage couples, but they are doubly important when dealing with cross-cultural situations. Appropriate communication is at the heart of successful marriages. If partners have difficulty communicating and respecting the ideas and opinions of the other during courtship, matters will usually not improve after marriage.

In their book *Building a Successful Marriage*, Judson and Mary Landis note that several danger signals often appear when couples are incompatible: repeated quarreling with a discernible pattern, repeated break-ups, a strong desire to change the other, feelings of depression and moodiness during the courtship, and a feeling of regression rather than of growth. These danger signals also apply to couples who are planning intermarriage.

Some couples might suggest that over time they will be able to work out their differences. In some cases they might, but not in most instances. "It seems," according to Landis and Landis, "that the differences in mixed marriages do not necessarily decrease with the passing of time after marriage. They tend to become magnified in the minds of the couple and their families. To achieve happiness in such marriages, individuals must be mentally and emotionally mature and must possess more than average understanding and tolerance."

Practical Wisdom from Church Leaders

Young people are justified in asking what the position of the Church is regarding intermarriage. The position has consistently been that wisdom suggests that intermarriage should be avoided. It is clear that intermarriage is not a sin or a transgression. In President Spencer W. Kimball's words, "It is not expedient."[2] President Kimball has emphasized the problem of different backgrounds. He, as well as other leaders, has emphasized the importance of creating homogeneous marriages. That is, young people (and others) are advised to seek marriage partners who come from similar religious, social, economic, and educational backgrounds. Speaking at Brigham Young University in 1976, President Kimball said, "We recommend that people marry those who are of the same racial background generally, and of somewhat the same economic and social and educational background (some of those are not an absolute necessity, but preferred), and above all, the same religious background, without question."

In Hawaii in 1978, President Kimball admonished the Saints "to marry within their own race. There is nothing wrong with any other course, but it is generally better if two people can have the same background and similar experiences before they're married."

Speaking at Brigham Young University–Hawaii Campus in January 1977, Elder Boyd K. Packer emphasized the importance of not being an exception, when following the rule is clearly the better course. He said, "We've always counseled in the Church for our Mexican members to marry Mexicans, and our Japanese members to marry Japanese, our Caucasians to marry Caucasians, our Polynesian members to marry Polynesians. That counsel has been wise." Elder Packer acknowledged that some intermarriages do work well, but he suggested that young people recognize that these marriages are exceptions and that no one should try to be the exception.

Speaking to the same student body a year later, Elder John H. Groberg told the BYU–Hawaii students that he would advise them not to intermarry. But he further counseled that if those who are contemplating intermarriage will gather "the facts," they might enter intermarriage with a higher chance for success. Study the implications and consequences of such a marriage, he said. "Please, as you make decisions in this most vital area, be prayerful, be certain that you have faced all of the facts and when a decision is made, don't have it a wishy washy decision. Have it a firm decision. Have the confirmation of the Spirit. And I am sure that confirmation can come in some instances within our own race, in some instances, without our own race. I don't think that one factor in and of itself makes it right or wrong, as long as we face the facts; as long as we're sure that we are willing to accept whatever limitations that marriage will impose upon us, and as long as we are willing to pay the price, to see ourselves, our children, our families, our husband and wife through to that greatest of all goals, eternal life."

There is yet another dimension that the Brethren have mentioned. This is the need for the various peoples of the world to remain in their homelands to build up Zion. A problem arises when priesthood bearers from Asia, the islands, or elsewhere marry women from America and then fail to return home to build up the Church. Sometimes American women go to the husband's land for a while but then conclude that they do not want to raise their children in a non-American or non-Australian or some other environment. The unhappy wife then places pressure on her husband to go to the land of her birth. Many men have found it necessary to leave their homelands to keep their intermarriages intact when they could have contributed much more to the Church if they had been able to remain home.

Intermarriage Counseling

Whatever the counselor's thoughts on premarriage counseling, marriage counseling requires the same sensitivity, understanding, and concern that exist in any other marriage counseling situation—plus a little more. Lay counselors should begin by studying Terrance D. Olson's chapter "Counseling Couples" in *Counseling: A Guide to Helping Others* (Salt Lake City: Deseret Book Co., 1983). Most problems can be handled by using the ideas taught in that chapter.

Problems of Intermarriage

There are a few problems that are peculiar to intermarried couples. For example, intermarried couples often attribute marriage problems to the matter of race. A Black/Caucasian couple visited with a counselor concerning their teenage son. He was moody, unthoughtful of them, somewhat rebellious, and aloof. They suggested that his problems stemmed from his failure to identify with either of their races. A wise counselor, having met with the boy, rightly suggested that he was a teenager with typical teen adjustment problems.

Sometimes one partner will blame the other for having peculiar habits. (And some habits can be peculiar.) But in most cases it is best to look for cultural reasons for "peculiar" behavior. Many habits can be explained in this way, and, once explained, will less likely be a source of irritation.

Within marriage, the lack of shared values is often the root of discord. Values are those ideas or material goods that a person considers true or good. We speak of the American value system. Americans value material wealth, competitive success, upward social mobility, individualism, private ownership, and so on. By contrast, in Polynesia, particularly in Samoa, people value cooperation, mutual interdependence, group ownership within the extended family, and patriarchal control. It is easy to see that American/Polynesian marriages can have value conflicts. Values are subtle. Intellectually a person can accept another culture, but emotionally one remains convinced that his native ways are best. In Markoff's words: "What makes the area of values so important a source of problems is not merely that cultures differ in their value systems, but that all of us tend to feel that our particular culturally ordained values are incontestably 'right' or 'true' or 'best.'"

The gospel provides the soundest basis for shared marital values. In a very real way, everyone who commits himself to the restored gospel agrees to shed the value system of his past. If all Latter-day Saints could do that and if all people throughout the world shared the same values and principles, most problems would be solved. Speaking of the special intercultural environment that exists at the Brigham Young University–Hawaii Campus and the goal of improving that environment, Eric B. Shumway said, "The gospel is the point of supreme reference which bridges ethnic chasms in ways

the principles of other international organizations cannot."
What he says is true of intermarried couples. The gospel provides the supreme reference for bridging marital chasms.
Shumway further suggests that harmony at BYU–Hawaii
can best be achieved by emphasizing similarities of people
rather than differences, "again with the gospel of Jesus Christ
as the common ground for understanding all men." Once an
intermarriage has been contracted, this is certainly the best
attitude to assume toward it from outside or within.

But it is also necessary for both partners to realize and to
believe that God created all men and women and that he did
not create them identically. God must savor variety, for he
made a great deal of it. People, too, should savor variety
by allowing their spouses to be different and to have, within
the bounds the Lord has set, different values, desires, tem-
peraments, and ideas. "Partners of divergent backgrounds,"
writes Emily H. Mudd, "bring conflicting values, expectations,
and behavior into marriage and hence have less common
ground on which to build. More consistent effort is therefore
necessary to establish a mutual basis of understanding and
functioning. When troubles arise, the sense of difference
magnifies the difficulty."[3]

Building "common ground" in a marriage comes from
working at communication and having shared experiences.
The Latin root of the word communication means "share."
Lay counselors should do all possible to help couples develop
communication skills. Language impediments are sometimes a problem. For example, in most East Asian countries
it is considered inappropriate to directly disagree with someone. Most Asians will not give a direct no. It is easy to see
that such a custom could cause misunderstandings in a
marriage. Encourage the learning of at least one language
that both partners understand well. Deep and sensitive issues, the kinds of matters married couples must ponder and
discuss together, must be clearly understood. Both partners
should be aware that nonverbal communication is also important and often causes more problems than verbal communication.

Children

The coming of children is often a time of dissatisfaction in intermarriages. One or both partners may have a difficult time adjusting to the physical appearance of their children. Children can magnify the cultural differences because child-rearing habits may be unusual and even obnoxious to one or the other of the partners. Sometimes children do not affect the marriage at all until they are in their teens and express resentment that their parents created a situation in which they have to accept the abuse—direct or subtle—of society. Children of intermarriages have no choice but to intermarry when they mature because they are not of a single race. They often find it necessary to choose between the culture of one parent or the other. Some children of intermarriages have to adapt to two distinct parenting traditions. For example, Ray, although reared in America, was the son of a British father and a Malaysian mother. He found it necessary to deal with his father regarding some aspects of his life and with his mother in others. His father gave little or no affection. His mother was warm and affectionate, as was her family. When he was old enough to date—by American standards—his father said he could not consider it until he was in his late teens. His mother's feelings were not so strict. When it was time for him to marry, he had to choose whether to return to his mission field in Southeast Asia and select a bride from his mother's culture or to select an American girl. He chose the latter because he was now culturally an American.

Experience has shown that children are usually adaptable, perhaps more adaptable than their intermarried parents. A key in successful counseling is to help parents establish norms that are acceptable within local society and also within the gospel framework. Generally, intermarried parents should rear their children so that they are well adjusted in whatever society they live. So-called international families—those who move around the globe because of employment—will have to seek some form of stability to help their children find cultural continuity. The gospel and the programs of the Church provide the best basis for such continuity.

Conclusion

The two foregoing sections may have a ring of inconsistency. The section on premarital counseling emphasizes cultural differences and the problems they bring to a marriage. The section on counseling intermarried couples stresses the importance of downplaying and respecting differences. However, both positions are consistent for the groups of people involved.

The counsel of the leaders of the Church is sound. Intermarriage is generally not "expedient." It is well to remember, however, that many other marriages are also not expedient. The degree of inexpedience can be measured largely by the degree of cultural difference that separates any two people who contemplate marriage.

Once a couple is married, lay counselors should do everything in their power to diminish the cultural chasms between them. Their marriage is as sacred in the eyes of the Lord as is any other marriage.

NOTES

1. Richard Markoff, "Intercultural Marriage: Problem Areas," in Tseng et al, *Adjustment in Intercultural Marriage* (Honolulu: Department of Psychiatry, University of Hawaii, 1977), p. 58.

2. Edward L. Kimball, ed., *The Teachings of Spencer W. Kimball* (Salt Lake City: Bookcraft, 1982), p. 302.

3. Emily H. Mudd with Hilda M. Goodwin, "Marital Problems and Marital Adjustments," in *The Encyclopedia of Mental Health* (New York: Watts, 1963), p. 669.

SUGGESTED READINGS

Landis, Judson T., and Mary G. Landis. *Building a Successful Marriage.* Seventh Edition. Englewood Cliffs, New Jersey: Prentice-Hall, 1977.

Tseng, Wen-Shing; John F. McDermott, Jr.; Thomas W. Maretzki; and Gardiner B. Jones, editors. *Adjustment in Intercultural Marriage.* Honolulu: Department of Psychiatry, University of Hawaii, 1977.

ABOUT THE AUTHOR

Dr. R. Lanier (Lanny) Britsch, professor of history and graduate coordinator of the history department at Brigham Young University, received his bachelor's and master's degrees from Brigham Young University and his Ph.D. from Claremont Graduate School.

He has served in the Church as a high councilor in the BYU Thirteenth Stake. His previous callings include first counselor in the Orem, Sharon Stake presidency, high councilor, president of the BYU Asian Students Branch, and elders quorum president.

He and his wife, JoAnn, are the parents of six children.

12

Intimacy
Christopher M. Wallace

Troubled couples often feel that it is impossible for them ever to "become one." It isn't realistic, they've decided. The ideal of intimacy is often criticized by those who argue that such "idealistic" thinking burdens with guilt or despair those who are struggling with "reality." But when ideals are discarded or discounted in the name of being realistic, the visions of what relationships between a husband and wife could be are eclipsed. Where there is no vision, people (and marriages) perish.

Faith and hope are the foundation of our ideals, of what we consider possible. The way humans hold ideals is what makes reality possible. Intimacy, the ideal relationship, is obtainable and real, but it rests on the willingness of a husband and wife to see that possibility.

What Is Intimacy?

An intimate relationship includes closeness, confidence, familiarity, and trust. In marriage, it is an ideal relationship sought by a husband and wife. It is a relationship that has much to do with a couple's spirituality, authenticity, and obedience. It reveals and bonds the deepest feelings of their hearts. Intimacy is a relationship that a husband and a wife actively work out *together*.

The Lord spoke to Joseph Smith on the subject of togetherness: "And again, verily I say unto you, that . . . marriage is ordained of God unto man." (D&C 49:15.) It is not without reason that the Lord stated that the only way a man and a woman should live together in a sexual relationship is within the bounds of marriage. God has set boundaries that will result in an intimate relationship if couples will stay within these boundaries. Marriage is merely an outward ordinance or exercise that reveals the nature of inward mutual commitments. Intimacy symbolizes commitment to one's spouse and to the whole marital relationship. Certainly neither a marriage ceremony nor a marriage certificate binds a man and a woman together; rather, it is their individual commitments to each other, to their parents, and to any children that they might bring into this world that binds them together. This means that intimacy cannot be fully understood outside the context of love over time, of commitment, of responsibility, of sacrifice, and of family relationships across generations.

From the beginning, God has spoken of intimacy in marriage in terms of oneness. He said to Adam and Eve, "Therefore shall a man leave his father and mother, and shall cleave unto his wife: and they shall be one flesh." (Genesis 2:24.) God pronounced this commandment and his other creations as "very good." (Genesis 1:31.) The phrase 'one flesh' has meanings on at least two levels, physical and spiritual. President Spencer W. Kimball noted this when he said, "The Bible celebrates sex and its proper use, presenting it as God-created, God-ordained, God-blessed. It makes plain that God himself implanted the physical magnetism between the sexes for two reasons: for the propagation of the human race, and for the expression of that kind of love between man and wife that makes for true *oneness*. His commandment to the first man and woman to be one flesh was as important as his command to 'be fruitful and multiply.'" (*Ensign*, May, 1974, pp. 7-8; italics added.)

This idea of working to attain oneness is analogous to the concept of becoming a soul, where a soul is oneness of flesh and spirit, where the flesh willingly complies to or is submissive to the spirit. As individuals are perfected through faith, repentance, forgiveness, service, and love, oneness is obtained through a wedding of flesh and spirit. This pattern cannot be discarded by couples seeking intimacy. As both individuals in the marriage strive to become like Christ by giving their hearts to each other in faith and love, they become one as a couple.

The Lord has counseled husbands on marriage and intimacy, commanding, "Thou shalt love thy wife with all thy heart, and shalt cleave unto her and none else." (D&C 42:22.) The Lord commands husbands to do four things in this verse. First, they are commanded to *love* their wives; not to just like, nor to merely be a friend, but to love their wives in the same spirit and willingness as they would love their God. Secondly, husbands are commanded to love their wives with *all* their hearts—not 80 percent or even 95 percent, but with 100 percent of their hearts. This may also mean that this loving is to be undertaken all the time. Thirdly, they are commanded to *cleave* unto their wives, to adhere closely to their wives in times of trouble, to love them when they are seemingly hardest to love. And, fourth, adding much to the initial three, the Lord commands husbands to cleave to *none* else, not to their mothers or fathers or friends, but only to their wives.

When a husband or a wife has a problem, a challenge, or a joyful experience, to whom should they go for help, for wisdom, or to share? It may very well be that when husbands and wives turn to each other to face problems and challenges, they will learn about how to love and become godlike in ways that cannot be learned by solving problems with people other than one's spouse. Joseph F. Smith addressed this idea when he said, "The lawful association of the sexes is ordained of God, not only as the sole means of race perpetuation, but for the development of the higher faculties and nobler traits of human nature, which love-inspired companionship of man and woman alone can insure." (*Improvement Era*, June 1917, p. 739.)

This does not mean that a wife or a husband cannot seek wisdom and learning from others; only that when husbands or wives seek answers to their problems *only* from others, these couples do themselves a disservice.

Intimacy or oneness has three inseparable and interconnected parts: one flesh, one heart, and one mind. Moroni wrote about faith, hope, and charity and their relationship. (See Moroni 10.) He wrote that followers of Christ needed each virtue to be saved in the kingdom of God and that they couldn't develop one without concurrently developing the other two. That is, in order to have faith, they must also have hope and charity. Furthermore, the degree to which a man or a woman has charity will be directly proportional to the degree of faith and hope they have obtained. In similar manner, a husband and wife can be of one heart only as much as they are of one mind and of one flesh. Or, they can be of one flesh only as much as they are of one mind and of one heart. It is interesting that all the virtues that could be listed that a husband and a wife need to develop to be of one flesh (fidelity, sacrifice, respect, love, patience, and so on) are the same godly virtues needed to become of one heart or one mind.

How Is Intimacy Achieved?

While intimacy is not a physical act, physical actions may be expressions of intimacy. For example, sexual intercourse is but one way that intimacy can be expressed physically, and other ways include a hug, verbal support, disclosure of personal commitment, a smile, or the shedding of a tear in sorrow or joy. While the physical expressions of intimacy may have much to do with becoming one flesh, sexual intercourse is, ultimately, more an expression of "psychology" than physiology. That is, the physical pleasure quickly fades, but feelings of closeness, trust, and intimacy are enduring. Moreover, it seems that intimacy is the by-product of obedient, virtuous marital relationships. This is a major reason why becoming one flesh will be accomplished in the same manner as becoming one heart and one mind. The spiritual dimension of intimacy transcends all others.

When God commands us, it is possible to obey with his help. (See 1 Nephi 3:7 and Moses 1:10.) If he commands us to develop godlike appetites and passions rather than carnal, sensual, and devilish appetites and passions, it will be possible. (See 2 Nephi 2:25-28 and Mosiah 3:19.) So the possibility of attaining oneness is real. It means becoming one in body and spirit; it means keeping appetites, behaviors, thoughts, and passions within the bounds that God has commanded.

Until a husband and wife are willing to take such a possibility seriously, there will be no escape from their lack of intimacy. When they spurn the possibility of the ideal, they remain helpless in the less-than-ideal world they insist on living in. Is intimacy possible? If so, where, or in whom, does intimacy begin? It begins in the heart of each individual working and striving toward individual perfection. Such individuals invite their mates to follow. This is the principle of "light cleaving unto light." (See D&C 88:40.)

What about Couples Who Have Problems?

How can these ideas be relevant to a man whose wife is constantly critical, or to a woman whose husband avoids giving her affection? Such circumstances do not come because the ideal is unobtainable, but because at least one of the individuals has abandoned the pursuit of that ideal. One indication of an individual's abandonment will be his insistence that it is his wife's fault that intimacy is lacking or nonexistent in their relationship.

Where only one spouse, wife or husband, is earnestly striving to be Christlike, oneness cannot be attained. Oneness must be actively worked out together. For instance, a husband and wife will not be able to be intimate when she is domineering, when he is hard-hearted, or when both are selfish. No matter how much energy they expend, the couple will not have intimacy unless each begins working to change. Of course, a criticized husband could have gained such virtues as long-suffering, meekness, and love unfeigned; a neglected wife could have gained compassion and charity. People in emotionally or physically distant marriages must focus first on their own attitudes and behaviors, not on their partners', if they are to pursue intimacy.

How You Can Help

If you want to help a couple who is troubled by the absence of intimacy in their marriage, then you can teach them the meaning of intimacy (teach correct principles), show them the difference between how the world sees intimacy and what God offers us concerning intimacy (offer them the ideal), and question them about their own attitudes and behaviors regarding the possibility of intimacy in their own relationship (invite them to *act* on correct principles).

Imagine a husband and a wife coming to you, each complaining that the other is emotionally distant. You ask questions to clarify your understanding of their relationship in terms of intimacy. You might ask about the strength of their commitments to their relationship, about being faithful and trusting, about their willingness to repent or forgive, and so on. That is, you invite them to ponder their own commitments and behaviors. Are they willing to acknowledge the possibility of becoming intimate? Are they willing to seek such closeness? What are they willing to do to achieve intimacy?

Only through their individual commitments to be willing to do what is necessary to become intimate can they begin to see each other honestly enough to help them solve their problems and develop intimacy. Your questioning will reveal the symptoms that express their lack of oneness. You can then teach the three facets of intimacy: one flesh, one heart, and one mind.

A bishop shared with me certain tasks that he assigns to couples that have problems concerning intimacy. After he has assessed that the problem is a relationship problem and not a medical one, he instructs the couple to read and discuss together a list of specific scriptures. (On occasion, your questioning will reveal that a sexual problem might be physical. In order to confirm this hypothesis, you will need to refer the couple to a competent physician [a gynecologist for the wife and a urologist for the husband]. Even when surgical procedures are necessary to correct the problems, you may still be in a position to help this couple grow in intimacy.) After they have read the scriptures, he asks them to examine their individual behaviors and attitudes in the spirit of the scriptures to ascertain how each personally adds to or detracts from their intimacy. Their final task is to write a letter (which is not mailed) to their parents, whether living or dead, sharing what they have learned about how it is possible to achieve intimacy in marriage.

I asked this bishop what results he obtained; he said the following case is typical. Jim and Barbara had come to him complaining about some problems in their sexual relationship. Infrequency and a lack of interest were Jim's accusations of his wife. Barbara countered by complaining about Jim's insensitivity, his begging to have sex, his never appreciating that she is exhausted after a long day with their four preschool-age children.

The bishop said he felt that any counsel he might have given at this time would not be readily received. His initial questions and suggestions had been met with, "Yes, but she never initiates anything sexual," or "Oh, I've tried everything. You don't know what it's like to live with a man like that!" So the bishop gave them his assignment. This is a partial list of the scriptures he handed them:
Genesis 1:27-28, 31; 2:24
Matthew 22:37-39
1 Corinthians 7:3-4
Ephesians 5:21-33
Titus 2:4-5
Doctrine and Covenants 25; 29:34-35; 42:22-24, 29; 64:8-10; 121:33-46
Moses 5:2-5

After the couple had pondered the verses and written their letters, they again met with the bishop. Here is an excerpt from Jim's letter:

> What I've learned the most from these last two days is that I've never really believed that the gospel had answers to our problems. Moroni speaks of faith, hope, and charity. He said that we must have each quality to be saved and that we couldn't have any one without the others.
>
> So if Barbara and I want to be of one heart, we have to be of one mind and one flesh also. Lately, we've been having more and more fights, and I have been blaming Barbara. As you know, the doctor told us that if Barb got pregnant again, it would probably kill her

because of the blood clots. Well, for the last two years we have not had sex unless I begged. And I resented the doctor giving Barb all the power in our sexual relationship. But when I read Paul's counsel about our bodies, I realized that I have been seeking my own gratification. Well, I went to Barbara to apologize, and one week later she came to me and told me that she would like to have another baby. I've got to think about that. I sure don't want to lose her.

Barbara wrote this:

I am so excited. Jim and I have been talking with the bishop, and he told us to read some scriptures and discuss them prayerfully and faithfully. I was so mad when the bishop asked us if we were having problems in our sexual relationship. The last thing I wanted to hear was some man telling me to submit to my husband. But the bishop didn't do that. He asked me if I was giving my heart (not my body) totally to Jim. Well, that night we were reading in the New Testament when it hit me that I've been using the blood clots as a way to blame Jim for our problems. I've wept bitter tears for the loneliness I have served myself. I never thought of myself as selfish, but I sure have been. We also talked about what it means to have God command us to have sex. We learned that we are of one flesh only as much as we are of one mind and one heart. When I accused Jim of never being willing to just hold me without always wanting to have sex, it was my way of avoiding sex. I've finally figured out that being one flesh is mostly spiritual, and that sex is only a physical expression of our closeness.

This couple discovered much about intimacy because they didn't give up on the idea. Often couples are unwilling to consider that real solutions to their lack of intimacy lie in the gospel. For the most part, those who are helped are the ones who return to the simple truths of the gospel. These people do not feel that the Church or those in authority are burdening them when they ask them to work toward becoming of one heart, one mind, and one flesh. They are willing to bring their ideals to bear upon reality.

What Keeps People from Becoming Intimate?

In these latter days, many have sought intimacy through spurious avenues. Some have sought oneness outside the bonds of marriage. Elder Boyd K. Packer has noted, "However much they hope to find in a relationship of that kind, they will lose more. Living together without marriage destroys something inside all who participate. Virtue, self-esteem, and refinement of character wither away. Claiming that it will not happen does not prevent the loss; and these virtues, once lost, are not easily reclaimed. To suppose that one day they may nonchalantly change their habits and immediately claim all that might have been theirs had they not made a mockery of marriage is to suppose something that will not be." (*Ensign*, May 1981, p. 13.)

Others are seeking intimacy but have confused it with sexual gratification. Yet others strive for oneness without seeking to develop in their relationship the principles the Lord admonishes his people to found their family lives upon. (See, for example, D&C 121:33-46.) Certainly such principles as honesty, respect, modesty, sacrifice, compassion, fidelity, commitment, forgiveness, and cooperation, to name a few, are essential for quality marital (and family) relationships. If even *one* of these principles is lacking, honesty, for example, the quality of every other principle is affected—changed. For dishonesty replaces honesty, and where there is dishonesty, respect, loyalty, understanding, and so on begin to erode away and are replaced by other less than ideal foundations. What does all this mean? What would marriage be without virtues? Is intimacy possible without commitment or compassion? When the quality of the principles and virtues is poor, the quality of the whole relationship will be poor.

How wise is it for a woman to marry a man who tells her that he would like to marry her, but who will commit himself fully only after an evaluation of the first five years of marriage? What problems are evidenced in marriages where commitment is less than total on the part of one or both partners? When commitment falters, intimacy will quickly flee. Evidence of waning commitment may surface in their communication, their sexual relationship, or their childrens' behavior. What is the solution if a spouse has not committed himself to such virtues as honesty, fidelity, trust, justice, forgiveness, repentance, and sacrifice? When either or both spouses withhold themselves from nourishing, protecting, or caring for their intimate relationship, what can be done to solve the problem?

Deal with Causes, Not Symptoms

It is by working with causes, not symptoms, that you can best help couples. When symptoms are the only issues dealt with, Band-Aids are applied and the more fundamental problems are evidenced in other areas of the couples' relationships. This is not unlike dealing with the symptom of tobacco-stained teeth by using tooth-whitening toothpaste. Such an approach assumes in advance that smokers are either unwilling or unable to give up smoking. The Lord said, "Wherefore, men are free according to the flesh. . . . And they are free to choose liberty . . . or to choose captivity." (2 Nephi 2:27.) Likewise, problems of intimacy are more an exercise of agency, not the result of incompatabilities. They are the result of selfishness and hardheartedness. The point is not that couples cannot achieve intimacy, but that they *will* not. They will find it impossible to become intimate precisely because they require changes in their spouse rather than attitudinal changes in themselves. One client said he could love his wife if she could just keep a pitcher of orange juice in the refrigerator. The counselor told this husband, "I can get your wife to keep the juice in the refrigerator and you will have your reward, but don't think it will be intimacy—it will be cold orange juice." When a husband or a wife falsely insists that intimacy depends more on their spouse's behavior than on their own commitments to their spouse, they will fail to achieve intimacy.

Asking couples the following questions will help you understand the fundamental issues pertinent to their problems:

1. Without worrying about what your spouse might do, what are *you* willing to do to become intimate?

2. If you were to give your heart and mind to your spouse, what would you do to develop intimacy?

3. If you were to see your spouse in a way that did not

blame him (or her) for the lack of intimacy, what would you then see and feel about your responsibility to become intimate?

4. Explain what you understand about having to repent of your hostile feelings toward your spouse (instead of insisting that your hostility is *because of* your spouse).

5. Explain how you see your responsibility to promote intimacy. What would it mean to forgive your spouse of any of his (or her) offenses against you?

6. Imagine that you are becoming the best possible spouse a person could have. What virtues, qualities, and habits do you have as you see yourself as this better spouse? Now, what would you have to do to begin this self-improvement?

7. If your spouse is unwilling to make the first step, what are you willing to do?

SUGGESTED READINGS

Mosiah 3:19; 5:2

Alma 5

Moroni 7

James 1:19-20

John 3:19-20

Luke 17:1-5

D&C 64:8-10

ABOUT THE AUTHOR

Christopher M. Wallace studied at Sarah Lawrence College and Brigham Young University. He has been curriculum director of a multistate project that teaches family life and ethics in the public schools. He is completing doctoral studies in marriage and family therapy. In the Church, he has served as a Sunday School teacher and in a bishopric. He and his wife, Debbie, are the parents of three children.

13

Families As Systems
James M. Harper

The family is the great eternal unit. It can be an unending source of love, strength, and growth for its members. When it functions well, the family is one of our most important human resources. President Joseph F. Smith emphasized the eternal nature of the family:

> Who are there besides the Latter-day Saints who contemplate the thought that beyond the grave we will continue in the family organization? the father, the mother, the children recognizing each other in the relations which they owe to each other and in which they stand to each other? This family organization being a unit in the great and perfect organization of God's work, and all destined to continue throughout time and eternity. We are living for eternity and not merely for the moment. (*Gospel Doctrine*, p. 277.)

Most of us assume that we understand how families operate because we have had "on-the-job" experience as a family member. However, what appears to be obvious about our own families may not help us understand how family processes go awry. A prerequisite to helping families is a working knowledge of the principles of family organization and functioning.

The Family as a System

Imagine Maria, a fifteen-year-old daughter in the High-strum family. Maria frequently fails to attend high-school classes, sneaks out of the home to meet boys even though her parents feel she is too young to date, and runs around with the "wrong crowd." At home Mrs. Highstrum constantly finds herself in battles with Maria and fears she will drive her away. The father voices his disapproval of his daughter's behavior, but he claims it falls on deaf ears. Both parents are terrified of Maria's involvement in drugs and her decreasing church activity.

To an outside observer it is easy to recognize that Maria is in trouble, but it is not as easy to recognize how Maria is constantly pulled into conflicts between other family members. An outside observer may have a great deal of information about Maria and her parents as individuals, but he may not know very much about the characteristics of their relationships with each other.

Visualize the following Saturday morning in the Highstrum home. Dad is reading the paper in the family room, and Mom passes by Maria's room and notices that it is a mess. She finds her daughter in the kitchen and proceeds to scold her, and Maria responds by screaming. Ignoring the commotion, Father continues to read in the family room. As the noise level escalates, he decides to leave the house to run some errands. Mom starts to feel guilty as she realizes that the intensity of her anger does not fit the deed—a messy room. But when Mrs. Highstrum discovers that once again Father has escaped the "trials of parenting," she flies into full-blown rage. At this point Maria is vaguely aware that her mother's explosion is an overflow of the underlying but unresolved tension between her parents. Mother is resentful of having to shoulder the full burden of discipline. Maria, too, feels victimized as she receives the brunt of Mother's emotion and resents her father's emotional absence, which prevents him from coming to her aid. When Father finally comes home, he cracks down on Maria.

What started as a focus on one troubled teenager shifts to a complex and powerful set of interconnections between family members. Who is to blame for Maria's delinquency? At one level, every family member has part of the blame because their individual behaviors fit together and feed on each other. However, on an individual level, Maria must be responsible for her choices as must other members of the family.

This characteristic of interconnectedness makes the family a system in that it is organized so that change in one or more parts of the family is usually accompanied by change in other parts. In the case of the Highstrum family, one cannot completely understand Maria's behavior without considering mother-daughter and father-daughter interaction. But one can't really comprehend the mother-daughter relationship or the father-daughter relationship except in the context of the marriage. Three basic principles will help in your attempts to understand and help families.

1. Understanding the personalities of each individual in a family does not mean you understand the family. Observing interaction in the entire family yields a more accurate understanding.

2. A change in one member of the family is usually accompanied by a change in other members.

3. Although it may appear that only one person in the family needs professional help, the entire family often contributes to the problem because of the "fit" of their behaviors. If professional help becomes necessary, it is usually beneficial to involve the entire family, not just a single individual.

Family Structure

Every family develops systematic ways of being a family with particular forms of solving problems, communicating, handling affection and closeness, responding to requirements for change, expressing emotion, and dealing with crises. These patterns of relationships among family members are referred to as *structure*.

One way of thinking about family structure is to focus on the composition of family groups across more than one generation. Examining a three-generational structure of grandparents, parents, and children can help you to help the family understand their current problem.

Intergenerational Structure: The Genogram

One of the themes that emerges in the study of families is the patterns that tend to repeat themselves over the generations. This led observers of family life to develop a diagram called the genogram that allows issues in a family to be studied in relation to one another. In reality the genogram is a "psychological" family tree.

Figure 1 is a three-generation genogram of the Highstrum family. It shows how Maria's behaviors fit with the rest of the family. Maria is the second of four children. By examining the relationships in the child generation, we discover that Maria and her younger sister, Chris, do not get along (as indicated by a wavy line). This is complicated further by the fact that Chris and Mom have a very close relationship (as indicated by parallel lines). Maria feels like an outsider because she experiences conflict with both Mom and Chris. Marital tensions do exist in the family, but the conflict is not out in the open. Father has a strong bond to

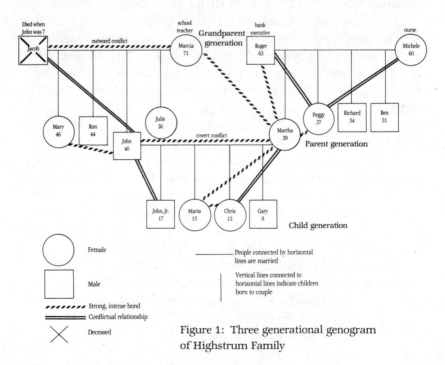

Figure 1: Three generational genogram of Highstrum Family

John, the oldest child, whereas Mother ties into Chris. One could infer that these strong parental bonds with John and Chris may do real harm to the marriage because the parents can avoid resolving their conflict by spending time with their children.

In looking at John, Sr.'s family of origin, we discover that he was also very close to his father, who died when John, Sr., was seven. His parents' marriage exhibited outward conflict, and his mother never remarried after his father's death. John, Sr., reports that his mother still disapproves of his marriage to Martha, who confirms his report by making derogatory remarks about her mother-in-law. Martha is the first child in her family. She reports poor relationships with her father and her younger sister, Peggy, who was the parents' favorite.

This genogram permits us to draw several conclusions about the Highstrums. First, John, Sr., the husband, repeats the pattern of marital conflict that he witnessed in his parents' family. One also has to wonder if the fact that John was in conflict with his older sister Mary doesn't influence his present behavior with his wife, who was the first child in her parents' family. Secondly, in examining Mom's relationship with her daughter, Maria, it is possible that unresolved issues with Peggy, Mom's sister, surface in the mother-daughter battles. Thirdly, in the closeness of their relationship, Mom and Chris unintentionally isolate Maria. Lastly, the parents don't have to resolve their marital conflict because they have children with whom they are close. Will a change in Maria's individual behavior help? It would, but a reorganization of several family relationships might facilitate change more quickly. It is usually very informative to construct a three-generational genogram when working with a family. The family can help bring meaning to the diagram and can teach themselves about the overall patterns in their relationships.

Boundaries: Who's Who in This Organization?

Boundaries are like invisible fences in families. You can't see them, but when you cross over them, they are forcibly brought to your awareness. These are the forces in the family that regulate the flow of people and ideas. For example, a father might say to his son, "I don't want to hear you talk that way again." A boundary has been set in which the son is expected to function. These limits are important because they give guidelines to prevent individuals from coming into contact with what the family considers undesirable.

There are six levels of boundaries in an intact family. The most basic is the individual. Each of us regulates the kind of information about ourselves that we allow others to receive, and we also screen out input that is offensive or irrelevant. The concept of interpersonal space assumes that each individual has a comfortable level of physical closeness to others. When someone crosses over that boundary, he retreats physically.

The second boundary involves two-person relationships such as husband-wife, parent-child, and sibling-sibling. It would be inappropriate for a child to discuss the same things with his mother that his father discusses with her; the marital boundary would be violated.

The third boundary exists when three people are together. The best example is the father-mother-child relationship. When parents are trying to talk with a particular child, and a brother or sister interrupts, the parents might ask the "intruder" to wait or even to leave the room. When this happens, the child quickly senses the boundary he was told not to cross.

The fourth boundary involves the relationship between the individual and the entire family. A family council imposing some family rules on a child would be an example. The fifth and sixth levels of boundary concern exchanges of information between individuals and the outside world and between the family as a whole and the outside world.

Families get into trouble when they fail to establish limits at each boundary, but, conversely, boundaries that are too strict make it hard for a family to adjust to new changes in their life. Suppose, for instance, that a mother and son form a relationship around which a strong boundary exists. The two spend a great deal of time talking and having fun together, but the other family members find it difficult to cross the boundary and interact with mother or son. The father eventually becomes resentful because he feels left out.

In another case, a family member might not share what she did at school or work. The boundary around her and the outside world is so impermeable that other family members have no idea what she does during the day. Such boundaries can lead to emotional isolation called *disengagement*. Disengaged families preserve separateness between people but handicap open communication and closeness.

However, it is possible for a family to have too much closeness. Members can have a powerful sense of belonging but give up their autonomy. This condition is called *enmeshment*, and it is similar to being glued to one another: it's great to be together, but you can't get unstuck.

A family with a greater degree of openness is able to accept messages from its environment and to adapt to what it hears. Some families tend to shut out or distort information in order to avoid upsetting an established pattern. For example, if an ecclesiastical leader suggests to a husband that he needs to treat his wife differently, can the family handle the message and change, or does the message become distorted? A family's ability to hear messages both within the family and from the environment is a primary indicator of its psychological health.

Figure 2 illustrates two characteristics of family boundaries. The horizontal line represents closeness, from disengagement to enmeshment. The vertical line represents ways of responding to information from the environment. A chaotic response could be inconsistent, random, irrational, or unpredictable behavior. Rigid responses are so unvarying and rule-bound that they seem to ignore changes in the environment. An example of a chaotic response to news of a child's suspension from school might be a mother throwing dishes or a father going to the photo album to look at pictures of the child when in kindergarten.

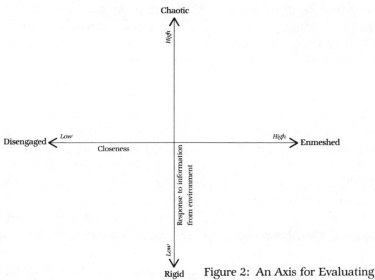

Figure 2: An Axis for Evaluating
Characteristics of Family Boundaries

The following questions will help you decide where a family fits on the diagram in figure 2.

Degree of openness within the family and in response to the environment:

1. What kind of leadership exists in the family (shared or just one person)?

2. Are family rules clear and stable (or seldom clear and change so often that things are chaotic)?

3. Are limits set at each boundary? Moderation in all things is the key. (Either too strict or too permissive boundaries will create family trouble. The guideline should be Doctrine and Covenants 121:34-46, where specific warning is given against compulsion, pride, control, unrighteous dominion, hypocrisy, and guile.)

4. To what degree will the family permit open flow of information between family members?

5. To what degree does the family relate to its environment? Can it receive new information from its environment and respond in flexible ways? (A good indication of this is how the family relates to the school system.)

Degree of closeness:

1. How often does the family spend time playing together?

2. How independent or dependent are family members?

3. How often do individuals make their own decisions?

4. Do family members share information with each other?

5. Are family members separated, close, or smothered?

Coalitions and the Marital Bond

Husbands and wives who put each other first in their lives offer children the greatest heritage they can receive, the example and security of a good marriage. Sometimes, however, parents become closer to their children than to each other. Children might even try to get one parent to side with them against the other. Spouses do not usually intend this to happen, but when they spend more time with children's concerns than with each other's, the result can be a weakened marital bond.

Consider the case of a young Latter-day Saint couple with two children. He was just beginning a promising business career and felt that extra time at work would give him the boost he needed. Papers brought home, business trips, general work stress, and church assignments all contributed to the husband's lack of time with his family. The wife didn't mind because she wanted to support him in his successes. As the children grew older, the patterns continued, and the mother became very close to both children because she spent so much time caring for them. Even when Dad was at home, the kids related better to Mom than they did to him, so he felt left out. This feeling of isolation at home led to his increased involvement with work and church.

In this situation a coalition had formed between the wife and children to the exclusion of the father. The couple were not aware of the consequences of their decision to follow these paths. Nevertheless, the coalition grew out of a situation their decisions had created. The only other bond that should be as strong as the marital commitment is our relationship with the Lord. When other coalitions form that are stronger than these two bonds, families experience trouble.

Likewise, people and activities outside the family can have a stronger hold on a member than the family. Work, church, leisurely activities, and friends can interfere with family relationships, especially the marriage.

Listening to a conversation at the dinner table can serve to identify coalitions in a family. When two family members carry on a conversation and ignore a third member, a coalition is in operation. When two family members make a decision for a third, coalitions are operating. Children who exhibit problems such as delinquency, drug use, and sexual promiscuity are usually on the low end of several family coalitions. Ecclesiastical leaders can strengthen family structure by encouraging husband and wife bonds as primary. Any other coalitions with children, grandparents, outsiders, or activities should supplement, and not replace, the marital bond. The Savior taught that when two people marry, they are no more two people but one flesh. (Matthew 19:4-6.) Their oneness does not imply that they are one person but rather that they are like the Father and Son, one in purpose, feelings, and goals.

Communication

Families should listen to one another and then question or comment in constructive ways on what they hear. When boundaries are rigid and closeness is lacking, it is more difficult for each member to hear the others even when positive things are said.

Family communication can be evaluated on dimensions of quantity and quality. A common cliche tells us that "quality time is what counts." Although there is some truth to that saying, the *amount* of time a family spends sharing information together is also crucial. A few minutes of "quality" time does not create the same feeling in families that more time can. However, all the time in the world does a family little good if it lacks quality.

How can the quality of family communication be evaluated? By considering the following issues:

1. Is there variety in the topics discussed? Ideally, topics might range from current events, good literature, movies, and politics to interpersonal relationships, feelings, and family dynamics.

2. Are topics discussed until they are resolved? One of the problems in dysfunctional families is that several topics are briefly discussed but no one topic is pursued to its finish. Interruptions, topic changes, and irrelevant issues distract the family from their task.

3. What do the messages imply about relationships? Are comments made in a loving, friendly manner or in an aggressive assault? A parent can say the same words to two different children, but one message may sound like an armed truce while the other implies tenderness.

4. Ratio of agreements and disagreements. In quality communication people are able to disagree without being assaultive, and differences are received as contributions. However, the total communication contains more agreement than disagreement. If a family has an expectation that everyone must be "nice," members may feel unnecessarily guilty about expressing their real wishes and needs.

5. Intensity of expression. Family members should be able to communicate emotions of fear, sadness, affection, and exhilaration, among others, but these expressions can be of such intensity that other family members become overwhelmed and appear insensitive.

6. Speaking order. Quality in this respect means that family members do not speak for each other and that every family member is allowed to speak. When you meet a family, you can watch who speaks to whom, who gets left out, and who interrupts. For example, the parents may try to talk to each other while the children interrupt. Or while the father talks, no one listens; but when the mother talks, everyone listens except the father.

7. Commitment. Do family members respond to each others' requests with clear messages about what they are willing to do? The healthy family is able to achieve results. If family members agree to do something but do not follow through, commitment is not strong enough or other prob-

lems are diverting the family from their decisions. Helping family members make clear, direct requests will minimize problems with follow-through.

Time Dimensions in the Family

Time plays an important part in family life because our daily schedules revolve around it. Most families are unaware of the effect that scheduling has on them, but nevertheless time has its influence. You should evaluate the family's daily and weekly schedules in your attempts to understand how the family functions.

Consider the family in which both the father and mother are involved in church and civic responsibilities. During a particular week, they are both very busy and away from home several nights. Toward the end of the week, their two oldest boys seem to argue about trivial matters, such as whether their forks cross an arbitrary line on the dinner table. In fact, all of the children seem on edge. What these parents may fail to realize is that the tempo of their life influences the mood and conflict in the family. By slowing down the fast pace of activities, a family can often reduce conflict between children.

In another example, members of a family were too busy to eat most meals together. With the convenience of microwave technology, teenage children heated the prepared food and generally ate alone. It was little wonder that the people in the family became isolated and emotionally distant from each other. It is always informative to chart by hour each family member's daily activities for a week. This type of record helps the family evaluate its use of time.

Behavior occurs in patterns, and it is not uncommon for families to experience cycles of conflict, mood, and communication. For example, a husband and wife were experiencing a period of discouragement. When a visiting teacher inquired about the wife's general welfare, she discovered that periods of discouragement occurred about every five months and lasted for two weeks. By asking about events that typically occur before these "down" periods, you can learn much about the cycle. It seems that this couple was very concerned about the school performance of their fifteen-year-old son. They received a report card usually about two weeks before their discouragement set in. Then for two weeks the parents discussed ways to help their son, but these discussions usually ended in disagreement, which created emotional distance in their marriage. With the loss of their usual support of each other, both marital partners became discouraged. Just understanding the events in such a cycle can be a starting point for a husband and wife to examine ways to break the cycle.

Another dimension of time in the family is the life cycle. Each family progresses through several stages, beginning with the marriage of husband and wife and ending with the death of both parents. The important thing to remember is that each stage requires the family to accomplish particular developmental tasks. In a family with mostly teenage children, a major task is balancing freedom and responsibility of the children. Many parents assume that the same forms of discipline that worked when the children were young will work when children are adolescents. The psychological task of the teenager is to become more independent, and when parents do not foster such growth, the families experience severe conflict. It is not the intent of this chapter to cover all of the family developmental tasks through the life cycle, but it is important for you to consider the developmental stages of the life cycle when working with families. You might ask yourself, What are the developmental needs of family members at a particular age and is the family organized to help meet those needs?

In one family a ten-year-old son was learning to play baseball, but his skills were not very well developed. The parents recognized that their son had two specific developmental needs that centered around playing baseball. First, he needed to learn the motor skills necessary to catch the ball with a glove, handle a bat, and run and slide to the bases. All of these skills would aid his physical development. Secondly, success in playing baseball would help him be socially accepted by his friends. The family was organized so that they could practice baseball together and help the ten-year-old develop his skills.

Functions of Family Behavior

As structure refers to the pattern of family relationships, function refers to the quality of family interaction. To evaluate function in a given family, you must determine the result of a set of interactions. In other words, what is the function or purpose of behaviors of the family members in regulating their relationships? The individuals cannot always tell you what the function is, so you must watch the entire family in action. To simply focus on the individual who has the problem is insufficient. All family relationships must be observed.

In the case of the Highstrum family cited earlier, the mother became hysterically upset with her daughter. What was the result of this interaction? One thing it did was to influence the father into the role of disciplinarian. He came home and cracked down on his daughter. Another consequence was that emotional distance in the marriage increased. Perhaps the episode even provided the mother with a sense of her parenting role. Although we're not completely convinced that these were the functions of the conflict, they are important guesses or considerations.

Often the function of family behavior is to maintain some long-standing pattern of relating to each other. Consider the marital bond in a family that was weak, and in which the predominant mood was anger. Whenever the parents began to fight openly, their four-year-old son went outside, doused himself with water, rolled in the dirt, and returned to his parents. Shocked by his appearance, the mother and father abruptly discontinued their fighting to attend to him. The child's behavior stopped his parents' arguments, and that was its function. Adolescent children often behave in such undesirable ways to maintain some degree of family unity. In such cases, it is important to focus on issues of family unity and not just the adolescent child.

When an outsider suggests that a family change in some

way, the response of the family can be defensive. Perhaps they become angry, silent, or even suggest problems that are not at the heart of the issue. The function of these behaviors is protection. The family has behaved in patterned ways for a long time and so seeks to remain that way. Outsiders can gently teach, illustrate, or demonstrate possible meanings of family patterns. They can point out structures and functions. They can offer knowledge to families that can provide the opportunity for the family to consider changes that are in the family's best interests.

SUGGESTED READINGS

Allred, G. Hugh. *How to Strengthen Your Marriage and Family.* Provo: Brigham Young University Press, 1976.

Galvin, Kathleen M. and Bernard J. Brommel. *Family Communication: Cohesion and Change.* Glenville, Illinois: Scott, Foresman and Company, 1982.

Miller, Jean R. *Family Focused Care.* New York: McGraw-Hill, 1980.

Willmot, William W. *Dyadic Communication: A Transactional Perspective.* Reading, Mass.: Addison-Wesley, 1979.

ABOUT THE AUTHOR

Dr. James M. Harper, associate professor and program director of the graduate marriage and family therapy program at Brigham Young University, received his bachelor's and master's degrees from that same university and his Ph.D. in counseling psychology from the University of Minnesota.

He is a licensed marriage and family therapist and has served as president of the Utah Association for Marriage and Family Therapy. His articles have appeared in a wide variety of publications.

He has served the Church as a mission president, a member of a bishopric, a high councilor, an elders quorum president, a Boy Scout leader, and a Sunday School teacher.

He and his wife, Colleen, are the parents of four children.

14

Spouse Abuse
W. Eugene Gibbons

Clearly the gospel neither teaches nor condones family violence, aggression, or abuse of any type. Yet some men justify and rationalize their physical abuse of their families on the basis of so-called religious principles. Often, in their defensiveness, they caution others that to interfere in their private life is the ultimate invasion of privacy and agency. They say that such an invasion is unconstitutional or even satanic. Still others protest that society authorizes them as fathers and husbands to discipline family members however they wish. Unfortunately, some Latter-day Saint parents also share these attitudes; Latter-day Saint families are not free of abuse. How can we who are counselors respond to those who abuse family members?

Attitudes Concerning Abuse

The counselor's task is complicated by the problem of differentiating between physical force and abuse. For centuries people have argued about whether a slap is a blow and whether a blow constitutes violence; and they argue whether it is right or wrong to strike at all. Thus, the most serious question a counselor may find himself struggling with is what constitutes abuse.

Because we live in a society where widely differing opinions about physical force are held, a lay counselor should not be embarrassed or dismayed if he realizes that the level of compulsion and force he has learned is out of harmony with what the gospel permits. He may feel that because society has "spared the rod," it has lost its ability to discipline and teach the present generation, or he may be horrified at the use of physical coercion and see such behavior as the ultimate expression of sin.

While there may be heated differences of opinion, Latter-day Saint counselors can find the only lasting answers in gospel principles. They must fuse those principles with careful study, deep commitment to family life, sorrow for the sinner, and change in the behavior of all involved in any kind of physical abuse.

Abuse: A Family Problem

A counselor needs to be concerned with the relationships that exist among the various individuals in the family. Sometimes the atmosphere includes a concern with the maintenance of power, control, and balance within the family unit. The abusive husband and the abused wife each represent a separate, distinct unit interacting within the larger family system, which is also a unique unit in interaction with broader society. When family violence occurs, it is possible that every family member is either a participant or a victim. Although all family members can usually be included in counseling, unfortunately some members sabotage change because, in their perverted view, the violence has come to serve a "necessary" function within the troubled family. Such a view has been found among many families suffering conflicts.

These families have developed a "system" of family abuse—a repetitive cycle or pattern where both the victims and the abuser "cooperate" in violence. Such patterns can even be transmitted across generations, and family members often become cynical about the possibility of change.

Professionals who work with family violence and spouse abuse have identified three characteristics of abusive and abused individuals. The first characteristic is low self-esteem (often rooted in past generations). It is characterized by the

violence that is a symptom of the pain that arises when a
person has a limited sense of personal worth. A second characteristic is the feeling of helplessness. A person with these
problems worries about how to control his life and environment. The abuser husband uses violence to "gain control."
Meanwhile, the victim lives in constant fear and is usually
convinced that she is powerless to do anything about the
problem. The third characteristic is that family members
find it difficult to identify, discuss, and solve their problems.
A typical abuser/abused couple sense that their dreams of a
happy marriage are slipping away. Their attempts to resolve
their difficulties sometimes result in violence and intensify
the problem.

Offering Help

There are a variety of issues and "dos" and "don'ts" that
lay counselors must keep in mind as they try to resolve problems of abuse. In addition, there are times when referral to
appropriate professional help is the only responsible course.

Abuse and violence must not be overlooked. They can be
life-threatening. *Violence is a criminal behavior that must be
stopped.* Protection of the abused person is the counselor's
first concern. It must be kept in mind, however, that the dynamics of chronic battering are usually complex. For example, a counselor's immediate reaction might be to encourage the abused wife and the children to either move in
with relatives or to move into a shelter for the abused. This
seems reasonable, but it does not take into account the possibility that such a decision may result in an episode even
more violent than any other episode previously experienced.
In addition, the wife may still feel that she loves or needs her
mate and that he doesn't really mean to harm her or the
children. She may be unable to see any pattern, sequence, or
cycle to the abuse and may sincerely believe it will stop. She
desires to end the violence but generally has no thought of
ending the relationship. Therefore, a lay counselor should
hesitate to suggest separation, even to a shelter or home, unless the victim rationally understands what she is doing, can

verbalize how she is feeling and thinking, and has weighed the consequences of her decision to leave the home. There are times when the abused individual needs to make a decision to leave home, but the decision must be hers, and it must include long-range plans. It must not be precipitous or impulsive. However, in cases of emergencies and violent episodes, short-term protection is essential. An abused wife may even need police protection or a place to relocate for a few hours. Even the ramifications of her remaining away overnight need careful evaluation. The abused wife needs help in understanding the consequences of her decisions; she must prepare to live with what might follow.

The abused wife needs understanding and support. Her view of reality must be respected. The counselor can expect her to be resistant and protective. She may feel that if change occurs the marriage will still eventually deteriorate. Usually, she is certain that help to stop the violence will not be forthcoming. She may not believe that there are helpers who really understand her situation. She fears that she is the only one who has ever experienced such a crisis. She is ashamed of her own inadequacy, of her inability to make decisions, and of the fact that her home is not happy. Because she is convinced that she must carry her burden alone, she needs empathic assistance in expressing and sharing her fears, pains, hopes, and ambivalent feelings about her husband.

One of the most helpful contributions a lay counselor can make is to help the abused woman reestablish control over her life. Her feelings of helplessness and hopelessness are devastating, but she can be counseled to see that problems can be addressed and that solutions can be found. She still has choices. Richard J. Anderson, a Utah social worker, suggests that the counselor should talk with the abused woman rationally, suggesting realistic choices, so that she may develop a new sense of control.[1] He should show her that she can gain by evaluating and selecting from a variety of alternatives. The counselor should help her to move away from all-or-nothing thinking, such as "Either stay in this relationship or have no relationship." Instead, she should be shown that she can leave, stay with the hope and commitment that things will change, seek individual or marital counseling, temporarily separate, stay and relinquish the hope that he will change, and so on. There are other options. The abused wife needs to feel that she has the power to change and control her life.

The abuser also needs help. If the primary purpose of intervention and counseling is to salvage the family, the counselor must not ignore or reject the offender. He needs the understanding, support, forgiveness, and counsel of someone who can influence him to change his behavior. He will probably not welcome this support, however. He will make it difficult for a counselor to counsel and may try almost anything to avoid a visit with a counselor. He is usually very resistant and does not believe anyone really cares about him or his side of the conflict. He will be extremely sensitive to any show of authority and will watch for attitudes and cues that suggest that the counselor's mind is already made up. The abuser needs to know that the counselor is committed to understanding his legitimate concerns, his pain, his anger, his isolation, his guilt, his frustration, and his disappointment about his marriage. Even though it may appear to others that he is out of control, he wants to believe that someone is willing to hear what he is attempting to do. He wants a valued person to understand his motives and hopes and not to view his behavior in isolation. Until he believes that the counselor understands him, he will not listen to counsel about his harmful behavior. It will be impossible to help him until he esteems the counselor as a friend. (See D&C 38:24-25.)

With trust established, a counselor can begin by teaching the family problem-solving and coping skills for dealing with everyday challenges. The counselor can show individual family members how to identify, talk about, and work through their stress, conflicts, and feelings. However, the counselor must remember that the abuser does not believe he can control his angry feelings. He invariably has difficulty expressing what he is experiencing and generally expresses emotions, such as frustration, guilt, and disappointment, in anger. He is convinced that he is victimized by his mate. He wonders why everyone is against him and why no one wants to hear his side of the story. In being angry and hurt, the abuser is bewildered that no one wants to nurture or comfort him. He is often unaware of his emotional conflicts and tends to express much of what he feels through exaggerated masculinity and violence.

The abused wife, too, has responsibility. She must be committed to change and not simply to a life of longsuffering. Her motto must be "I may be his excuse, but I will never be the reason for his abuse." The cycle cannot be changed if she continues to visualize herself as a helpless victim of her husband's rage. Even though the wife needs protection, empathy, and support, the counselor does her no favors if he charts a course for her that permits her to continue in the victim's role.

A Warning

Working with couples in abusive situations is a complicated process that should not be taken lightly. However, when a person does decide to work with and counsel a couple, he needs to remember that anger and stress are central factors in abuse. The counselor must work with these problems with the couple in a systematic way. In his article, "Structured Conjoint Therapy for Spouse Abuse Cases," John W. Taylor suggests that it is the responsibility of the counselor to promote personal responsibility for anger and stress; to show the connection between stress build-up and volatile anger levels; to point out and to begin to change the pattern of escalation of mutual anger and frustration; and to use rising anger and stress levels as warning signals that are preliminary to more harsh or violent behavior.[2]

Behavioral Hints of Stress or Abuse in Families

As a result of many years of counseling abusers and their families, Richard J. Anderson has developed a profile of the male abuser and the abused female.

Profile of the Abusing Male
1. Has low self-esteem—feels dependent, feels inferior, feels inadequate, sees self as a personal failure, has feelings of helplessness and abandonment.
2. Able to hide his failures, fears, and inadequacies from others. Has good social skills in public.
3. Is emotionally dependent, but usually this is recognized only by the family.
4. Is self-centered and does not delay gratification.
5. Harbors fears of being cheated by his wife (jealous, accusative). Disbelieves her protestations of innocence.
6. Uses spy tactics to control her (contains mate—restricts her social contacts more and more).
7. Expresses no sense of violating another's boundaries.
8. Insists forceable behavior is justified in that it is aimed at securing the family good.
9. Seems to have no guilt about incidents of abuse. Talks about them on an intellectual level.
10. Is sexually demanding and assaultive (experiences impotence at times).
11. Controls others by threatening homocide or suicide. Often attempts one or both when spouse leaves.
12. Often has a history of family violence as an abused child or as a witness of his father abusing his mother.
13. Has a poor relationship with his father.

Profile of Abused Female
1. Endures frustration.
2. May exhibit depression and stress and have psychosomatic complaints.
3. May be a high risk for home accidents. May secretly use drugs and alcohol.
4. Seems to possess unlimited patience to "solve" marriage problems. Clings to minor promises as a hope for change in the future.
5. Describes herself only in terms of her family.
6. Expresses low self-esteem.
7. Has poor social skills.

8. Feels restricted and trapped.

9. Often accepts blame for husband's wrongdoing, believes her own behavior is provocative, and does not assess the degree of her danger.

10. Clings to the belief that acceptance of violent behavior will lead to long-term resolution of the problem.

11. Has a poor sexual self-image. Assumes the role of rape victim in marriage.

12. Frequently considers suicide and makes minor attempts. Thinks about homocide, but more rarely.

13. Loves husband but is afraid of him—does not understand her ambivalence and feels crazy.

14. Wants to stay in the marriage. She is not ready to give it up, but she does not want to be hurt.

Review of Abusers' Attitudes

A general profile can be drawn of the husband and wife in abusive interaction. Invariably, the male abuser tries to confuse the issue of abuse and to legitimatize his actions by suggesting that his experience is unique to him and his family. He needs to be affirmed as a unique, worthy individual, but a counselor must not become distracted or sidetracked by his denials or rationalizations. The abuser is usually much like other abusers, and the abused is quite like others who are abused. Often, when abuse is a pattern, couples set up implicit or explicit rules that govern their behavior as well as a subset of rules about how each partner may behave with respect to those rules. Thus, if a couple sets a rule about fidelity, they also set a rule about which partner may define, violate, or change the rule.

Conclusion

If couples are serious in their desire to stop the abusive pattern and to improve their marital relationships, they will begin to take responsibility for their individual behavior and to acknowledge the many little games they play and the skill with which they provoke one another. Only as couples begin to treat their mates with respect, and only as they begin to give one another positive attention and nurturing, can they change.

Summary of Counseling Guidelines

1. Abuse must stop immediately—you must not accept a couple's suggestion to "taper off."

2. Abuse is a complex problem. You should help the family implement a variety of changes as well as new attitudes and skills. Teach problem-solving skills. Understand certain emotions as signals of problems.

3. The abuser needs to be loved and understood so that he can change. In addition, however ambivalent the abused wife may appear, she probably still loves her husband and is committed to the marriage.

4. The victim must work toward change and make a commitment not to endure abuse. She must agree to help restructure the husband-wife and family interaction.

5. The abuser must be helped to see that he can learn to deal with his anger and frustration in ways that do not hurt others.

6. Abuse is but a symptom of deeper emotional problems—usually neither the abuser nor the abused feels very good about themselves.

7. Members of a family need support to change.

8. At some point the family must be addressed as a unit. They need help in understanding their relationships, their attitudes, their communication, and their skills of negotiation and problem-solving.

9. Don't take abuse lightly. At the point you feel you are no longer being effective, refer the family to a professional immediately.

NOTES

1. Modified from Richard J. Anderson, M.S.W., clinical social worker employed as a protective services worker in the state of Utah in community operations.

2. John W. Taylor, "Structured Conjoint Therapy for Spouse Abuse Cases," *Social Casework* 65 (January 1984): 14.

SUGGESTED READINGS

Gelles, Richard J. *The Violent Home: A Study of Physical Aggression Between Husbands and Wives*. Beverly Hills: Sage Publications, 1972.

Langley, Roger and Richard C. Levy. *Wife Beating: The Silent Crisis*. New York: Pocket Books (Simon and Schuster), 1977.

Martin, Dee. *Battered Wives*. New York: Pocket Books (Simon and Schuster), 1976.

Walker, Lenore L. *The Battered Woman*. New York: Harper and Row, 1979.

ABOUT THE AUTHOR

Dr. W. Eugene Gibbons, chairman of the social-work department at Brigham Young University, received his bachelor's, master's, and doctor of social work degrees from the University of Utah. Dr. Gibbons has worked as a psychiatric social worker at the Utah State Hospital and as director of outpatient and social services for Timpanogos Community Mental Health Center in Provo, Utah. He is presently chairman of the Utah state board of mental health. He has authored several professional articles and is a member of a number of professional and honorary societies.

In the Church, Dr. Gibbons has served in a variety of callings, including bishop, stake executive secretary, YMMIA president, elders quorum president, and first counselor in the Orem Utah Stake presidency.

He and his wife, Evelyn, are the parents of six children.

15

Remarriage and Combined Families
Blaine R. Porter

Combined families, also referred to as blended, second, reconstituted, step, or rem (remarried) families, are those families where at least one, if not both, husband and wife have been married before and have had children. Remarriage resulting in combined families is an increasingly common phenomenon that affects millions of men, women, and children. More than 50 million remarried people are currently living in the United States, and in 1975 one in every four marriages involved someone who had been married before.[1] In 1982, 41 percent of all marriages were remarriages for one or both partners.[2]

Approximately one out of every five children under the age of eighteen currently lives in a single-parent family, and the best estimates from census data now predict that one out of every two children born in the 1980s will live in a single-parent family before the age of eighteen. Since approximately 80 percent of all persons remarry following a divorce or widowhood (especially younger ones who tend to still have children at home), most of these children will experience a combined family. Conservative estimates indicate that there are over fifteen million children living in combined families with stepparents and another four to five million children between the ages of eighteen and twenty-two who are living in and out of combined or blended families. It is further estimated that there are, at a minimum, twenty-five million husbands and wives who are step-mothers and stepfathers. Most of the increase in single-parent households is due to divorce. The percentage resulting from widowhood has remained about the same, but there has been a substantial increase in unwed parenthood.

The formerly marrieds come from all walks of life, all socioeconomic backgrounds, all religious affiliations, and all cultural and ethnic groups. According to Paul Glick and A. J. Norton, formerly marrieds tend to be young and in their twenties when they first reunite. The average age is twenty-seven for women and twenty-nine for men. Divorced persons tend to marry other divorced people. They gravitate toward partners whom they perceive to be quite different in character from their first spouse.[3] Two other studies found that over 50 percent of remarried subjects said they were not at all attracted to the same kinds of persons they first married.[4] Remarried individuals sought traits of warmth, maturity, and the capacity for commitment, as opposed to traits of attractiveness and wealth, which characterized their earlier choices. Jesse Bernard concluded that those who remarry often consider their first marriage as an "apprenticeship" and, as a result, bring a greater capacity for commitment and maturity to their second marriage.[5]

Reasons for Remarriage

Around 80 percent of people who divorce remarry within three years.[6] This suggests that while the first marriage relationship obviously was a disappointment or did not prove to be satisfactory for a permanent union, most people who divorce do not become disenchanted with marriage itself. Many widowed persons also remarry. The most frequently offered reasons for remarriage include the desire for companionship, satisfaction of emotional needs, and opportunities for legitimate sexual expression. Other reasons that are mentioned less frequently but still may play important roles in the decision for remarriage include seeking financial security, yielding to family pressure, and desiring to establish a two-parent home for the children. If divorced, some

people also may want to prove that they can succeed; therefore, they try again. In addition, some people may want to
prove that they are still attractive.

The seeking of security, both emotional and financial, is
a primary factor in remarriage for both men and women.
The desire to have greater financial security is especially
common among women, whose financial resources are
often limited. Data indicate that 80 to 85 percent of men do
not provide financial support for their children following a
divorce. Yielding to the desire to be relieved of the pressure
of earning a living and being taken care of financially can become a paramount reason to remarry, especially for women.
However, if one is willing to get married just to avoid work
or the responsibility of single parenthood, one may enter
hastily and carelessly into a relationship. A strong desire to
escape an existing problem may mean that other serious
considerations may be overlooked or their importance
minimized.

While widowhood usually elicits sympathy or at least
genuine concern from others, divorce is still accompanied
by social stigma, although that is less true now than was true
a few decades ago. Some people feel that being a divorced
person in their church, neighborhood, community, or social
set is a real liability. This creates pressure to remarry in
order to reduce or, hopefully, eliminate the stigma. But getting married to escape from or to run away from a situation
will probably not lead to success and is not a healthy reason
for marriage.

Most of the above reasons for remarriage fall within the
category of "seeking" and "getting." Serious consideration
should also be given to remarriage as an opportunity to find
fulfillment through giving. This is a healthy reason for marriage and remarriage, but one must consider it carefully.

Issues to Be Considered

If you are counseling someone who is considering remarriage, he should give the following issues careful attention.
It is important that these questions be responded to as hon-

estly and as objectively as possible. We often rationalize our decisions in order to obtain quick, easy, and emotionally desired situations and then discover that we must live with undesired consequences for months or years. The chances for a successful remarriage will be increased through serious, patient consideration of the following questions:

1. How successful and satisfying was your first (or other) marriage? Did satisfying, rewarding, and growth-promoting events outweigh disappointments and unresolved problems? Did earlier experiences contribute to personal growth and development, or did they contribute to feelings of inferiority, inadequacy, or guilt? If the experiences were primarily negative, did you learn enough from them so that you are capable of creating something better in a new relationship?

2. Are you basically a happy, positive, growing, productive person? Do you have something constructive to offer another person and a new relationship, or are you seeking marriage as an escape from an unhappy, unpleasant, and overwhelming situation?

3. If children are present in the home, will remarriage lead to a better situation for them? Have you taken them into consideration and discussed the pros and cons with them? (This will need to be adjusted to the age of the children). Are they sufficiently aware of the consequences of remarriage and the adjustments that would be required of them when combining families?

I recall one client who informed me that she was planning to get married after a three-week acquaintance with her prospective husband. When I suggested that was a very short period of time for testing a relationship and that further testing would be in order, she responded, "Well, I had him and his children over for dinner Sunday, and our children had a wonderful time playing together. They really enjoyed each other and want to be together." I suggested that sharing an afternoon of fun and games is very different from sharing a closet, dresser drawers, and a mother's time and love.

4. What will it take to blend children from separate families? Do you have the skill to establish more cooperation than competition among children from different families? Can you promote willing and harmonious sharing, helping, caring, and loving? These qualities are often difficult to achieve within an original blood-related family. It is not possible to project with complete accuracy what the results will be, but the question of the success and happiness of combined families and the impact that combining may have on each person involved should be raised and carefully considered.

5. How much commitment can be elicited from everyone concerned? The desire of a mother or a father or both may not be enough to accomplish the desired goals if children are not committed also. Is the degree of commitment between the two adults fairly equal or is it mostly one sided? If it appears at certain times that goals are not being achieved, how will the situation be handled, and how will both partners feel? Do those who will be involved have the skill and commitment to resolve conflicts in a productive way?

6. What are the risks involved, and what are the potential rewards? If remarriage is occurring after a divorce and it does not succeed to the degree you want and hope for, will you interpret it as "another failure"? If the marriage is reasonably satisfactory but the relationships between a child or children and a stepparent are disruptive and negative and children leave home earlier than otherwise would have been the case in order to escape from an unhappy home situation, will this result in regrets on your part?

7. Are you looking primarily for a marriage companion or for a parent for your children? Both roles must be given serious consideration; but if you are looking for an eternal relationship, perhaps it is appropriate to give greater weight to marriage companionship than to parenthood. This is a difficult issue because your potential partner's ability to perform both roles is desirable and must be carefully evaluated.

8. As you look at your past personal and married life,

what "ghosts" will accompany you into a new marriage? Do you have numerous unresolved problems, or have you carefully considered them, resolved them, and put them into proper perspective? Have you discussed appropriate past problems with the potential marriage partner? Have you discussed these issues with a spiritual leader or a professional who can help you determine the state of your emotional and mental health and who can help you evaluate the degree to which you have resolved problems in a constructive, objective, and healthy manner?

It is easy to rationalize our thoughts so that we arrive at the answers we want. We can even interpret answers to prayers the way we want. All problems and issues do not have to be and probably never will be totally resolved. But being aware of problems and acknowledging the possibility of undesired events occurring is helpful. Anticipating the possibility of difficulties and having plans to constructively handle them is a great asset. It is when difficulties occur that we can link our faith with our works. But if we refuse to acknowledge the possibility of future problems, we may be surprised and overwhelmed when they come.

People who remarry often dream or hope to heal former hurts through the new relationship. However the loss of a former spouse occurred, remarriage carries the expectation that the "new family will be just like the old one or better." People in remarriages hope that old problems will disappear. Seldom do they acknowledge that problems may continue or that new ones might arise. One of the most common myths is that if a person loves another person enough to marry him, he will also love the person's children.

Challenges Facing Combined Families

Remarriage covers a number of different types of marriages:
1. Divorced man/single woman.
2. Divorced man/widowed woman.
3. Divorced man/divorced woman.
4. Single man/divorced woman.

5. Single man/widowed woman.
6. Widowed man/single woman.
7. Widowed man/widowed woman.
8. Widowed man/divorced woman.

Each previous marital status brings with it certain experiences and expectations and sometimes pain, guilt, remorse, anger, bonds, and attachments. Add to this the many combinations of involvement of children such as number, age, sex, relationship with other parents, and so on. The child of divorced parents who both remarry will have two biological parents; two stepparents; a range of possible combinations of biological siblings, step-siblings, and half-siblings; up to eight grandparents (even more if any grandparents are divorced and remarried); and any number of extended relatives through the new spouses of the biological parents. It is easy to see the complexity in combined families and the challenge of anticipating the kinds of problems or fulfillments that may be encountered is overwhelming. The difficulty of trying to establish any single model is obvious, as Emily and John Visher point out:

> When a number of persons of varying ages and stages of development suddenly come together from a variety of previous family and household backgrounds, each one already has ideas about how the television set should be used, where the dog sleeps, who prepares breakfast, how the laundry is folded, and how the hamburgers are cooked. The problem, of course, is that there is no agreement. Everyone brings different family traditions from their former family experiences—most of them given below conscious awareness until the startling experiences of trying to mind a parent who allows watching television before dinner or finding the dog sleeping at the foot of the bed.
>
> In addition, family alliances form, with outsiders and insiders vying for positions because of the parent-child relationships that preceded the new couple's relationship. An only child may suddenly have three sisters. A biological parent may remain in memory if not in actuality. The children may be members of at least two households—going back and forth, experiencing culture shock. A stepfamily is a complex family with a large cast of characters—a family forest rather than a family tree.[7]

Combining families requires a great deal of patience, kindness, generosity, and forgiveness on everyone's part.

Children, especially, may be hesitant to offer loyalty and affection to a newcomer. They may feel they are being disloyal to a biological parent. They may feel caught in an uncomfortable situation, realizing that they should establish a warm, creative relationship with new siblings and a new parent, but they do not know how to do that while still trying to maintain previously existing bonds. Ambivalent feelings and unwelcomed behavior can be dealt with more effectively if they are acknowledged and understood. Children should be helped to understand this.

It is a mistake to expect a stepfamily to function as a normal family. It does not, and it cannot. What happens when one moves from the role of friend to that of spouse and stepparent was described by one stepparent as "like being plunked down, a stranger, in the middle of rural China, speaking the wrong language and yet torn all the while by too many people asking unanswerable questions."

When parents discipline their biological children, the children may not like the discipline or even the parents. However, when a stepparent disciplines a stepchild, the magnitude of these feelings is much greater. The stepchild may respond, "You are not my father!" or "You are not my mother!" or "You wouldn't do this to your *own* child!" Almost daily one is reminded that the relationship is "step" and not biological. A child may say, "I don't have to do this because you are not my mother!" or "If you were really my mother, you wouldn't make me do this!" or "Why did you have to come into our lives? Everything was fine until you came along." These feelings exist on the part of adults, too. A woman may say, "Well, I care about my stepchildren almost as if they were my own, and yet I resent them because they remind me of something I do not want to remember."

A spouse may feel that a new husband or wife in a remarriage is fine, but that the marriage is greatly complicated by children. Most remarried people report that right from the start things were much harder than they had anticipated. The tendency is to expect, to act, and to react as though the stepfamily were a biological family.

People are frequently surprised at the changes in the

families before and after a marriage. Many women have indicated that they established a good relationship with the children of a prospective husband—they had long conversations and found that his children would share things with them they would not share with their father. Yet, after the marriage, something happened to this closeness; the children became more distant and seemed to feel that someone was taking the place of their mother. Such behavior is not easily understood by either generation. The challenge is even further complicated if some of the children are not living all the time with the family but visiting occasionally or on weekends. The wonderful, big family gatherings that one might have dreamed of just do not come about. Children may visit and want to have time with their parent but not the stepparent. The parent will probably feel sad about this and may even be critical of the stepparent for not being more successful in being able to establish a close, meaningful relationship with the children. The children may resent the parent, the stepparent, or both for creating this situation.

When possible, it is best for a combined family to start out in a new house. Too often, stepparents and their children move into the home previously lived in by the other adult and his or her children. It is difficult not to feel like a guest or an intruder for those who move in. It is also difficult for those who have previously been there not to resent changes that will be made—sharing things that have been private and feeling that someone else is taking over things or responsibilities that belong to a present family member or to a departed parent who no longer lives there.

In cases of divorce, noncustodial parents often complicate life. They justifiably may wonder whether a stepparent will move in and do a better job of parenting than he or she had done, especially since they may see their children so little. They may feel particularly helpless if they feel the new stepparent is not doing a good job with the children. It is difficult to accept the feeling that someone else is taking one's place. If children are living part of their lives in a second household, their loyalties will be divided. They may feel confused and frustrated. They may feel used if they have become pawns between their parents. Wise adults will do everything possible to avoid putting children into these difficult situations.

Children who spend part of their time in at least two households find they are confronted with different rules, regulations, traditions, and ways of doing things. They often become skillful in manipulating parents and in playing one against the other.

Preparing for Remarriage

If you or someone you are counseling is a formerly married person involved in a second or subsequent marriage, some of the following problems may be confronting you:

1. *Discarding excess baggage.* It is not unusual for people to carry into another marriage unresolved issues from an earlier marriage. These unresolved issues may be both conscious and unconscious. In more extreme cases it may be wise to seek professional help in an effort to understand and resolve as many past issues as possible. Unresolved issues frequently become hurdles to one's personal adjustment as well as relationships with others.

2. *Establishing realistic expectations.* Most people entering a first marriage do so with unrealistic expectations. After marriage, however, they review those expectations and adjust them appropriately. Failure to adjust one's expectations may result in great disappointment and sometimes may even precipitate a divorce. Likewise, people may enter a second marriage with unrealistic expectations. For example, they may expect a second or subsequent marriage to be like a first one or to be like a first family. But a combined family may never be like a first family. As a lay counselor, you should observe the person you are helping, and if his expectations seem to be seriously unrealistic, it may be wise to refer him to a professional who can provide guidance by reviewing what expectations are realistic for a combined family.

3. *Being patient.* It may take a long time—months or even years—to achieve a healthy, creative relationship with stepchildren, especially in their teen years. This, of course, depends on the personalities involved, but trying to force a relationship too soon may complicate life considerably and may even postpone or prevent the relationship one is seeking. Children are often reluctant to allow someone to "take the place of" another parent. With older children, it may not be realistic to expect to become a second mother or a second father. A good friendship may be the most one can expect.

4. *Integrating two or more family units.* In a natural or first family the membership is well-defined, and family boundaries are clearly delineated. Family expectations, rules, roles, tasks, and goals are usually clear. In contrast, membership in a combined family is more complicated. There may be multiple relationships and bonds. Some members of the family may feel that they belong to two families or that they do not belong at all. For example, a combined family consists of two units that used to be single but are now joined. However, in a combined family there may still be a single family unit for the children, who may be spending time with a single parent as well as with the new combined family. In addition, there may be two combined family units, where a child's biological parents have each remarried. The child's parents may not only be involved with a new spouse but still have certain bonds and ties, pleasant or unpleasant, with a former spouse. These multiple networks add stress, strain, and demands upon individuals and may be complicating factors in a combined family.

5. *Adjusting to a newly acquired family.* Suddenly acquiring a full-grown son or daughter or several of each may be a positive experience or an extremely difficult challenge. Suddenly becoming a grandparent by marriage presents new challenges, not only in relationships but also in self-concept. This is especially true if one's age is considerably younger than when he or she anticipated being in this stage of life. Becoming an instant mother-in-law or father-in-law may not be easy for one who is still psychologically and bio-

logically in the stage of childbearing and preschool parenthood.

6. *Handling financial matters.* In a second marriage,
each partner has already established financial status. Pre-
sumably, each has a source of income, and each has habits
of dealing with money that may be quite unlike the habits of
the other. Patterns regarding who pays the bills, whether or
not there will be allowances for spending money, and dealing
with childrens' financial matters may be difficult to resolve.
Expecting financial support from an ex-spouse, or assuming
financial responsibilities for "someone else's" children also
present difficulties.

If someone has come to you for help in considering the
issue of remarriage, as you review these concerns it is important that you create safe and trusting conditions so that the
person will be relatively free to discuss issues with you. Be
understanding, warm, and objective. Be very cautious in giving advice. Try to help the person think through issues. Raise
questions to find out whether he has actually thought about
them or not; and, if so, encourage him to be as honest and
objective as possible. You may be helpful in raising questions he has not yet considered. It may be possible for you to
help him see an issue or a question in a new light. Avoid
being trapped into making a decision for him.

The New Family System

Families do not exist in a vacuum. The cultural myths
and expectations that surround combined families complicate the period of transition and integration, which, to quote
one stepmother, "does not take months—it takes years."
When a newborn baby arrives in a first marriage, it comes
with no expectations of what its world will be like. The parents have time to gradually combine their own family traditions and ways of doing things into a pattern that is taken
for granted by all family members. But in combined families, each family member brings a legacy of traditions and
a set of definite ideas about such diverse things as how holi-
days are celebrated and how children are disciplined. Both

children and adults hold to the familiar customs of their former households. They find it hard to make adjustments, and many combined family members face feelings of bewilderment, frustration, hostility, and failure. Negotiation and concern for others is necessary in all families, but it is particularly important in combined families.

Family happiness is possible, but it takes time, effort, and skill. Family councils or family meetings where each person can express his feelings and feel that he is accepted and that his ideas are freely discussed can be helpful to the family that is trying to work out acceptable regulations and traditions. Families can even find that the very task of combining traditions from the past or of creating new patterns for special occasions can be exciting, interesting, and rewarding. This is possible when members feel excited about change rather than upset by it.

Many individuals who have combined families agree that it was well worth the efforts that were involved. For them, remarriage brought increased happiness. In fact, some found it so rewarding that they wished their second marriage had been their first so that they could have enjoyed it longer.

Approximately 40 percent of second marriages end in divorce in the first four years. If a couple who remarry have children from their previous marriages, the likelihood that the marriage will end in divorce is increased. The second marriage can be successful, but it requires even greater skill, patience, and effort than the first marriage. The family members must avoid comparing a second spouse with a first one, or a second mother or father with a first. In addition, they must prepare for marital happiness. There are courses, books, manuals, seminars, and workshops to help people prepare for marriage, for childbirth, for parenthood. However, there are many problems involved in combining families that are different from and do not exist in first marriages and first families. Couples who are unprepared for the combined family adventure are the most likely to face disappointment and struggle. It is best to face the new challenge with eyes wide open, with a deep commitment to seek appropriate help, and with the determination to do what is necessary in order to succeed.

As we better understand combined families and accept the fact that combined families are not like biological families, we can offer better help. We must accept combined families as legitimate kinship units. To the degree that we are able to do that, we can help those in combined families to achieve rewarding and deeply satisfying relationships.

Resources

If you are living in a combined family or if you are counseling someone who is, the following may be useful sources of help:

1. Your bishop. If he is not able to give you the help you need, he will probably be in a position to make intelligent referrals.

2. LDS Social Services or similar social agencies in your community.

3. The Stepfamily Association of America (900 Welch Road, Suite 400, Palo Alto, CA 94304). This organization publishes a quarterly newsletter, *Stepfamily Bulletin,* for those who are interested in step relationships. This association also sends book lists and reprints to its members, provides training workshops for professionals, helps chapters and state divisions form mutual support networks, and is engaged in community education.

NOTES

1. Paul C. Glick, "Children of Divorced Parents in Demographic Perspective," *Journal of Social Issues* 35 (1979).

2. Margaret Crosbie-Burnett, "The Impact of Remarriage on Labor Force Participation, Divorce Decree Modification, Ex-Spousal Relationship, and Extended Family Reorganization," paper presented at the Annual Meeting of the National Council on Family Relations, St. Paul, Minnesota, October 1983.

3. Paul C. Glick and A. J. Norton, "Number, Timing, and Duration of Marriages and Divorces in the U.S.: June 1975," *Current Population Reports* (October 1976).

4. M. Hunt and B. Hunt, *The Divorce Experience* (New York: McGraw-Hill, 1977); Leslie

A. Westoff, *The Second Time Around: Remarriage in America* (New York: The Viking Press, 1977).

5. Jesse Bernard, *Remarriage: A Study of Marriage,* 2nd ed. (New York: Russell, 1971).

6. Paul C. Glick and A. J. Norton, "Marrying, Divorcing, and Living Together in the U.S. Today," *Population Bulletin* 32 (1977).

7. Emily B. Visher and John S. Visher, "Stepfamilies in the 1980's." In *Therapy with Remarriage Families,* James C. Hansen and Lillian Messinger, eds. (Rockville, Maryland: Aspen System Corporation, 1982), pp. 105-120.

ABOUT THE AUTHOR

Dr. Blaine R. Porter, former dean of the College of Family Living and university professor at Brigham Young University, received his bachelor's and master's degrees at BYU and his Ph.D. from Cornell University. A well-known family life educator, he has served on numerous regional and national committees. Dr. Porter is the author of many professional books, monographs, and articles.

His service in the Church has been wide and varied. He has served as a bishop, in a stake presidency, and in a number of Melchizedek Priesthood assignments.

Once a widower, Dr. Porter is remarried and lives in Provo with his wife, Barbara, and their daughter. He has four grown children by his first marriage.

16

Childlessness and Adoption

Harold C. Brown

My earliest recollection of adoption was as a young boy visiting a cousin who had been adopted. Having never known anyone adopted, I asked my cousin many questions about what it was like to be adopted. I discovered that he was prepared for my questions, but finally, after one too many, he must have taken my inquisitiveness personally. "My parents chose me," he said. "Your parents had to take what they got!" End of conversation!

One out of five American couples can't have children.[1] The feelings of infertile couples vary from depression, anger, and frustration to exhilaration upon conception or adoption. Emotions run high, and the need for help often exists. Few who have not endured them are aware of the feelings childless couples suffer.

But much can be done to help couples with the challenges of infertility. Friends, Church leaders, and others in a position to help should be aware of the challenges and frustrations that accompany infertility and adoption.

Although much could be said about the baby that is adopted or the parents who relinquish a child for adoption, this chapter will focus on the childless couple.

Adoption Opportunities

Only a few decades ago many more children were available for adoption. Orphanages were not uncommon, and it was difficult to find enough families interested in caring for homeless children. (This is still true for children with physical, social, or emotional handicaps.)

Today, however, there is a growing number of families wishing to adopt and a decreasing number of available infants. The foremost reason for this lack of infants is that in 1969, 90 percent of unmarried females bearing children relinquished their children for adoption. But in 1979, just ten years later, 90 percent of this same group kept their children rather than relinquishing them for adoption. The percent of unwed mothers who keep their children is even higher today. This trend to keep infants has been dramatic and has shown no sign of reversing itself.

This has led to frustration for many childless couples, and it has also widened the door for black-market and other illegal or unethical adoption practices. Some couples wishing to adopt have paid large sums of money for supposedly "legitimate" adoption expenses that later turned out to be illegal. Some have paid in advance and after an expenditure of considerable time and money have found that no child was forthcoming. Because fewer children are available for adoption, this experience has become more common. There were approximately 65,000 adoptions in 1983 in the United States. But with one in five couples unable to conceive, the "baby gap" continues to grow.

Sterility

Most couples wishing to adopt do so because one of the partners is sterile. Sterility may exist in either the man or the woman. Approximately 40 percent of sterility is related to the male and another 40 percent to the female. Twenty percent of infertility cases are related to both people in the partnership.

There are numerous causes of infertility. The most common cause in women is infection. In men, varicocele is one of the most common causes. Varicocele is a varicose vein near one of the testicles. Though there is some question on exactly how varicocele causes sterility, it is felt that the added temperature brought to the testicle by the varicose vein causes a lack of sperm development. Couples who have infertility problems should be referred to a physician.

Because a couple has not been able to have children it should not be assumed that sterility is permanent. Numerous couples have been helped to have children through accurate information and competent professional help. For various reasons, couples may hesitate to seek such assistance, but they should be encouraged to do so. A lay counselor may help couples overcome feelings of embarrassment or inadequacy so that they are willing to receive the best possible medical care available.

Problems Facing Childless Couples

Society values children. This is especially true among the Latter-day Saints. The Church teaches that a major reason for earth life is to marry, have a family, and live faithfully so that family associations may be eternal. Church lessons, activities, and programs are geared toward the family and child care. This can be frustrating to couples without children. Their feelings are not always rational, but examples of how some childless couples have viewed their situation might help you understand their problems. One woman said, "I never had such a black period in my life. Being unable to have children was very difficult for me to resolve. I was very depressed and everything seemed black."

These are the words of an adoptive mother recounting her feelings after discovering that she could not conceive and bear children. Most childless couples experience periods of hopelessness and loneliness. They often feel misunderstood and depressed.

Another woman noted, "I was very much aware of babies and other people with babies. I was conscious of the need for my son to have playmates. [This particular woman delivered one child before discovering she could have no more.] Though at the time my feelings were exaggerated, they were nevertheless real and frustrating."

It is common for couples who are unable to have children to have feelings of frustration, especially when visiting with couples who are rearing children. They watch their friends hold, cuddle, feed, and care for their new babies. They long to have the same sweet experience and often find friendships strained by their feelings. Their experiences and interests begin to vary, adding to the loneliness. One woman said, "I began hating pregnant people. I would ride the bus to work, see a pregnant woman, and want to slap the person sitting next to me."[2]

Often childless couples generate feelings of guilt. While no obligation to explain childlessness exists, couples often want to do so. They often feel a need to say, "We are trying! We want children too."

One couple explained that they felt the accusing glances, real or imagined, of friends and neighbors who commented, not so subtly, about the freedom and selfishness of not having children. The wife felt guilty for working. She thought at times that her friends were accusing her of a lack of commitment to children and family life.

This same couple indicated that family gatherings were often unpleasant. Each of the wife's brothers and sisters had several children. Family discussions revolved around child-rearing and the growth and development of each child. Grandparents cuddled, held, and spoiled grandchildren. Mothers were busy changing diapers and feeding and caring for little ones, and they would laugh about the latest accomplishment or stage of life. And although the couple were happy for their brothers and sisters, they felt left out and lonely: "We would see our brothers and sisters with their babies, holding them. It really tore my heart apart. I felt that we were on the outside looking in through a window."

This couple wondered if being childless was some form of punishment or discipline—perhaps they were unfaithful or in some way undeserving. They sought many answers but found few to comfort them.

"We felt there was no one to talk to," they said, "no one who understood enough to say, 'How do you feel?' Even one of the adoption agencies we called left us with the impression that they cared about the child more than us. And while we understood their position, we wanted someone to understand us so we wouldn't be all alone." This couple has since found the joy of having children through adoption.

Couples often look back and realize that their situation wasn't as desperate as they felt at the time, yet their feelings were real. Much can be done to help couples deal with such feelings. A counselor can usually do little to actually provide children, but listening, understanding, and providing support can do a great deal to help.

How the Lay Counselor Can Help

Often counselors want to solve all the problems of those who come for help. But a counselor can best help by providing perspective and balance. One of the questions often asked by those unable to have children is "Why can't we have children? Why us?" The question bears eternal import in the mind of the person asking it. While usually such questions have no direct answers, much can be done to help couples focus on what they can do rather than on what they cannot understand.

A counselor should not give false hope to a childless couple. Many couples will never have biological children of their own. On the other hand, modern medicine and technology have increased the chance of conception. The American Fertility Society claims that specialists can help 70 percent of infertile couples.[3] Couples should be aware of these facts and be encouraged to seek competent help.

Listen and Understand

Most counselors have had the experience of listening to someone seeking help and after the interview being thanked generously by the one seeking help. Often little has been said by the counselor, but the person felt relieved that someone listened and cared.

Counselors can convey a feeling of understanding by expressing sympathy and understanding. Comments such as, "It must be difficult at times to want children so much," or

"You probably don't always feel that your friends understand," or "At times you must feel all alone" can be helpful. Such empathic comments can give hope and courage to the couple who may feel that someone important finally understands how they feel.

Reaching Out to Others

It is important to remind childless couples that they are worthwhile and capable of doing good for others. The problem of infertility can be attended by feeling sorry for oneself and by turning inward. This in turn can add to the loneliness and frustration and isolation. Happiness comes from reaching out and serving others. There is much adoptive couples can do. Service can be in the form of Church callings or community service. Some couples might consider taking care of a child on a temporary basis. Numerous infants and children need shelter and foster care for brief periods of time. Such service can be rewarding personally and might provide good training. Losing oneself in the cause of serving others can lighten burdens and broaden perspectives.

President Kimball's counsel has meaning in this regard:

> Should we be protected always from hardship, pain, suffering, sacrifice or labor? Should [God] immediately punish the wicked? If growth comes from fun and ease and aimless irresponsibility, then why should we ever exert ourselves to work or learn or overcome? But if we look upon the whole of life as an eternal thing stretching far into the pre-mortal past and into the eternal post-death future, then all happenings may be in proper perspective and may fall into proper place.
>
> We knew before we were born that we were coming to the earth for bodies and experience and that we would have joys and sorrows, ease and pain, comforts and hardships, health and sickness, successes and disappointments, and we knew also that we would die. We accepted all these eventualities with a glad heart, eager to accept both the favorable and unfavorable. We were willing to come and take life as it came and as we might organize and control it, and this without murmur, complaint or unreasonable demands.[4]

Adoption

If it is determined that sterility is permanent, then pursuing the adoption route may be desirable and rewarding.

Even though there are not many infants available, adoption is within the reach of most couples who are persistent and show adequate parenting skills. A counselor can encourage the couple to seek a professional, reputable adoption source. Because the desire to have children is often so great, there is a temptation to seek a child from any source. Careful selection is important to assure competent help and to avoid pitfalls that may lead to frustration, undue expense, and possible legal and ethical complications. Help in selecting an adoption source is one of the greatest aids a counselor can offer.

Selecting an Adoption Source

There are several pitfalls that should be avoided by prospective adoptive couples. A careful check of adoption agencies and individuals offering adoption services is essential. A call to the state or county family or social services office can help. Respected church, community, or other private agencies can also provide helpful information. Latter-day Saints can inquire at their nearest LDS Social Services agency.

International Adoptions

Once a couple called me indicating that they had been promised a child from another country. They had paid a large sum of money in advance and had made additional payments over more than a year's time; the costs had exceeded their original commitments. Much time had passed, and there were many "reasons" why the child had not arrived. This couple's hopes were alternately raised and then shattered by promises and disappointments. They had been persuaded that there was a particular child in great need, and that they were the ones to help. They could imagine a child needing them and could see themselves offering that needed love. Eventually they stopped their pursuit of empty promises. There were legal, immigration, and other problems. The person promising the child eventually disappeared with their money. They were left with empty arms and heartache. Unfortunately, this story has been repeated all too often.

There are reputable international agencies who can and do provide safe, legal adoptions. Again, the best source of information is a local Social Services office. International adoption requires competence and knowledge. Complex and varying laws often make international adoptions a challenge. If they are not handled properly, immigration and legal problems may lead to unwarranted expenses and disappointments.

For example, on one occasion a family in the United States had been contacted by someone in another country, telling them a child was available for adoption. They were most eager to respond. The child had been relinquished by its father when his wife died unexpectedly. The father was emotionally upset and confused. He was worried about how he could care for his large family. There were problems trying to get the child out of the country. The couple wishing to adopt the child called me for help. Under the circumstances my advice was to no longer be involved with the situation. The legal and immigration problems were serious. The circumstances surrounding the relinquishment of the child raised serious ethical questions. Would this father regret giving up his child after his emotions settled and his circumstances changed?

Intercultural adoptions often bring additional challenges to the family and child. It is critical that international adoptions be approached cautiously and preceded by a thorough investigation of the adoption source.

Confidentiality

Confidentiality about the adoptive child's family must be assured. Today a controversy exists over whether or not or under what conditions adoption records should be opened. Some advocate that an adopted child has a right to know who his or her biological parents are and the circumstances surrounding the adoption. This same group generally argues that the biological parents also have a right to know where the child is placed and to learn of its growth and development.

Others feel that the relinquishment given by biological

parents is final and that contact between the parties should not be made. In the Church, most adopted children can be sealed in the temple. The Church member must consider this fact carefully.

It can be argued that the adoptive parents have worked and sacrificed to raise their adopted child. They have made the financial and emotional sacrifices required to be a parent. Many resist having a biological parent come into the picture. Adoptive parents often fear that contact with the biological parent could weaken or destroy the relationship they have with their child.

The compromise position most often advocated is one of allowing mutual registration by both the adoptee and the biological parents when the adoptee reaches a certain age, usually eighteen. If both register and agree to a contact it would then be arranged by a neutral party. To allow contact of either party without the consent of the other has many potential problems. Often the biological parents do not want their identity revealed. Relatives, friends, and sometimes immediate family members of the biological parents may be unaware that another child ever existed. While some argue that total revelation of all information in such cases is preferred, such solutions are not always simple. Biological parents, adoptees, and adopting parents have rights, feelings, and circumstances that need careful consideration. Counselors should exercise great care when exploring this matter. The right of confidentiality is sacred and should be approached cautiously.

This controversy is still alive and far from being settled. A great deal of federal and state legislation is still in progress. This issue will undoubtedly eventually be decided in the courts.

On one occasion a couple adopted a child from a woman in the same ward in which they lived. An attorney assisted with the adoption, and although he was competent in his speciality, he was not fully aware of the adoption laws in the state in which he lived. He also expressed to the couple that there was no reason to have a serious concern about the confidentiality with the natural mother, who knew the couple.

She had assured him she had no desire to raise the child, and she had given her word not to interfere or disrupt the child or the adoptive parents' lives. However, it wasn't very long until the natural mother changed her mind and wanted the child back. Although the adoptive couple moved to another state, the biological mother—with the help of an attorney— found a flaw in the adoption proceedings and eventually got the child back after six years in the adoptive home. There were heartache and tears, with the greatest tragedy being that the child was caught between a biological mother and adoptive parents.

While this example may be somewhat unusual, such tragedy and heartache occur too often. Confidentiality is imperative.

Legal Protection

An adoptive couple should be assured of the best legal protection when adopting a child. While there is no guarantee that litigation will not be pursued with any adoption, careful selection of an attorney can minimize legal exposure. Not only does federal legislation affect adoptions, but laws vary from state to state, and often smaller government entities have laws that affect adoptions. Even individual courts and judges are given a great deal of latitude in child placement decisions. Presently, adoption laws are rapidly changing, and couples should take extra care or they may be caught in painful legal technicalities.

Professional adoption agencies provide excellent protection. When agencies who have placed children face litigation, they often do so without even contacting adoptive parents. Inquiries from biological parents are handled in a sensitive but routine manner. A great deal of protection for the families and children involved comes from these professional, licensed agencies.

Education and Preparation

A couple wishing to adopt should prepare adequately to receive a child. This includes learning about agencies and adoption procedures. It also includes commitment to the child who is to be theirs in every sense but biological. Granted, millions of couples have children biologically without counseling and help. This is natural, normal, and usually desirable. However, when mortals become involved in the placement of infants, they should take care to assure that the adoptive home is prepared. Counselors should not be extreme or be overinvolved in an adoptive family's life, but taking time to prepare a couple by having them imagine the future, examine goals, and assess priorities can be very beneficial to them.

Some of the circumstances surrounding adoption produce additional concerns and challenges. Several years ago, the wife of a couple who had adopted a child came to me for help. Their child was very active and full of life. These parents had adopted through a physician who sincerely tried to help them. However, they had had only a limited opportunity to discuss possible problems and challenges they might face with an adopted child. This couple struggled for a great deal of time before they finally sought assistance. During the course of the interview, the adoptive mother finally admitted believing that because the mother of the baby had conceived out of wedlock, that perhaps there was a strong tendency for the child to be hard to handle and discipline. They had actually come to believe that there was little that could be done to help and control him. After some discussion and counseling, they came to understand that their child was not really any different from most children born to parents every day. Through some basic education, training, and prayer, they gained confidence and began to enjoy their parenting experience.

Often the adoptive couple needs very little information and help, but it is important that help be available. Licensed agencies provide this service as part of their normal duties. Some couples may be hesitant to seek help, fearing that they will be seen as inadequate. Adoptive parents are usually more concerned about appearing to be capable than are biological parents.[5]

No one can guarantee there will be no problems, but careful preparation and continuing education can help assure the happiness of the adoptive couple and the child.

Matching the Child and the Parents

The sacred nature of some adoption stories makes them difficult to tell, for there is often a spiritual side to matching children with adoptive couples. In professional agencies, great care is taken to match the background, interests, and characteristics of the adoptive parents and the biological parents. As much as possible the height, weight, hair and eye color, size, and characteristics of the biological parents are matched with the adoptive parents. Background, education, and interests are all taken into account. It is surprising how often a couple is able to delight in the comments of an unknowing friend or relative who says, "Oh, he looks just like his father!"

The frustrations and challenges and worries of adoption melt away when those who have the opportunity to adopt finally receive their child. As one woman expressed it, "It was the most exhilarating day of my life! I can remember every detail of that day. I felt complete joy! It seemed so impressive. Such a surprise. I could not understand that I could be that happy. My husband couldn't stop calling people— people we had not seen in years. To walk into that room and then hold the baby for the first time—there are not words to describe that feeling!"

NOTES

1. "Infertility: New Cures, New Hope," *Newsweek* (December 6, 1982), p. 102.

2. Ibid.

3. Ibid., p. 103.

4. Spencer W. Kimball, "Tragedy or Destiny," in *Faith Precedes the Miracle* (Salt Lake City: Deseret Book Company, 1975), pp. 95-106.

5. Janet L. Hoopes, *The Delaware Family Study: Prediction in Child Development* (New York: Child Welfare League of America, 1982).

SUGGESTED READINGS

"Barren Couples." *Psychology Today*, May 1979, pp. 101-12.

Behrman, S. J., M.D. and Robert W. Kistner, M.D. *Progress in Infertility*. Boston: Little, Brown and Co., 1975.

"Infertility: New Cures, New Hope." *Newsweek*, December 6, 1982.

Menning, Barbara Eck. *Infertility: A Guide for the Childless Couple*. Englewood Cliffs, New Jersey: Prentice-Hall, Inc., 1977.

Smith, I. Evelyn. *Readings in Adoption*. New York: Philosophical Library, 1963.

ABOUT THE AUTHOR

Harold C. Brown, director of Social Services, Employment, and Rehabilitation Services for the LDS Church, received his bachelor's degree from Brigham Young University and his master's of social work degree from the University of Utah. Formerly he has taught seminary and worked with various parts of the social, Indian Placement, and welfare programs of the Church. He is a member of the advisory board of the Graduate School of Social Work at the University of Utah.

He has previously served in the Church in elders quorum presidencies and as a bishop, and he presently serves as a member of the Salt Lake Cottonwood Stake presidency.

He and his wife, Penny, are the parents of eight children.

17

Dealing with Physical and Mental Handicaps

June Leifson

As Eldon Watson watched his young wife, Ann, bring their first child into the world, he hoped, as every parent hopes, that his baby would be well and whole. But his wishes were shattered when he looked at his child—the baby girl had a cleft lip and palate. A thousand thoughts rushed through his mind at once. What about his wife? Would she accept the baby? Would the child be able to play and dance and sing and date and . . . ? He looked at the doctor, but the doctor seemed to look everywhere but at Eldon. The nurses had tears rolling down their cheeks. Even though these people were obviously aware of the problem, they offered no support nor any encouragement. Fortunately, however, Eldon and Ann had caring families who gave help and support. They were lucky; not everyone has family, friends, and others who can help. Also, the Watsons had a good health insurance plan. But not everyone has good family support and good financial backing. Nor is everyone capable of giving competent help in times of difficulty such as this.

How can you, as a lay counselor, offer help to parents, to families, and to friends of the handicapped?

Every Situation Is Unique

First, remember that each physical and mental handicap is unique; no two families have the same problem. Do not assume that the same or a similar medical diagnosis presents the same problems to two different families.

Like Eldon and Ann, Allen and Carol Franz had a child with a cleft palate, but their child had other more severe problems. It was born with microcephaly—an abnormal smallness of the head. It had no eyes and was severely retarded. The Franzes had no health insurance and little or no family support. Carol stated that her mother had died just a few months before the baby was born. "When I really needed her, she wasn't here," she said.

Not only will financial conditions and family support vary, but also reactions and feelings toward a handicap will be interpreted and felt differently by each individual. A mother with a child born with Down's Syndrome stated, "I just wanted to scream. I was in shock. I just couldn't believe it could happen to us." A father's response when he had a child born with Down's Syndrome was: "I was stunned— shocked. My head was rolling. I felt sorry for myself; I felt sorry for the boy. I wanted to ask the Lord, Why me? What have I done? I had a sense of deep depression." Clearly, depending on family circumstances, finances, reactions, and feelings, a lay counselor will have to provide different kinds of help to each family.

Lay counselors can expect parents to exhibit a certain amount of guilt, depression, anger, grief, and frustration when confronted with a disabled child. The birth of a disabled child may be viewed as the death of the "normal and perfect" child who was to realize their personal aspirations. But expressions of reaction and emotion are seldom simple and clear-cut. A person's reactions are frequently blurred when he is first told of physical or mental problems; there may even be two or three reactions at the same time. One minute a person may feel guilt; the next minute he may feel guiltless but angry. The family may feel they should pull themselves together immediately, but intense emotional reactions usually require *time* to heal their pain.

Someone Somewhere Can Help

Lay counselors do not have to have all the answers, but they should let the family know that there is someone somewhere to help them; you and they together can find the answers and help. The hardest problem to overcome is fear of the unknown—not knowing where to obtain help. Eldon's situation in the delivery room could have been helped greatly if someone had immediately said, "There is help for this condition. There are operations and therapies that can help." When a doctor or a nurse does not provide this help, a lay counselor should add support and comfort. In every state, in every town, in every ward and branch there are resources to help families. These resources include medical specialists, county health nurses, books in the local library, and home teachers who can give special priesthood blessings. There are many support and resource groups who can give individuals and families the opportunity to hear from others who have gone through similar experiences. They can give honest, straightforward answers to tough questions. For those who become disabled later in life—from adolescence onward—there are hospital rehabilitation centers, the Division of Rehabilitation, or the Governor's Committee on Employment of the Handicapped that can give assistance. There *is* someone somewhere who can help. As a counselor, you should assure the family that they are not alone.

Accept the Situation for What It Is—Go On

Help the family (and the individual, if he is mature enough or mentally capable) to accept the situation for what it is and go on. Trying to move forward is important. The handicap may be difficult to accept, but families need to objectively look at their circumstances. They (and others) often look at the person with the disability and see only the disability; they do not see the person. As one mother said, "In reality, my child is 90 percent normal, only 10 percent handicapped."

Another counseling problem may be the guilt of the parents. Even though a child's disability may come from the parents through a genetic defect, drug use, sickness, or an accident, their guilt must be resolved. Bishops and priesthood leaders can offer advice and direction. The lay counselor can help parents accept the situation, seek forgiveness if appropriate, and go on to build their lives.

The family and the disabled person, when capable, need to realize and emphasize the strengths and possibilities they and the disabled person have. Families have great strengths that can be developed. These strengths may be the physical or emotional ability of the family members to help the handicapped person. They may be the family's willingness to communicate, to be united, to show loyalty, to cooperate with each other, and to show love. Because some families consider accepting help a weakness, counselors can help such families realize that to accept help when needed is actually a strength.

In addition, families with handicapped members need to have a sense of security—a sense that they are working together to provide encouragement and support for each other. They also need to provide genuine praise and recognition for each other for every task performed (even small, simple tasks). As the family succeeds in its quest for strength, it will be able to give strength and help to the handicapped person. An important part of this supportive family climate is humor. Families and individuals need the relief that humor gives. But all must be sensitive. All must understand the difference between ridicule and humor and know the disabled person well enough to realize when humor will help.

Actions That Do Not Help

One common concern expressed by families who have members with physical and mental handicaps has been the negative reactions and responses of other people. One father said about his son, "His problem is obvious, and people don't know what to say or how to act. It is hard to accept their reaction. It's hard to go out in public with him. People want to have everything perfect. It makes it hard dealing with one's own ego." Not only adults but also children can be cruelly insensitive. For example, the first time one couple took their child to church, one of the Boy Scouts ran down the aisle, pulled the blanket down off the deformed baby, and said, "See."

It doesn't help when well-meaning individuals are more curious than concerned, when sympathy is not true sympathy, or when others don't really understand the problem. One insensitive person said to a mother of a mentally retarded child, "Well, your child is fine now." This mother wished that her child were "fine," but she realized that the child would be mentally retarded for life. Failure to accept the facts does not change reality.

Similarly, handicapped people do not want to be compared with others. Disabled people are unique. They do not want to hear about other handicapped people who succeeded where they cannot. Likewise, the parents of the handicapped do not want to hear about other handicapped people when the comparisons are not appropriate. Encouragement is necessary, but it must be given at the right time, with the correct facts, and in a sensitive way. By staying alert to such things, the lay counselor may be able to protect the troubled family from unintentional abuse at the hands of well-meaning but uninformed people. For example, the lay counselor could explain the situation to neighbors, friends, Church members, and others. This can remove the problem of morbid curiosity and place everyone on a more equal footing.

Neither the parent of a handicapped child nor the handicapped person himself (regardless of age) wants the disabled person to be treated as an object. An example of this is when a handicapped person goes with his parents or a friend to the supermarket to buy something. Because the clerk feels uncomfortable, he communicates with the parent or friend rather than with the handicapped person who is shopping. When a handicapped person has one disability, even a slight one, people often treat him as if he has many or more severe handicaps. For example, blind people are sometimes treated as if they are not only blind but also hard of hearing, unable to speak, and mentally incompetent. Lay counselors can help by explaining this human tendency to the family members and to the handicapped person, if he is capable of understanding. In addition, the lay counselor should be careful not to make this mistake himself.

All handicapped people do not have identical needs. Meeting the needs of a person with one disability differs from meeting the needs of another. We all have unique needs, wants, and desires. It is also important for the lay counselor to realize that most handicapped persons are not primarily in need. Many disabled persons are professors, doctors, bank managers, church leaders, home builders and so on. They can not only take care of themselves, but they can also offer valuable service to church and community.

Actions That Help

To help families and their handicapped members, the lay counselor needs to try to see the world from their viewpoint. This is called empathy. It involves both sympathy for their difficult situation and the attempt to see things the way they do. One of the best ways to understand how a disabled person and his family feel is to become well acquainted with them. A less direct, but helpful, approach is to read literature written from the viewpoint of the disabled and their families. Negative attitudes can be changed; positive attitudes can be intensified. Concern, caring, love, and kindness go a long way toward bridging any gaps that may exist between you, the family, and the handicapped person. Realize that although through the resurrection the person will someday be whole, the future promise of a perfect body will not solve the present problems of the disabled. The here and now of the situation also must be confronted. Disabled persons must learn how to manage their physical problems as well as they can. They must also learn to handle possible failures and painful interactions with others.

This places a responsibility on the lay counselor to be both empathetic and honest. The lay counselor should learn to speak the truth gently. The greatest barriers to disabled people are the attitudes of those around them. The lay counselor needs to take a hard look at his attitudes toward the disabled and to discover those feelings and incorrect ideas that may impair counseling.

Be practical in your help. For example, if a person with a white cane is standing on a street corner, ask him first if he would like your assistance before you take him across the street. If you plan to visit a disabled person, realize that the person who has disabilities is usually more susceptible to respiratory diseases and illnesses than others. Visit him when you are well. If the family of a disabled person states that they are doing just fine, but you can see that their world is crumbling around them, seek concrete ways to help them. You could take in a hot meal or two, take some of the children for an afternoon, do the washing and ironing, shop for needed items, or sit with the disabled person so the family can have a free afternoon or evening.

Your practical help is necessary, but you must allow the family or the handicapped person to be independent, at least as much as possible under the circumstances. When handicapped people develop their strengths and become self-sufficient, they gain confidence to face and enjoy life more fully.

The counselor should not only help the handicapped person and his family be self-reliant, but he should also help them understand that God is mindful of them and that handicaps can have a purpose. About a blind man, Jesus taught, "Neither hath this man sinned, nor his parents; but that the works of God should be made manifest in him." (John 9: 2-3.) President Spencer W. Kimball has said, "In the face of apparent tragedy we must put our trust in God, knowing that despite our limited view, his purpose will not fail. With all its troubles life offers us the tremendous privilege to grow in knowledge and wisdom, faith, and works, preparing to return and share God's glory."[1]

In the Book of Mormon, Jacob teaches us that we are not to counsel the Lord, but that we are to take counsel from his hand. (Jacob 4:10.) The Lord does understand why we have the disabled, the blind, the deaf, and the deformed even if we, his children, do not have all the answers. We do not need to ask why, but we do need to seek faith in and support from the Lord.

What can a lay counselor do? You must pray for those with special challenges; then you must be willing to let the Lord answer prayers in his own way. He knows which ways are best—he is a caring Father. President Kimball has said, "The Lord has not promised us freedom from adversity or affliction. Instead, he has given us the avenue of communication known as prayer, whereby we might humble ourselves and seek his help and divine guidance, so that we could establish a house of prayer."[2]

Have Hope and Faith

What else can a lay counselor do? He can stand in for the Good Shepherd. He can help the families have hope—an anchor to hold onto during the inevitable times of trouble. Hope provides the inner reassurance necessary to go forward.

Teach the families and the handicapped person to have faith in the eternal perspective of the gospel. President Kimball has said that when elders bless and recoveries do not follow, often there is not only disappointment but also a diminishing of faith. He noted that not all the sick and afflicted were healed in other dispensations, either. "Even the Savior, with all power on earth and in heaven, did not heal them all. He could have done so . . . but many did not have the faith to be healed . . . others he did not heal because they were not to be healed."[3]

President Joseph F. Smith wrote that a person will not always be marred by scars, wounds, deformities, defects, or infirmities, for these will be removed in their course, in their proper time, according to a merciful providence of God. President Smith said, "Deformity will be removed; defects will be eliminated, and men and women shall attain to that perfection of their spirits, to the perfection that God designed in the beginning. It is His purpose that men and women, His children, be born to become heirs of God, and joint heirs with Jesus Christ, shall be made perfect, physically as well as spiritually, through obedience to the law by which He had provided the means that perfection shall come to all His children."[4]

NOTES

1. Spencer W. Kimball, *Tragedy or Destiny* (Salt Lake City: Deseret Book Company, 1977), p. 12.

2. Spencer W. Kimball, "Fortify Your Homes against Evil," *Ensign,* May 1979, p. 6.

3. Spencer W. Kimball, *President Kimball Speaks Out* (Salt Lake City: Deseret Book Company, 1981), pp. 80-81.

4. Joseph F. Smith, *Improvement Era,* June 1909, p. 592.

SUGGESTED READINGS

Darling, Rosalyn and Jon Darling. *Children Who Are Different.* St. Louis: C.V. Mosby Company, 1982.

Despain, Goldie. "Does the Church Provide Curriculum or Resource Material for Handicapped Members?" *Ensign,* August 1981, pp. 28-29.

Ensign, April 1976. This issue contains a number of articles related to various handicaps and how members handle them.

Guidebook for Parents of Handicapped Children (currently being written to help parents understand the position of the Church on handicaps). Special Curriculum Office, 50 East North Temple, Room 2445, Salt Lake City, Utah 84150.

Hawkes, Mary Jane. "Sharing Sarah." *Ensign,* June 1981, pp. 32-34.

Komatsu, Adney Y. "After Much Tribulation Come Blessings." *Ensign,* November 1979, pp. 68-69.

For general information regarding Church programs for the handicapped write: Director of Handicapped Services, Personal Welfare Services, 50 East North Temple, Salt Lake City, Utah 84150.

ABOUT THE AUTHOR

Dr. June Leifson, assistant dean of the College of Nursing at Brigham Young University, received her bachelor's degree from BYU, her master's degree from Wayne State University, and her Ph.D. in family sciences from BYU. She has been selected for numerous honors and awards, including Outstanding Young Woman of America. In 1977, she was a delegate to the White House Congress of Handicapped Individuals. In 1982, she received the Beatty Award, the Utah Public Health Association's highest award. She has served the Church as a missionary, as a Young Women's president, as a stake Special Interest leader, and in many other ways.

18

Coping with Challenges in the Adult Life Course

Kenneth R. Hardy

> "To everything there is a season, and a time to every purpose under the heaven: A time to be born and a time to die; a time to plant, and a time to pluck up that which is planted." (Ecclesiastes 3:1-2.)

A common misconception as we are growing up is that once we are adults, having finished school, obtained a job, or gotten married, life proceeds pretty much on an even keel, without much change, until we are old and feeble. But those of us who have lived through adulthood know better. There are lots of ups and downs, good times and not so good, quiet times and hectic times. Sometimes we feel sure of ourselves; at other points, we are filled with doubts and, perhaps, misgivings about the choices we have made. For few, if any, is adult life a bed of roses. For most, there is a full share of challenges to be met.

Life Seasons and the Life Structure

Unless our lives are cut short from our three score and ten years (the American life expectancy being about seventy-one years for men and seventy-seven for women), each of us experiences a life course of four major seasons, like the seasons of the year, which overlap and merge into each other: (1) pre-adulthood, those growing-up years of infancy, childhood, and adolescence; (2) young adulthood; (3) middle adulthood; and (4) late adulthood. Although each of these periods lasts about twenty-five years, because they overlap they run their full course in eighty years or so. Again, as the four seasons of the year may run a somewhat different course from year to year, so there are individual differences in our life course. For some, adulthood comes early, perhaps precipitated by parental death; for others, it is delayed; for some, young adulthood is stretched out like an Indian summer; while for others, fall comes early. These transitions may come out of phase for some of us, earlier or later than for those around us. Some of life's challenges we can expect, since they happen to most of us, for example, the slowing speed and reactions with age (we just can't keep up with the young adults on the basketball court anymore). Other events are not anticipated, such as the sudden death of a spouse at age thirty-five. Unanticipated events more often assume crisis proportions, partly because they catch us unprepared; though if they are negative in character, we may perceive them more readily as unjustified or tragic.

The challenges of adult living come not only with "significant" events, but also with the day-to-day demands of life when things seem to be going more routinely. Perhaps we can do a better job of coping through planning and preparation if we have a better awareness of the possibilities that lie ahead.

Our "life structure" is built around the major choices we make and the course we then follow as we act upon those choices. Our choices and actions will be affected by the limits our world imposes upon us and by the actions of people around us. Our lives are centered around several life themes, areas in which we commit our energies and make our choices. Some common life themes include our life "dream"; our work; our relationships with others; our family life; our beliefs about life's meaning and purpose; and our life "clock" or expected life span. Generally, we could say that for a person's life structure to be "adequate" at any given time, it should provide at least a modicum of personal satisfaction and should be prized and rewarded by society. Sometimes, though, we will struggle through the more difficult periods of life if we can sustain our hope that things will improve and that our dreams can reach fruition. For example, a husband and wife may willingly submit to years of subsistence living to complete an education, expecting that circumstances will improve after the schooling is completed.

As time passes, we may question the adequacy of our choices and actions in one life theme or another. Perhaps a child gets into serious trouble; our employer offers us a promotion that requires a move to another state; a life-threatening illness occurs; or we are called to or released from a demanding Church position. Perhaps the ticking away of our life clock or the cumulative impact of personal and world events causes us to reexamine what we are doing, wishing, and believing.

If several major themes are affected at once, we enter a crisis period that requires important readjustments. A change in one thematic area may produce effects in others. For example, a job transfer may create disruptions in marital and family relationships if the spouse and children don't want to move; it may sever friendship ties and lead to a change in Church callings. Crises can initiate significant personal growth as we stretch ourselves to cope with them; on the other hand, if we are overwhelmed by them, their effects can be devastating.

Life Themes in Adulthood

Let's now consider each of the life themes in turn, noting how each theme appears in different periods of the life course.

The Life Dream

The life dream is the vision of what we might do or become, what we might bring to pass in our lives. It excites us and helps us sustain our efforts as we try to bring to fruition the anticipations for the future contained within the dream.

One of the tasks of early adulthood is to form and make specific that vision out of the shapeless longings of youth and then to set a course of action to bring it about. For example, John Goddard, the well-known explorer, constructed a list of some forty adventures or explorations he wanted to complete in his life, such as traveling the Nile from its source to the Mediterranean Sea. Another person might dream of becoming a gentleman farmer, complete with mansion and large, productive acreage. Someone else might envision being a fulfilled mother at the center of a loving home, surrounded by adoring children and a devoted husband. Yet another woman might not have crystallized a dream and may drift along for years, perhaps being a part of others' dream fulfillment, without any clear sense of her own desires. The dream usually includes within it elements of the other themes of work, of love and friendship, of growing older, of religion and life purposes.

Youthful zest, enthusiasm, and the vitalizing idealism associated with the life dream are great aids in carrying the person into and through the young adult epoch. For there are momentous changes associated with moving out of the parental home, performing missionary service, establishing oneself in a new social group, getting into the world of full-time employment, and creating and solidifying new personal relationships. These often reach fruition in marriage and the creation of a new family unit.

As we continue our lives, there will be times when we reflect upon our experiences, appraising whether our dreams are being realized, whether they are "pipe dreams" that are totally unrealistic, whether our dreams need revision since they may not represent what we now want, and so on. Actually, this appraisal is continuous, but most of the time we ignore or suppress it as a disruptive intrusion in the onward course to which we are committed. Periodically, though, we will engage in a more conscious, deliberate, and sometimes agonizing reappraisal. Many seem to experience this at mid-life (roughly, ages thirty-five through forty-five). For example, a husband who has been buried for years in his work and career advancement may be shocked into the realization that he doesn't know his children and that his marriage has gone sour. Sometimes a poignant event (such as the death of a loved one) causes our feelings to surface, precipitating such a review. At such times we may rearrange the relative importance of our various life themes, with some assuming a new importance and others being relegated to a minor role.

Work, Occupation, Career

A central theme for most of us deals with the kind of work we will do as a vocation, including the "unpaid" vocation of homemaker. There are two common misconceptions we should consider here. The first is that after some initial indecision people decide upon their vocation, usually by their early twenties, and then stick with that commitment for life. The second misconception is that a person should remain with a given occupation for all of his or her working life. In actuality, there is wide variation in how quickly and certainly vocational decisions are made; furthermore, permanence in a vocational pathway is not necessarily related to a "successful" work career. In an analysis of persons listed in *Who's Who in America*, Sarason found that about 40 percent had made some kind of career change, and, of these changers, about one-fourth had made one or more major career shifts. This was true for persons listed in the 1930s, in the 1950s, and in the 1970s.[1] One example of a man who took a long time to find his niche in the world of work is James Michener, one of the most widely read authors of our time. He knocked about doing various things for many years. He was thirty-eight years old before he settled down to serious writing. Perhaps a few examples of persons I am aware of, all of them devoted Church members, will give some flavor of the variety to be found.

One man began teaching school at age twenty and taught in the same school district for forty-seven years before retirement. He did painting and wallpapering on the side to help support his family.

Another man (N. Eldon Tanner) also began teaching school at age twenty. He too engaged in business activities on the side to help support his family. However, at age thirty-seven, he was elected to the Alberta provincial legislature, and two years later he became a cabinet officer of the provincial government. At age fifty-five he became president of a business firm; at age sixty-two he was called as a general authority, remaining so until his death at age eighty-four.

Still another man entered military service after high school graduation during World War II. Returning to civilian life, he went into the business world and became financially successful through a variety of enterprises. Called as a bishop, he felt very inadequate to counsel ward members. Following his release, he sold out most of his interests, moved his family to a university community, and started college in his late thirties. He graduated in three years, went on for an advanced degree, and is now a professional psychologist.

One woman was a full-time homemaker, rearing several children. In her early forties she returned to college, graduated, completed a doctoral degree, and now works full-time as a professional.

As a final example, a young man went to college immediately after high-school graduation, but he dropped out after two and one-half years to try his hand in business. He became an insurance agent, did very well at it, and was promoted to a managerial position. Unsatisfied with that line of work, he returned to college, graduated, and then went on to law school. He is now a practicing attorney.

Career shifts are likely to increase in the years ahead. In the midst of the computer revolution in our highly technological society, the pace of change has been stepped up, and the already bewildering array of occupational specialties is increasing. More and more, we will need periodic retraining to keep current and to take advantage of new opportunities as well as to avoid unemployment due to obsolescence and other economic causes. Additionally, Americans today believe that work should be personally fulfilling. All of this suggests that both men and women will find it more difficult than ever to settle into one line of work and remain in it for a life-time. Thus, we can anticipate more frequent job or career changes. It is improbable that the stresses associated with such changes will disappear. If we anticipate that they will happen and plan for them, however, we can reduce the stress and better cope with it.

As we consider whether or not it is necessary for us to stay in one career path, a little thought experiment might prove enlightening. Suppose you were given a bonus on your life span. Let's say you had 150 years to live, and that you would have reasonably good physical and mental function-ing for that period of time. Would you want to continue in the same work in which you are now engaged for the rest of your life? If not, what would you like to do? Would you like to pursue several additional careers? This experiment might suggest that there is nothing inevitable about having just one career in one's life. Additionally, a belief in eternal life suggests an extended sequence of possible careers, though we know practically nothing about career opportunities on the other side of the veil!

In the season of young adulthood, a major task of living is that of finding a work niche, settling into it, giving it a (perhaps extended) try, and progressing within it. By middle adulthood we have ordinarily established our credentials; now, however, we may reappraise our job choice and our progress within it, our future prospects, and our possibilities for making a change before it's "too late." As suggested by the work histories above, some may opt for a change. Others may stay where they are, either out of choice or necessity. Women today often confront tough choices as they ap-proach mid-life. The woman who has remained single or who has chosen a childless marriage while pursuing paid employment may reconsider the possibilities for children before her child-bearing years pass. A woman who has cho-sen marriage and motherhood in her early twenties without concomitant paid employment may experience a reap-praisal as her children grow up and may consider entry into the labor force in some way.

As we enter our sixties, we anticipate changes in our work status. For most, there will be no more promotions, the person having reached his terminal position. Retirement or partial retirement, early or delayed retirement, what to do with more free time, and adjustments due to changes in income must be considered as we move into late adulthood. Some enjoy, indeed relish, the retirement years; others, for whom the work theme is vital to their self-definition, put off retirement as long as possible and are miserable when it comes. The self-employed, not locked into a standardized retirement age, often work beyond the normal retirement age.

Personal Relationships

Another major life theme centers upon our relationships with other people—not the casual or superficial interactions we have with acquaintances or work contacts, but rather relationships with others with whom we have more powerful emotional attachments. Usually these are members of our family of origin (parents, brothers, and sisters), friends of both sexes (most commonly about our own age), possibly a few work associates, marriage partners, children, and grandchildren. The foundation of these relationships is formed, of course, in preadulthood. Beginning with our dependence upon our parents in infancy, we work out adult-child relationships; then with brothers, sisters, and playmates, we develop ways of relating to peers, most commonly of the same sex; in our teen years, we struggle through the exciting and anxious process of forming attachments to peers of the opposite sex. Through all of this development, our affectional needs, our social skills, our tendencies to be distant and wary or open and trusting are molded.

As we become adults, major shifts occur that affect these relationships. Typically, we move out of our parents' home, and as we do so, we find that our child-parent relationship changes. Managerial care by our parents is less direct. Gradually, parents and children may develop a new relationship as peers and friends. Brothers and sisters, no longer vying so much for parental attention and favor, may find their relationships changing, frequently for the better. Casual relationships with opposite sex friends give way, through the years of young adulthood, to more lasting, committed friendships and relationships. For most (90 percent), marriage results. In America today, that first marriage is often followed by divorce and remarriage before midlife. Also, in our geographically mobile society, we lose contact with the friends of youth. Adult men typically report having few close male friends; many report having none at all. As the adult years proceed, if children enter our lives, they may provide a major focus for our emotional attachments.

It is interesting to note where people invest themselves emotionally; which relationships, if any, they will focus upon. It is instructive to consider how these concerns might change over the years of early, middle, and later adulthood, and to contemplate how the importance of these relationships might change as the life course proceeds. Some observers suggest that young adult men typically focus their energies on job and career to the relative neglect of family. In our Latter-day-Saint society, men strongly committed to the Church may compound the situation by giving devoted service to time-demanding Church callings after the work day is over. The Church has recognized this problem, and the Brethren have striven in various ways to encourage men to give appropriate attention to the cultivation of family relationships.

Traditionally, we have conceived of men as being concerned with activities and things as they pursue achievements in the world, while we have conceived of women as being more concerned with feelings and people. Whether or not this is a culturally prescribed and thus self-fulfilling phenomenon, it has been true more often than not that women have given more care to the cultivation of relationships than have men. It has been noted, for example, that women provide the bulk of intergenerational helping in our society; that is, if older parents need help, the women (daughters or daughters-in-law) usually step in; if children need help, the women (mothers, grandmothers, aunts) generally provide it. Through such help, relationships are solidified.

Some observers have suggested that as adults move into

the era of middle adulthood, men may reexamine their priorities and may shift toward a greater focus on interpersonal relationships, mending the marriage (or perhaps trying out a new one), trying to get closer to their children, and so on. They may also invest more in their relationships with their parents, as they see parental vigor and health decline, and recognize more vividly the limited time of the mortal life. Conversely, women who have immersed themselves in the care of home and family through the young adult years are sometimes reported to experience an opposite reaction to that of men as they enter midlife. Some, at least, turn outward from the family with a new or renewed interest in education, employment, and community involvement.

Those who do not marry, as well as those who return to singlehood through divorce or death of a spouse (and who do not remarry), may focus on peer (usually same-sex) relationships, sometimes sharing living quarters. They often develop special relationships with other family members (parents, nieces, nephews, and so on). Some evidence suggests that single women are happier with their lives than married women of corresponding ages. The evidence also suggests that single men are less happy than single women. Perhaps this is due to less adequate domestic arrangements and to less satisfactory or meaningful peer associations.

One other relationship should be mentioned, as it is one of considerable significance for many adults: the mentoring relationship. In young adulthood there may be someone, usually five to fifteen years older, who may provide sponsorship, guidance, support, and inspiration, usually in a personal and direct way, for the person. The mentor may open doors, teach the person the ropes, model appropriate behavior, and build the person's self-confidence. In time, as the person achieves experience and maturity, the relationship must change; at times, there is a stormy break, especially if the mentor needs the relationship to continue.

As the life course continues toward and into middle adulthood, the person may take his own turn at mentoring.

Mentoring occurs in many settings: in the trade, business, or profession; in the sports world; in child rearing and home management; in the Church. Bishops, stake presidents, and auxiliary and quorum presidents often serve as mentors to their close associates. Youth leaders and teachers may also function as mentors.

Personal relationships of depth and stability greatly enrich our lives. They provide much of the stuff that makes our lives seem worthwhile. When those relationships end or become disturbed, much grief and agony ensue. The vicissitudes of these relationships tell much of the story of our lives.

Life Meaning and Purpose

The theme of life's purpose is the larger context into which we place the events of our lives. It includes the things we believe in and to which we commit ourselves, the people and institutions toward which we feel a sense of loyalty or obligation, and our ethical and moral sentiments. This framework provides direction and meaning in our lives. Through it we may come to envision our life as having some mission or purpose against the larger backdrop of history. Throughout our lives we form and then modify our system of making sense of our life experience. For Latter-day Saints, the gospel provides an encompassing framework, a focus for our devotions.

It is quite characteristic that from the midteen years through the twenties we are searching for a value system. During these years, typically, conversion and commitment to religious, political-economic, and other ideologies occur. Some youth may passively or vigorously disavow the values of their parents, opting perhaps for an attractive alternative, or perhaps floundering for a more or less extended period of time until a substitute is found or created. And, of course, after a period of rebellion or noncommitment, some may experience an upsurge or renewal of faith in a belief system that didn't "take" in their earlier years.

Once we have worked out our values and beliefs, it is difficult for us to change them, at least in any major way. As a missionary church, we are well aware that the great bulk of our converts come from the youth and young adult groups. While substantial numbers may come from those in their thirties, relatively few are forty or beyond. Similarly, for those who are lifetime members of the Church, activation or reactivation occurs more readily in the twenties and early thirties; it is less likely after forty. Of course, at any age, each of us may come to the point when our present belief system is so unsatisfying, untenable, or incomplete that we become quite receptive to new options. Generally, this is more likely before our patterns of commitment are firmly rooted, or when life events create upheavals within us, causing us to question anew our earlier assumptions and beliefs. Such was the case for Thomas L. Kane, a noteworthy example because of his role in early Church history. The son of a noted federal judge, he led in his youth a privileged life of education and travel and had entertained a future that would fulfill political ambitions of fame and public prominence. But what started out as a casual encounter with the Mormons led him soon, at age twenty-four, to visit the beleaguered Saints, following their expulsion from Nauvoo, in the year 1846. He wrote of this experience four years later, "I believe there is a crisis in the life of every man, when he is called upon to decide seriously and permanently if he will die unto sin and live unto righteousness. . . . Such an event, I believe . . . was my visit to [the Mormon camps on the Missouri]. . . . It was the spectacle of your noble self denial and suffering for conscience' sake, [that] first made a truly serious and abiding impression upon my mind, commanding me to note that there was something higher and better than the pursuit of the interests of earthly life for the spirit made after the image of Deity."[2]

While Kane did not join the Church, he stated, "But now, I have lost almost entirely the natural love for intrigue and management that once were a prominent trait of my character." His commitment to loftier ideals was demonstrated in many subsequent acts of public service, most particularly in his assistance to the Mormon cause.

The "Life Clock"

At all ages, we have some sense of the passage of time in relation to the running out of our life course, but that awareness changes drastically over the years. The baby's focus upon the immediate present enlarges to the daily pattern of the child, who gradually comes to look forward to the time when he or she is grown up and able to do the things adults can do. As youth and young adults expand and crystallize the life dream, it seems that life stretches out almost endlessly before them. Growing old and dying seem almost hypothetical, something that happens to others. The young, at the height of their bodily vigor and mental agility, push the awareness of death aside; the fulfillment of plans and the achievement of goals occupy center stage. But with the passing of the years, we become more conscious that our life span is limited, that time will run out for us. While our bodily faculties diminish only gradually, the modest loss is noticeable enough to prick our consciousness. The deaths of our grandparents, then of our parents and their generation, and perhaps of some of our peers makes much sharper the recognition that our turn, too, is coming, and that we must come to terms with the reality of death. As we go through middle adulthood and into late adulthood, time seems to speed up, the years passing by ever more swiftly.

Young adults experience a tug-of-war between their desire to explore, to have adventure, and to be "free" and uncommitted and the conflicting wish to settle down, to establish roots through marriage, home, family, and steady employment. Those who settle down early may later wonder if they missed out on the excitement of young adulthood, while those who postpone settling down until their thirties may wonder if they passed by golden opportunities in job entry or marriage. As time passes, we have some sense that if we are going to marry, buy our first dwelling, and so on, we should do so about a certain point in time.

During the years between the mid-thirties and the mid-forties, as we pass the anticipated midpoint of our life, we look back upon the past and also look forward to the future. We consider the things we still might change in our family relationships, our careers, in our personal habits, and in our value systems.

In the forties and fifties, we tend to experience a greater sense of urgency to make amends for our neglect of or damage to others, and to accomplish things while we can. At the same time, we engage in a more studied reflection of what we are about. These are the "solid citizen" years, where we experience ourselves at the center of society, the anchor generation between the older folks and the younger ones we are shepherding. For most of us, these are the years of fruition, when our careers reach their peaks and when our children mature and leave the nest, giving us some evidence about how they have turned out. Many experience these years as "the best years of our lives." We also begin to wonder what our legacy will be, what we will leave for our children and the world, what social impact our lives will have made.

In the sixties and seventies, the scales have definitely tipped on the side of being old rather than young. Now we spend much time reviewing the past. While we may initiate new projects, these are usually of more modest dimensions than those of young and middle adulthood. As health and vigor permit, we may try to bring to a satisfactory conclusion unfinished business or projects, though at a more measured pace than formerly. Those who feel particularly robust may initiate ambitious new projects, and some may bring these to a satisfactory conclusion.

In our eighties and nineties, should we survive in reasonably good health, we may experience as a bonus granted to us before it is our turn to leave. By now, we have outlived most of our peers and perhaps some of our children.

Throughout adulthood there abides the persistent wish for life after death. Unless quenched by despair, cynicism, sin, or hopeless misery, the flame of faith enlightens our path with the promise of reunion with those who have preceded or who will follow us through the veil.

Gospel Helps

We have now partially reviewed the course of five themes, those of the life dream, work, personal relationships, life meaning and purpose, and the life clock. These themes don't tell all the story of our lives, of course. Our hobbies and recreational pursuits, our ethnic background, and community and other involvements in society are some, though not all, of the other threads that complete the tapestry of our lives. But having discussed what we have, let us now look at some of the contributions the gospel framework might make in helping us and those around us cope with the challenges in the adult life course that we have considered.

A central value of the gospel is that it provides an eternal perspective. It shows us that this mortal probation, our life on earth, is but a brief way station on an eternal journey, and that life has a wise and glorious purpose. I think it significant that in all dispensations, God has provided his prophets with transcendant visions of space and time, parts of which have been shared with the people and which we find in our scriptures. He has also revealed commandments, principles, and teachings to guide us in making decisions and in acting consistently with eternal goals and righteous purposes. This perspective can help us work out life themes that will lead us to joy rather than to bitterness and regret. It can help us keep our priorities properly ordered so that pursuit of goals in one life theme will not crowd out others to which we should attend. As President Spencer W. Kimball has said, "If we live in such a way that the considerations of eternity press upon us, we will make better decisions."[3]

This suggests that proper planning through the gospel vision can prepare us for the inevitable vicissitudes of life and can prevent us from making some serious mistakes. It can also make us resilient against the stresses of expected and unexpected crises. But, generally, a gospel vision does not come easily or early in life. For many, the gospel perspective is not prized in early adulthood, and for many more it is lost farther along the way. All of us make mistakes, some of them bad ones. Fortunate it is, then, that the gospel teaches us that life's conditions are redemptive and educative rather than condemnatory and punitive. We can repent; we can change; we can seek to make amends and to correct our course at any age. The parable of the prodigal son, the parable of the laborers in the vineyard hired at different times of the day, the Savior's treatment of the woman caught in adultery—all are examples of God's willingness to help lift us sinners out of old mistakes and start us on a better course.

The eternal perspective of the gospel also comforts us in our declining days. As we experience the diminution of our powers and the waning of energy, as our bodily mechanisms wear out, we can accept this in good spirits, being assured that on the other side of the veil we shall pick up the unfinished business of life with full vigor and continue on the pathway of eternal growth.

Making Good Decisions

But a view into the eternities does not necessarily illumine our short-range decisions. It is a condition of mortality that we live by faith, seeing darkly into the days and years ahead. Obtaining a patriarchal blessing, especially as we enter young adulthood, may provide us with some glimpses into the book of our life possibilities and give us some general direction. Wisely, perhaps, such a blessing is rarely specific enough to guide us in day-to-day decisions. Instead, it paints with broad brushstrokes.

Our lives are not fully programmed in advance; rather, they are open-ended to allow the full exercise of agency. The choices we make are real. One of our probationary tests seems to be to check our willingness to place ourselves in the Lord's hands, trusting him to help us in our daily walk as well as at life's critical junctures. Another test is to give ourselves fully into his service. At times, specific guidance may come in answer to fervent prayer, perhaps after fasting; it may come through a father's blessing or other special priesthood blessings. At such times, there may be a special calling for us to fulfill or a virtuous reason for us to pursue a certain course. Yet, in many cases, it is probably true that it doesn't matter to God which of several options we exercise as long as we operate within righteous guidelines. But a life guided by faith is perhaps designed to keep us humbly attuned to the promptings of the Spirit, thereby leading us to discern when our own best judgment is quietly ratified and when another course might better be followed.

Missionary Service in Young Adulthood

Participating in missionary service, particularly for those on the threshold of young adulthood, can help to establish one upon a favorable life course. Therein are provided opportunities to give oneself wholeheartedly and fully to a life of Christian service, to develop love for other people of varying ages and circumstances, to make decisions guided by the Spirit, to form and cultivate mutually beneficial companionships, to organize one's daily activities for maximum effectiveness, to enhance a scripturally-based gospel knowledge, and to make good choices based upon well-ordered priorities. A successful missionary is much better equipped to complete the transition into young adulthood.

The Special Friend

A special friend is someone who shares our vision, our dream; who believes in us and who supports us in our struggle to achieve our dream, who participates fully in it. A mentor cannot fulfill all these requirements. For those who marry, it is particularly fortunate if one's spouse is someone with whom they can go hand-in-hand toward the actualization of the dream they share. A wise marital choice is valuable in this regard, but equally important is a continuing mutual commitment and willingness to work as a team to achieve common and individual purposes.

For those who do not marry, it is most beneficial to have a good friend who can fulfill the requirements just mentioned, at least to some degree. Possibly a series of such friends at different periods may partially substitute here.

The Gospel in Home Living

Through all the years of early, middle, and late adulthood, the consistent implementation of Church standards and programs within our personal and family life can greatly help us cope with the changing stresses of life. For example, the use of family councils, personal interviews, family home evenings, and parental planning sessions can resolve conflicts and foster love, unity, and close relationships within the family. Personal and family preparedness programs can prevent many problems and help with emergencies. Continuing educational and vocational development can increase career opportunities and employment security and enrich life; sound financial management, including food production and storage, adequate insurance coverage, and a savings and budgeting program can provide for economic resilience; developing esthetic and avocational talents and appreciation can add much to life; involvement as individuals and as family groups in service to others—in neighborliness, missionary work, genealogical and temple work, and Church callings—can foster character development and spiritual growth.

Writing entries in a personal journal in a thoughtful, consistent manner can provide opportunities to review our actions in relationship to our goals. Summarizing these in our personal history gives us opportunities to reflect upon the broader purpose of our lives and to revise our course as needed. As we participate in activities with our extended families—in genealogical research, in family reunions, and in family projects—we can, if we will, place ourselves in the broader sweep of family and human history, in the great drama of mortal existence. We can cement ties with our kin, drawing closer to those to whom we owe much, with whom we share much, and to whom we can give much.

For many, great opportunities open up in the retirement years that can fill late adulthood with satisfying and ennobling service, years that might otherwise be filled with aimless busywork, loneliness, self-pity, or a surfeit of recreation. Full-time missionary work may be a possibility, as may temple work. Continued genealogical research and the development of family histories can produce generational ties. A variety of other voluntary service options, if exercised, can make the retirement years as busy and meaningful as we care to make them: welfare projects, foster grandparenting, sub-for-Santas, neighborly visiting of the home-bound, and so on.

Gospel Service

In serving others we find much of the meaning of life. Those others are found everywhere: within the walls of our own home; among our ancestors; in our neighborhoods; indeed, wherever our influence might reach. In the larger sense, our life task is to grow toward sanctification, and the most important virtue toward that end is that of Christ-like love. We foster and demonstrate the love of God and of his children through a life of consistent service. The Church formalizes many opportunities for service in the callings we receive, but our service should not be limited to formal assignments. As we extend ourselves in love, we reap a harvest of trust, mutual respect, caring, and true friendship, whether within the home or outside it.

An important service we can provide adults of any age is to extend empathy, compassion, and gospel reassurance as they experience the challenges of the adult life course. When they are agonizing over seemingly endless vocational decisions or are experiencing marital distress or family conflicts; when they are crying out against the injustices, tragedies, and seeming futility of life; when they are discouraged about insufficient worldly success or wondering if their life has made any difference; when they are filled with remorse or misgivings over past mistakes—in all such cases we can help. At these times, we can help people understand that difficulties in adult living are normal. We can share our gospel perspectives to help the person with his decisions and struggles. Since we ourselves are trying to find our own way, we can extend empathy. Finally, we can extend compassion, patience, long-suffering, and kindness—in a word, love—as we support the efforts of others to work through their difficulties.

NOTES

1. See Seymour B. Sarason, *Work, Aging, and Social Change* (New York: Free Press, 1977), pp. 245-51. Sarason discusses the belief, especially strong for professional people, that one must remain in a single career until retirement. He labels it the "one life–one career" imperative.

2. Letter from Thomas L. Kane to Brigham Young and others, July 11, 1850, LDS Church Archives; quoted in Leonard J. Arrington, "In Honorable Remembrance: Thomas L. Kane's Services to the Mormons," *BYU Studies* 21 (Fall 1981): 392.

3. Spencer W. Kimball, "The Things of Eternity—Stand We in Jeopardy?" *Ensign* 7 (January 1977): 3.

SUGGESTED READINGS

I have drawn heavily from what I consider to be the best single reference to the adult life course: Daniel J. Levinson, *The Seasons of a Man's Life* (New York: Knopf, 1978); the book is also published in paperback (New York: Ballantine, 1979). His general conception of the life course, the elements of the life structure, and the temporal processes affecting that structure I find very insightful. In this work, Levinson postulated a rigid sequencing of periods of stability and change affixed to precise ages, an idea that has not received general support.

Of course, I have also relied upon the work of many other contributors to adult psychology. A good general treatment of this field is the text by Judith Stevens-Long, *Adult Life: Developmental Processes*, 2nd ed. (Palo Alto: Mayfield, 1984).

ABOUT THE AUTHOR

Dr. Kenneth R. Hardy, professor of psychology, has taught at Brigham Young University for over thirty years. He received his bachelor's and master's degrees from the University of Utah and his Ph.D. from the University of Michigan. He has been a consultant in interpersonal relations and community development and has published articles in both professional and Church periodicals.

He has served in the Church as bishop, bishop's counselor, high councilor, ward executive secretary, and in many other teaching and administrative callings.

He and his wife, Mary, are the parents of six children.

19

Helping Those with Religious Questions and Doubts

D. Jeff Burton

> To some it is given by the Holy Ghost to know that Jesus Christ is the Son of God. . . . To others it is given to believe on their words, that they also might have eternal life if they continue faithful. (D&C 46:13-14.)

Mormonism is known, among other things, for its emphasis on personal conviction and strong testimony. Members often expect to receive a manifestation or confirmation that the essentials of the gospel are true. Partly because of this expectation, Latter-day Saints with unresolved religious questions and uncertainties may experience agonizing introspection, emotional difficulties, and even self-imposed alienation.

One aspect of the problem is that while some Latter-day Saints are patient in their search for understanding and are willing to seek additional insights into unresolved questions of faith, others are troubled by their unanswered questions. They seek a complete fulfillment and understanding, and when this ideal is not achieved, such seekers often experience feelings of unworthiness or guilt. Perhaps some of their religious colleagues even question their tendency to question, further suggesting that there must be something wrong with their faith.

Although many Latter-day Saints live comfortably close to an unruffled ideal, others have not achieved such serenity. For example, some seekers repress their natural urge to question in order to maintain an unruffled image, and they may settle for the appearance of belief in place of actual conviction. Such self-deception creates emotional conflict and is attended by feelings of guilt and hypocrisy. They may say to bishops, priesthood leaders, Relief Society presidents, and friends such things as "I'm living a lie," "What's wrong with me? I can't live up to the expectations of others," or "I feel so guilty. The Lord must hate me."

Some Latter-day Saints feel caught in a circle of attempts and failures to gain a testimony. They may feel frustrated, discouraged, and unworthy.

They may say, "I've prayed and fasted but I still have questions. Why don't I get the same answers as others?" or "I just can't accept a calling while I have these nagging doubts," or "I don't deserve blessings because I have uncertainties and questions inside."

Furthermore, members desiring to discuss their questions and doubts often find communicating about religious issues difficult or impossible. With no exchange of ideas, their emotional, spiritual, and intellectual growth may suffer. If others feel uncomfortable talking with them about their questions, they may become emotionally alienated from the Church and even stop all Church activity. They may tell you something like, "If I can't have the same assurance as others, I don't want to participate," or "I can't talk to anybody about this," or "If it weren't for the kids I'd just quit it all."

People with unresolved doubts may experience marital conflicts, denial of reality, weakened ability to deal with feelings and emotions, and reduced motivation to learn. They may say, "My wife keeps saying, 'Why can't you just believe? Why do you have to question everything?' She thinks I'm not trying, that I'm somehow unworthy of the blessings of a sure knowledge. Why can't she just understand that I do have questions?"

Interestingly, the struggle of a doubter reveals a degree of faith. Without some religious faith, there would be no reason to seek or to be dissatisfied with not understanding it all. People do not seek to understand that in which they have no faith. It is the recognition or hope for truth that helps guide those who are troubled about religious matters.

Religious doubt may arise at any age, but it is more typically seen during the years of intellectual maturation. Counselors should be particularly sensitive to this problem among young adults, and especially among college students.

Counseling Those with Doubts

Many of the problems associated with religious questions and doubt grow out of misconceptions concerning the relationship of knowledge to faith and the roles these play in our lives. By sharing the following perspectives on the nature of religious conviction and commitment, counselors can help struggling members to see their circumstances in a more positive light and pave the way to personal growth and emotional satisfaction.

1. *Mormonism and society have different meanings for the terms* faith *and* belief. Latter-day Saints often see the terms *belief* and *faith* as synonymous, both being the natural result of learning truth. The scriptures often equate the two words. However, in our present-day society, particularly in the sciences, the terms *belief* and *faith* have come to have distinct, mutually exclusive meanings.

In the contemporary sense, belief is a mental state that tells us something is true based on experience, information, evidence, or authority. For example, if we flip a coin fifty times and tabulate the results of heads versus tails, we are likely to *believe* from the evidence that each comes up about equally. Of course, no one person's interpretation of the evidence will prove satisfactory to everyone. A mother looks at a newborn baby and has sufficient evidence to believe in the existence of God. But a biochemist looking at the same child may marvel at the power of evolution.

The term *faith*, on the other hand, refers to a feeling, a

trust in "the evidence of things not seen." (Hebrews 11:1.) Belief is learned; faith is evidence yet to be learned. Belief is what we really think; faith is what we are willing to accept in the absence of proof.

Also, *faith* implies an active personal commitment. Thus, under these definitions, it is possible to question aspects of our religion yet live the gospel by faith.

Accept the possibility that you and the person you are counseling may be operating under different definitions as you discuss belief and faith. Define your terms to assure clear communication.

2. *Doubt is not necessarily a rejection of God.* Again, it is important to recognize the multiple meanings of the word *doubt*. In its modern, constructive sense, it means to be unsettled in belief or opinion; to be uncertain or undecided. It implies a lack of information or evidence upon which to base a belief. Doubt, according to this usage, is an inevitable consequence of a maturing, inquiring mind and should be managed, not denied. In contrast, the more traditional meaning of doubt includes the notion of distrust. In a religious context, doubt is associated with a rejection of God and a thankless denial of his goodness. Is there any wonder the word *doubt* has such a strong negative connotation? Sincere questioners can be encouraged to disclose their commitment to learn at the same time they reveal their questions. They can also avoid being hurt or offending others by choosing their words carefully and defining any likely-to-be-misunderstood expressions.

3. *No one knows everything.* We in the Church often use the words *I know* to describe our testimonies ("I know the Church is true.") Most often, we mean that we have received a witness of the Spirit. That kind of knowledge comes by means other than what science or technology subscribe to, and it is possible to receive this sure witness from God. But no mortal can know everything about God and his ways. (See Moses 1:5) And sometimes people use the word *know* to mean strong belief or faith (in other words, "I intensely believe the Church is true," or, "My faith is strong that the Church is true.")

To know, in its technological sense, is to have a clear understanding, to be relatively sure. Knowledge is familiarity with or awareness of facts and evidence. But in mortality *nothing* can be known by scientific criteria with perfection, only in degrees of confidence. While science and statistics have developed elaborate methods for testing, verifying, and strengthening the evidence upon which beliefs and knowledge are based, not even scientific tests produce perfect knowledge. Furthermore, scientists themselves use faith when they rely on their own methods or unproven assumptions.

Questioners can be shown that since no one can claim perfect knowledge in everything, it is only reasonable to expect a degree of uncertainty in this mortal life.

4. *Most Latter-day Saints have questions about religious matters.* Wondering is a common and natural reaction to all but the most commonplace information. Probably nearly every Latter-day Saint, for example, has had one or more of the following questions cross his mind at some time: Why would God command Adam and Eve not to eat of the tree of knowledge of good and evil? Why did he command Nephi to kill Laban? Why did he command Joseph Smith to practice polygamy? Did Joseph Smith truly translate gold plates and papyri? Is my bishop really inspired in this call?

A popular approach to dealing with such questions is to blame Satan or the weakness of the questioner. But if wondering is natural, if seeking more light and knowledge is a legitimate gospel activity, and if one so seeking is obedient to gospel principles, then guilt and repression of questions are unnecessary and only serve to cause pain and to divert attention away from dealing responsibly with real religious issues.

5. *Everyone is a believer to some degree; our uncertainties vary in strength.* Latter-day Saints who are uncertain about particular tenets of their religion should not be hasty in applying negative labels to themselves. Such negative self-labeling undermines self-esteem. A little belief is like a seed: nourishment and care may produce a tall, strong tree of knowledge. But that takes faith, time, and work.

Point out that varying strengths of belief in different facets of the gospel are not uncommon, and that questions are not the same as unbelief; indeed, it is highly unlikely that any two people will share exactly the same convictions on all issues. Help the person with questions or doubts to see himself as an integral part of a diverse Church rather than as an outsider.

6. *When properly approached, questioning is a vital part of the learning process.* Having questions implies a desire to expand the information upon which beliefs are based. Mormonism celebrates intelligence as "the glory of God" (D&C 93:36) and proclaims that man is saved no faster than he gains knowledge. Obviously, such commitment to learning cannot be served by suppressing inquiries about the kingdoms of heaven and earth.

On the other hand, a philosophy of sincere inquiry does not license questions asked in a spirit of challenge or accusation. Suppose a Church member has trouble understanding why the Lord would command Nephi to kill Laban. How does he seek information and express his true feelings without sounding distrustful, negative, or dissenting? Such threatening overtones can frequently be avoided by prefacing questions with honest statements of feelings, such as "I'm troubled by . . . " "It bothers me greatly, but I am skeptical of . . . ," "This is a question that has caused me a lot of turmoil. I want to talk to you because I respect you. I wonder if you could tell me what you know about . . . ?"

Counsel the person that the pursuit of truth is rarely harmed by sincere questions made in the spirit of humble curiosity.

7. *The blessings of the gospel come through faithfulness and obedience; particular beliefs may vary within certain bounds.* Some Latter-day Saints assume that there is only one way to believe in Church doctrines. Quite to the contrary, a great deal of freedom exists on matters of belief in religious matters. Joseph Smith, as reported in the *History of the Church* 5:215, said, "The most prominent difference in sentiment between the Latter-day Saints and sectarians was that the latter were all circumscribed by some peculiar

creed, which deprived its members the privilege of believing anything not contained therein, whereas the Latter-day Saints have no creed, but are ready to believe all true principles that exist."   .

Similarly, President Joseph F. Smith testified before the Congress of the United States that Latter-day Saints "are given the largest possible latitude of their convictions, and if a man rejects a message that I may give to him but is still moral and believes in the main principles of the gospel and desires to continue in his membership in the Church, he is permitted to remain." In the same setting, he observed:

> Members of the Mormon church are not all united on every principle. Every man is entitled to his own opinion and his own views and his own conceptions of right and wrong so long as they do not come in conflict with the standard principles of the Church. If a man assumes to deny God and to become an infidel we withdraw fellowship from him. But so long as a man believes in God and has a little faith in the Church organization, we nurture and aid that person to continue faithfully as a member of the Church though he may not believe all that is revealed. (*Reed Smoot Hearings*, pp. 97-98.)

The priority of faithfulness over particular beliefs is further demonstrated in the temple-recommend interview, which stresses a person's behavior, obedience, attitude, faithfulness, and commitment.

It is possible to show that questions and uncertainties concerning religion need not keep a person from participating in all facets of the gospel and need not prevent him from full enjoyment of gospel blessings. Through faithfully living the gospel, one may gain a witness that the gospel is true.

8. *Not all information is correct; no source of information is complete.* No single source of information (except God himself)can exhaust the facts concerning any gospel issue. Furthermore, some sources are wrong and others are written to deceive. Still others are well-intentioned but misleading. Historical studies, for example, are subject to many limitations because they involve not only the acquisition of sometimes scarce factual information but also the dubious process of correctly interpreting that information.

Caution the person against jumping to conclusions

based on inevitably inadequate information. Reemphasize the need for faith while he is gathering information and knowledge.

9. *Personal responses to questions and doubts can be controlled by the individual.* We need not be ashamed of or concerned about authentic emotions. We need not avoid sadness when a friend dies; we do not try to avoid joy when we are blessed; and we need not avoid feeling unsettled when we do not understand something important. We can keep seeking understanding, or we can give up. Our *reactions* to our feelings are as important as the feelings themselves, and we can manage our behavior. Control and positive management of difficult emotions are always helped by understanding the emotion—its origin, its reason for being, and what we can do about it.

It is possible that a person's troubled response to doubt and questioning is related in part to the way he was reared. Suppose, for example, as a young boy he innocently asked, "Did Joseph really see God?" If his parent or teacher responded with horror, "Of course he did! How could you ask such a thing?" the child may have concluded that questions are unimportant or bad. As he grew to adulthood, he may have come to see skepticism and curiosity as defects in his character. Personal doubts may have been seen as inappropriate temptations rather than as challenges to be explored and investigated. Thus, leaders, teachers, and parents may have unwittingly planted the seeds of trouble years ago.

A person may also be influenced by local responses to perceived skepticism. The people in his community may encourage guilt as a response to his doubt and inculcate the notion that questioning is a sign of sin, slothfulness, or error. Such negative reactions represent the fears and weaknesses of individuals and are not part of the gospel.

Help the person to understand himself and those around him, and urge him to accept others with patience and love while learning new ways to manage questions and doubts. After all, compassion for the uncompassionate is central to the Savior's mission.

10. *Religion has a spiritual component that is essential to*

learning spiritual truths. As the Doctrine and Covenants tells us, some are given to know, and others are given to believe on their words. We have no way of discerning in advance who will know and who will live by faith until they know for themselves. We don't even know which of the two is more blessed, but we do know that to those given to continue faithfully in the absence of knowledge, there is a promise of eternal life.

There is a spiritual dimension to religion, sometimes called the supernatural or metaphysical, that cannot be explained by contemporary empirical methods. And a person's spirit and mind can be taught truths by God that cannot be learned otherwise. But this requires obedience, faith, and a sincere heart. We are to learn by faith as well as by study. (D&C 88:118.)

So explore with the "sincere doubter" the possibility of giving the spiritual side of life a better chance to succeed. Sensitively explore the possibility that the person's attitudes or sins may be blocking his spiritual learning.

In Summary

As in all counseling, Church leaders, parents, and friends need to show concern, compassion, and understanding for the pain and difficulty the religious doubter may be experiencing. In addition, there are a number of practical suggestions the counselor can offer:

1. Look within yourself, analyze your feelings, and determine your true beliefs; don't be afraid of what you find.

2. Work to be worthy of building faith through obedience, prayer, study, and good works.

3. Establish personal study programs to expand the information and evidence upon which your beliefs and knowledge are built.

4. Give spiritual methods a chance.

5. Seek help when it is needed and admit your fallibility.

6. Talk about your questions in tactful, nonthreatening ways. Be willing to listen to the insights of others. Don't forget to express your positive beliefs and faith, too.

Finally, counselors should leave their charges with hope.

James Francis Cooke said, "The most welcomed people of the world are never those who look back upon the bitter frustrations of yesterday, but those who cast their eyes forward with faith, hope, courage, and happy curiosity."

SUGGESTED READINGS

Faith. Salt Lake City: Deseret Book Co., 1983.

ABOUT THE AUTHOR

D. Jeff Burton, an industrial hygienist, received his B.A. from the University of Utah and his M.A. from the University of Michigan.

He and his wife, Alice, have served as lay counselors and resource persons in the Salt Lake Winder Stake, where he is a high councilor. Brother Burton has published several articles on the problem of doubting.

He has served as a missionary in Japan, as a stake missionary, as a counselor in two bishoprics, and in other Church capacities. He and his wife are the parents of four children.

20

Retirement: Its Opportunities and Challenges

Phileon B. Robinson, Jr.

Evan T. Peterson

Gary D. Hansen

"Age is opportunity no less than youth itself though in another dress. And as the evening twilight fades away the sky is filled with stars, invisible by day."

Henry Wadsworth Longfellow

Retirement is a relatively new development on the social scene. A century ago there were virtually no retired persons except for the very wealthy. Some Americans think of retirement as the beginning of the end, and the career-oriented person may experience severe depression and withdrawal after retiring. The male suicide rate for many years has been highest for those age sixty-five and older.

Research shows that about half of older employees would prefer to continue working even if they had a chance to retire. Being able to work produces feelings of pride, accomplishment, and creativity. Work provides structure and order to one's life.

Obviously, work is much more than a source of income, as it partially regulates lives, provides social relationships, and offers a variety of important experiences. But retirement years can be filled with opportunity and meaning in spite of the losses associated with withdrawal from the labor force.

Retirement and the Law

Mandatory retirement is undergoing a transformation in this country, largely due some humanitarian concern and to the financial strain placed on the Social Security system. The Age Discrimination in Employment Act (1967) protects workers between the ages of forty and sixty-five from discriminatory practices in employment. In 1978 the act was amended to include workers up to the age of seventy. In July 1977 Maine became the first state to end all mandatory retirement.

Early retirement became increasingly popular during the 1960s. It was originally promoted by labor unions for industrial workers, but the trend has been changing because of the demands of the aging population on the Social Security system, accelerated inflation (which has a severe impact on those with a fixed income), and the fact that older people are now in better health and are capable of working longer.

Retirement Expectations

Some scholars and counselors have tried to identify the phases of retirement. Before retirement, many people develop fantasies about what their lives in retirement will be like. When retirement actually takes place, they go through a honeymoon phase in which they attempt to live out these preretirement fantasies. They plan to get a lot of things done around the house; to study music or art; to be of more help to their spouse; or to visit their children and grandchildren more frequently. They may plan to serve a mission or two or to get caught up on their temple work, genealogy, or life history. If their ideas for retirement are based on realistic information, they could well experience success and move into a period of stability. However, if their expectations are unrealistic, they will be unsuccessful in their retirement until they develop a realistic understanding of it.

Adjustment to Retirement

Adjustment to retirement can be a challenge. As you help people approaching this stage of life, consider their

situation. First, the person will lose his job as well as his related work and social roles. Second, he will have reduced income and loss of purchasing power. He may have problems
associated with advanced age, such as declining health and
the illness or death of his spouse. For some Latter-day Saints,
another loss occurs about the same time as retirement from
the labor force: retirement from Church activity. Many older
Church members are not called as bishops, Primary
teachers, stake presidents, Sunday School teachers, Relief Society presidents, and so forth. As a matter of fact, many are
released from a variety of different positions. Those in positions to help the retired maintain active Church service can
bless their lives by doing so, and the retired have much to
offer the Church as well.

Four factors (income, health, family and friends, and
spirituality) largely determine the options that retired people
have. Income is usually the most important factor. People
who adjust most easily to retirement are those who have
made adequate provision for financial security and who
have achieved their job-related goals. Those who have
looked forward to retirement and who have plans and activities that will keep them involved tend to be happier. Retirement satisfaction is also related to certain occupations. Professionals and those from upper management show the most
satisfactory adjustment to retirement.

Typically, health does not decline because of retirement,
but, a person's health can determine much of the quality of
his life. Family and friends also have a profound influence
on his well-being. Money cannot buy friendships nor the
love that exists among close family members.

The four factors are interrelated. For example, good
health can help to produce a strong financial situation. Conversely, a good financial condition can help to maintain adequate health.

Spiritual well-being enhances adjustment to retirement.
Those who are spiritually secure tend to view life more positively than do those who are spiritually insecure and uncertain.

Financial Preparation

Latter-day Saints preparing for the economic needs of their advanced years may be faced with some especially important challenges. Mormons have a longer life expectancy than most people, so economic planning is especially important. They often have larger families, with a commitment of resources to children continuing even after the children leave home. Indeed, it is not unusual for a Latter-day Saint father to retire before his last child has left home, so in some cases retirement funds will be supporting more than just an elderly couple. Also, Latter-day Saints make substantial financial contributions, especially for tithing and missions.

Financial preparation for old age is extremely important for everyone. We don't know how long we will live. We don't know with certainty what our future financial obligations will be. For example, an extended illness can use up all of the savings that a couple has accumulated. Also, we don't know what the rate of inflation will be in the future.

Here are a few practical suggestions about financial preparation:

1. As much as possible, make major home repairs (such as a new furnace or roof) before retirement. Identify what housing would be appropriate and affordable for the future.

2. Plan to have the best possible car, clothing, and furniture at retirement.

3. Don't invest in long-range investments that will mature after your time of need has passed. Having money readily available for use in retirement is far more important than the earnings you might receive from such investments.

4. Avoid get-rich-quick schemes. If you lost your money, how would you live?

Some type of private pension is usually required in order for retirees to have sufficient income. As recently as 1950, only about 10 percent of American workers were covered by some form of private pension. Today more than 30 percent of workers are covered. Most of these private plans have begun since the creation of Social Security and are designed to supplement it. Unfortunately, the majority of current retirees receive little or no pension beyond their Social Security income. Authorities agree that retirees need about 75 percent of their preretirement income to avoid a drop in their level of living. Savings are often inadequate, and many American retirees have to live on about half of their preretirement income. This is likely to be very difficult, especially in advanced old age and in widowhood, when the potentials for poverty and dependency are so high.

Older adults, before and after retirement, should acquire and use the best consumer information available. Such publications as *Consumer Reports*, *Changing Times*, and *Money* can be helpful. Inflation increases the probability that continued work will be essential for many, and second careers have been satisfying to both older men and women because of the added income, the satisfaction of productivity, and the involvement with others that they afford.

Investments should include assets that will respond favorably to inflation, such as real estate and some stocks and mutual funds. Those planning retirement should maximize their Social Security earnings, develop a substantial private pension or IRA or Keogh account, and have a combination of fixed- and variable-return assets in their savings and investment portfolio. Those who take these steps will enjoy more security and prosperity. They will be able to maintain an enjoyable life-style without the dread of deprivation, compromise, and dependency.

Those who want a secure future should regularly review their insurance programs, Social Security benefits, private pensions, and other savings and investments. They will use the best professional financial, tax, and legal counsel available. They will preserve their estate through proper planning and appropriate transfer arrangements. Only judicious attention can minimize unexpected losses and disappointments.

Health and Retirement

When old people are asked to list their problems they consistently rate health at or near the top. In a recent national survey in which respondents were asked what their most serious problem was, three times as many mentioned health as loneliness, the next most serious problem. Good physical health, like financial security, seems to be important not only because its absence brings suffering, but because it determines the limits of the other areas of life.

The old are usually afflicted more with long-term health problems than are the young. Common examples are heart trouble, arthritis, diabetes, rheumatism, and hypertension. On the other hand, old people suffer less than young people from temporary illnesses such as the common colds or pneumonia.

Although sickness tends to increase with age, fewer than 5 percent of the elderly are hospitalized at any one time. However, more than 20 percent of them spend time in hospitals or care institutions before they die. Compared with those under age sixty-five, they have three times as many hospitalizations, and their hospital stays are three times longer.

Supportive families and friends can play a significant role in the health care of the retired. Their help often delays institutionalization. When the aged go to institutions, their physical needs are cared for mainly by professionals. But even then, home teachers, visiting teachers, family, and friends can continue to contribute to their social and emotional well-being. Since these moves often take old people from their own families and neighborhoods, special effort is usually required to serve their needs. The help of those living near the new residence of the elderly may be required to give the necessary support. The tragic depression of the elderly in nursing homes can be radically changed by the visits of a loving wife or husband. A caring friend or church leader can also reinforce a person's sense of self-worth and strengthen his courage and ability to endure his trials. Of course, a person's own attitude toward life influences the benefits he can receive from loyal friends and family. Elder LeGrand Richards noted the importance of a good mental attitude when he wrote, "The only reason I can give for my long life is that

I am a very happy man and have been all my life." Professionals could easily note other influences that would help to explain his long life, but probably no one would deny the benefit that came from his enthusiasm for living. If it didn't add years to his life, it certainly added life to his years.

As people age and their hearing and vision deteriorate, they become increasingly accident prone. They should take precautions against slick floors, sliding rugs, and steep stairs. They might consider installing handrails and bright florescent lights. They may need to avoid driving after dark, and older pedestrians may need special help to avoid accidents. The fact that the period of convalescence is usually longer for old people following illness or accident emphasizes the need for more precautionary measures. Unfortunately, in some cases older patients never do fully recover from the effects of a serious fall or other accident.

When Latter-day Saints think about achieving good health, their minds naturally turn to the Word of Wisdom, which includes much more, of course, than the oft-mentioned exclusions from our diet. The spirit of the revelation speaks to us about our emotional and intellectual health as well as our physical condition. The spiritual, physical, intellectual, and emotional forces in our lives are all interrelated. We need regular physical examinations, adequate nutrition, daily exercise, and appropriate intellectual and cultural stimulation. Starting vigorous physical exercise late in life should be done with caution after consultation with a physician.

Family and Friends

Our most significant social relationship is usually with our spouse. If there is a good marital relationship before retirement, there is more likely to be a good marriage after retirement. A good marriage is one in which the couple knows how to enjoy each other and how to solve marital problems rather than one in which there are no problems. However, if the couple has not learned how to work out their problems, and particularly if they have both used their work as an escape from confrontation with each other, then the added time they spend together after retirement will indeed seem burdensome. Some women complain that their retired husbands seem to be always "underfoot." Others say they have "twice as much husband and half as much income." Many retired couples are alone together for the first time since the early years of their marriage. They may need to rebuild the relationship they used to have or create new bonds and shared activities. By trying new things while keeping a good sense of humor, they can solve many difficulties.

Children and grandchildren are another source of joy and satisfaction to many older people. Those who have achieved a good relationship with their adult children and with their grandchildren balance their love and concern so that it is not interpreted as interference or pressure. Most older people have frequent contact with their children, but for the day-to-day activities, they rely more on their friends and neighbors. Their children are, in a sense, an emotional reservoir for them. They can get help from them if they need to, but they prefer not to. The giving and taking between older adults and their adult children seems to be best when it is reciprocal. The older person does not want to be considered only when babysitting chores are needed, and the adult child does not want to be thought of only when his parents need something. Both cling to their independence while they continue to cherish each other.

Loneliness is a serious problem for many elderly who live alone with no family members nearby. Especially at night, on weekends, and on special occasions such as Christmas or the birthday of a loved one, visits and telephone calls from family, friends, and home teachers and visiting teachers are very important.

Spirituality and Learning

Latter-day Saints know that the mind is a gift from God and that man has stewardship for its use. This is important for aging Church members because never before in their lives have most of them had such a fine opportunity to read, study, and develop the mind. As physical activities become less attractive, intellectual pursuits become more important. Actually, relatively few older people participate in formal education programs. Many of them, however, do engage in learning activities alone or in other informal ways. Personal study projects of various kinds are becoming increasingly popular with adults of all ages. Sometimes nonparticipation in formal education is due to declining health, a lack of transportation, or some other similar reason.

While some older people say they are too old to learn, research clearly demonstrates that healthy old people can learn all they want or need to learn. The capacity to learn in old age can be greatly enhanced by a strong desire to learn. Learning skills will be more effective if educational activities have been engaged in regularly over the adult years. "Use it or lose it" applies to both physical and intellectual abilities.

From a leader of the American Association of Retired Persons has come the following statement about adult participation in learning activities: "The most pragmatic reason for improving one's mind is that this is the place where one increasingly lives as one grows older. As external pleasures diminish with age, a sparsely furnished mind becomes a prison cell when it should be a lounge, a library, and a balcony upon the world."

Members of the Church have a special responsibility to continue to grow in knowledge. We are told to "seek . . . out of the best books words of wisdom." (D&C 88:118.) We are also commanded to study all things that pertain to the kingdom. (D&C 88:79.) We might learn a language, learn to play the piano, learn to write, or learn hundreds of other things that are available to us. The Church provides many excellent study aids.

Many universities, including Brigham Young University, offer home-study courses. There are excellent adult-education programs in many areas of the country. Many people have access to schools that offer evening courses as well as day courses. Many classes can be taken without having to pay for academic credits. Even those who live in isolated parts of the country usually have libraries from which they can select good books.

Activity in Retirement

Members of the Church have many opportunities to be involved in worthwhile endeavors following retirement. Many of these activities are a continuation of the things the people enjoyed before retirement. These may include writing personal and family histories, doing genealogical work, serving frequently in the temple, working in the name-extraction program, working on a welfare farm, serving a mission, organizing and promoting family organizations, studying the scriptures, and, of course, continuing with ward and stake assignments and church attendance. Our work as Latter-day Saints is never finished.

Opportunities for public service are also available. There is work to do in senior centers, in chapters of the American Association of Retired Persons, in the Red Cross, in community hospitals, and in many other organizations.

Counseling Others about Retirement

Those wanting to help people in retirement might ponder the things they would do in their own family to help aging relatives. Then, keeping in mind the suggestions in this chapter, they can apply their insights to those people they are counseling.

SUGGESTED READINGS AND RESOURCES

Clark, Harold Glen. "How to Get Better as You Get Older." *Ensign*, December 1975.

Featherstone, Vaughn J. "The Savior's Program for Care of the Aged." *Ensign*, November 1974.

Hansen, Gary D. "Growing Older: Everybody's Challenge." *Ensign*, November 1973.

Publications from the American Association of Retired Persons, 1909 K Street NW, Washington, D.C., 20049.

Resource Center on Adult Development and Aging, 303 HCEB, Brigham Young University, Provo, Utah 84602.

ABOUT THE AUTHORS

Dr. Phileon B. Robinson, Jr., director of the Resource Center on Adult Development and Aging at Brigham Young University, received his bachelor's degree from BYU, his master's degree from Northwestern University, and his Ph.D. in adult education at the University of Nebraska. Prior to his present position, he was assistant dean of the Division of Continuing Education at BYU for twenty years. He has served in the Church as a mission president, a stake presidency member, and a counselor to a bishop, and in many other callings. Phil and his wife, Hortense, are the parents of seven children.

Dr. Evan T. Peterson, professor of sociology at Brigham Young University, received his bachelor's and master's degrees there and his Ph.D. degree from the University of Michigan. He has held numerous positions at BYU, including chairman of the sociology department, director of the Survey Research Center, and acting dean of the College of Social Sciences. He has taught as a visiting professor at a number of universities. Dr. Peterson is the author of over fifty books, chapters, articles, and other publications. He has served in the Church as a bishop, in bishoprics, as a high councilor, as a missionary, and in other priesthood callings. He and his wife, Gail, are the parents of six children.

Dr. Gary D. Hansen, a financial and tax-planning consultant, received his bachelor's degree at Utah State University, his master's degree at the University of Minnesota—Minneapolis, and his Ph.D. from the University of Oregon. He has taught at BYU and the University of Nebraska. He has served in the Church as a bishop's counselor, and a ward clerk, and in other priesthood callings. He and his wife, Bonnie, are the parents of seven children.

21

Chronic Illness

William G. Dyer

> Remember in all things the poor and the needy, the sick and the
> afflicted, for he that doeth not these things, the same is not my dis-
> ciple." (D&C 52:40.)

A central part of the message of the Savior has always
been to look after the sick and afflicted. The parable of the
Good Samaritan examined the response of the hated
Samaritan who attended to the wounds of an afflicted Jew.
For such service, the good Samaritan has become the em-
bodiment of the person who truly loves his neighbor as himself.

Most members of the Church and most bishoprics, Relief
Society presidencies, home and visiting teachers, and neighbors probably feel with some justification that they respond
immediately and generously whenever there is illness in the
ward or branch. Whenever a mother has a new baby, someone has an operation, or serious illness or injury strikes a
member, the other members rally around and attend to the
needs of the sick person and his family. However, a number
of sick people are neglected, ignored, mistreated, and misunderstood. These are those who suffer from chronic illness,
who have illness or disabilities that persist, that do not get
better. A chronic illness is a great trial for the sufferer, who
often feels great emotional stress, for the debilitating condition goes on and on without an apparent end. The chroni-

Figure 1: Cycle of Normal Illness

cally ill person, his family, his neighbors, and his church leaders often need to learn how to cope with this type of situation so they may all be able to bear their infirmities.

Normal and Chronic Cycles of Illness

Illness or injury come to all of us, and we usually expect to follow a pattern that is characteristic of most illness. Figure 1 shows this pattern. The person has an illness and falls from the path of normal health. Then comes a period of diagnosis and treatment followed by a period of convalescence. Finally, the person returns to good health again.

The person who is ill and his family, friends, and neighbors are used to this cycle and generally move in to help during the illness, treatment, and convalescence, assuming that at some point the person will return to normal health and that their assistance will no longer be needed. However, in the case of the chronically ill, this cycle does not occur. Figure 2 shows the pattern of chronic illness. The person becomes ill and loses his normal health. He too goes through a period of treatment and sometimes a form of convales-

Figure 2: Cycle of Chronic Illness

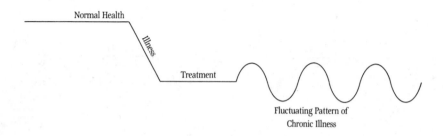

Fluctuating Pattern of
Chronic Illness

cence, but for a number of reasons, depending on the illness, the person does not return to a condition of normal health but continues in a fluctuating pattern of chronic ill health. The person may have periods when he feels better or worse, but at no time does he ever return to complete good health.

Unfortunately, family members, friends, and neighbors do not know how to respond to this unfamiliar pattern, and usually they shift their attention away from the chronically ill person as others with the more normal cycle of sickness occupy their attention. It is at this point that the person with the chronic illness feels that he no longer gets the support, understanding, and assistance he needs to help him endure his continuing pain, depression, and anxiety.

The Patient

The person who finds himself in persistent poor health must make adjustments. Since he, too, is used to the normal cycle of illness, he often cannot accept his illness but, in an increasing state of anxiety, frantically turns from one doctor, treatment, or proposed cure to another. This may be interspersed with periods of depression and apathy where the patient feels completely hopeless and wants to "give up." It is at these times that the patient especially needs support and encouragement from family, friends, and Church leaders.

The patient may also fluctuate between two opposing ways of handling his illness. He may say, "I'm not going to let this get me down; I'm going to try to live my normal life." He may then try to assume normal duties in the home, community, or Church, but he really is not well. People surrounding him are, in a sense, relieved that the person seems to be well and they then ease their support, let the patient take over his former duties, and are glad he has returned to "normal." But the person is not back to normal. He still feels sick. He feels a need to have people understand him and be sensitive to his struggle to live a normal life, but he is distressed to find that others now assume he is well and let him take over all the old responsibilities he really is not capable of handling.

Or, the chronically ill person may find that the only way to keep from being reburdened with all the old duties is to make his illness seem worse than it really is. If he stays in bed and appears to suffer, then others can accept the person as being ill and will move in to help.

One chronically ill mother reported that her teenage children would help wonderfully around the house if she stayed in bed, but if she got up and tried to work, the children expected her to assume all her duties again. It is as though people think that one is either sick or well. But, there are intermediate degrees of sickness and health, and the person in that twilight zone, along with his family, friends, and others, needs to learn how to live in that intermediate state.

As a person lives with illness from year to year, regaining his health naturally becomes a major preoccupation. His treatment and symptoms become the center of his thoughts and actions. Others often cannot understand this single-mindedness and may begin to avoid the patient. The patient himself may need to try to plan other interests and activities that broaden his world and allow for a wider range of discussion and interaction with others.

Something as ordinary as everyday greetings may create a problem for someone who is chronically ill. Someone greeting him may naturally ask, "How are you doing?" The sick person doesn't want to complain, so he responds with something like "I'm all right" or "I'm feeling better." This seems to satisfy the inquirer and is also what he may want to hear, for most people want to hear that people who are ill are improving. A more honest response from the patient would be, "I'm about the same, but I appreciate your concern."

Also, a patient may appear well, and may even feel well for a time, but his appearance may be at variance with his actual feelings. One bishop remarked that a man in his ward worked five days a week but never came to church or filled an assignment. The bishop felt for a long time that the man, who claimed to be a faithful Church member, was really something of a hypocrite. This bishop, however, spent time finding out more about this man and discovered that he was chronically ill but mustered all of his strength to go to work to make a living for his family and then used the weekend to recoup his meager energies. What this man needed was understanding and support, not condemnation, and when the bishop finally understood the situation, he was able to give the man and his family the help they needed.

Many chronically ill people find it difficult to live with their illness. They fight it, hate it, and give in to it; they feel abused and picked on, abandoned, and rejected by everyone, including the Lord. Learning to cope with their condition is a major challenge. It is possible to learn from long-term illness, to grow with the burden rather than be diminished by it. However, only a person who has had such an affliction can really appreciate the struggle of another.

The Family of the Chronically Ill

When illness strikes a person, the other family members move in, and, expecting the normal cycle of illness to occur, plan rather unconsciously to handle an illness of limited duration. They assume the extra duties, wait on the sick person, and see this as a challenge and a responsibility that they are willing to handle. If the illness becomes chronic, however, the family is often not prepared. Strains and disturbances may occur. Sometimes there are subtle and hidden feelings of resentment toward the sick person, a kind of blaming him for not getting better and allowing the whole family to return to normal. The sick person often senses this resentment and tries to reduce that by struggling to resume a normal role, which often results in even worse health. Sometimes family members slip into a pattern of isolating and ignoring the chronically ill person. They cope with the problem by blocking it out of their minds and even gear their activities to avoid and ignore the ill person in hopes of reducing some of their distress and strain. This may leave the sick person feeling unwanted, rejected, and alienated from the family. This, in turn, contributes to the stress in the family.

This is a difficult situation, for with the loss of the normal functioning of any family member, role relationships are disturbed and a new balance must be established in the family. If the mother or father is ill, someone else must pick up their duties in addition to providing care for the sick person. When a son or daughter is ill, the family loses whatever their contribution was to the family activity and work pattern. This shifts the person's responsibilities to other family members.

The family needs to establish a new set of duties and expectations about what each family member will need to do to accommodate the illness of the sick person. A daughter may have to prepare family meals; a son may have to do the washing; and the father may have to be the family chauffeur and shopper—all in addition to their regular activities and with the expectation that this will continue indefinitely. This is a great deal to ask of family members, and it takes a great deal of understanding, discipline, discussion, love, and faith to accept this new way of life. Chronic illness can disrupt and divide a family, or it can provide the family with an opportunity to grow in understanding, patience, sacrifice, and love for one another.

Friends, Neighbors, and Church Leaders and Members

Surrounding the chronically ill person and his family is the social world of friends, neighbors, and the Church. These can either be a source of support and help or a source of feelings of neglect, rejection, misunderstanding, and frustration. Most people help at the beginning of the illness. But when the person does not get better, they become confused and slowly begin to shift their attention away from the person. This loss of support often makes the sufferer feel neglected and rejected. Many chronically ill people who suddenly develop a more visible health problem like a heart attack or have an operation find that other people begin to respond with warmth and support that had been denied during the chronic period.

Since chronic illnesses are foreign to the experience of most people, it is often unclear to them how to respond. Many chronic sufferers have emotional illness that others find upsetting or difficult to respond to.

People in a ward or branch who wish to help bear the infirmities of those who are ill might consider the following ideas:

1. Survey the ward through home teachers and visiting teachers and identify all those who have a chronic illness—any physical, mental, or emotional condition that leaves the person at a level of health below what could be called normal.

2. Discuss in some detail with the person how his illness is affecting him and his family and find out what his needs are.

Don't just thoughtlessly ask, "Is there anything I can do for you?" Some people do not like organized branch or ward assistance—they prefer only spontaneous support. Others welcome an organized and sustained support program.

3. Make *short* visits. Many patients get tired or over-stimulated from long visits. A cheery visit for twenty to thirty minutes is best.

4. Send a card or note or make a short phone call to the sick person. These remembrances are always appreciated.

5. Look for ways to help with young children. Take them to your home to bake cookies or make candy, and send the goodies home with them. Take them to church activities or provide transportation to various functions.

6. Send a cake, a loaf of bread, a bowl of cherries, or some tomatoes. The feeling of being remembered is more important than the gift.

7. Tape record a sacrament meeting or Sunday School class and take it to the patient.

8. Under the direction of the bishop, take the person the sacrament.

9. When the patient does get out to a Church function, visit with them pleasantly. Avoid saying things that will make the person feel pressured, such as "We hope you can come every time now."

10. Older people who have a rather constant state of lowered health and energy might like young people to visit and share their fun and spirit.

11. Drop off an article, clipping, or book that you find uplifting, or stop and share a special experience you have had.

12. Don't brag or recount to the patient all of your accomplishments, travels, and so on. Illness tends to reduce the patient's feelings of competence and self-worth, and he isn't helped by hearing how good, important, or busy you are.

13. It is important that the bishop or branch president visit the patient and acknowledge and accept the illness. One bishop was heard to brush off the condition of a chronically ill person by saying, "It's all in your head." That may be true, but illness in "the head" can result in as much or

even more suffering than physical pain. Mental illness is not exempt from our compassionate response.

14. Don't ask, "What can I do to help?" People do not like to have to ask for support. Be sensitive and imaginative and go ahead and *do something* rather than just ask.

There is Hope with Endurance

One sister who was afflicted with multiple sclerosis reported how being remembered by others and being treated "normally" was important to her. When asked what her greatest source of strength was, she said it had come from the gospel, either from spoken words of leaders or from the scriptures. She noted two very comforting and strengthening articles: "Sweet Are the Uses of Adversity," by A. Theodore Tuttle (*Improvement Era*, December 1967, p. 47), and "The Crucible of Adversity and Affliction," by Marion G. Romney (*Improvement Era*, December 1969, p. 66). Once when she was feeling low, President Joseph Fielding Smith had given a talk in June Conference on the MIA theme for that year: "Search diligently, pray always, and be believing, and all things shall work together for your good, if ye walk uprightly." (D&C 90:24.) She noted, "President Smith said this doesn't mean that we'll necessarily be free from trials and difficulties, but that if we do what is right the Lord will turn our trials and difficulties into blessings. The Lord has done just that for me. Sometimes I see it more clearly than at other times, but I do believe he makes all things work together for our good."

Chronic illness may be difficult to bear, but it can be used as a source of strength. At a time when many of the Brethren who have counseled us regarding adversity are now suffering from it, we might redouble our efforts toward our neighbors who are similarly suffering. We can help the chronically ill endure to the end of their adversity. We thus become a part of those things that will work together for their good.

ABOUT THE AUTHOR

Dr. William G. Dyer, past dean of the School of Management at Brigham Young University, received his bachelor's and master's degrees from BYU and his Ph.D. from the University of Wisconsin. He is a noted authority on behavior change, having been consultant or trainer for numerous large corporations. Dr. Dyer is the author of thirteen books and monographs and over sixty-five articles.

In the Church he has served on the general board of the Sunday School, as a bishop, a high councilor, and a missionary, and in many teaching positions.

He and his wife, Bonnie, are the parents of five children.

22

Fears and Phobias
M. Gawain Wells

All of us have known feelings of fear. Often such feelings teach us of situations to avoid. We sometimes experience fears about specific objects or situations where we feel uncomfortable, but such fears do not significantly interfere with our lives. But phobias, which are excessive and persistent fears, can seriously interfere with our lives.

Development and Changes of Normal Fears

From birth, infants are startled and cry when exposed to sounds or other stimuli that are sudden, intense, or novel. Their eyes and mouths open widely and they reach out to clutch reflexively, even though there may be nothing to grasp. Most parents notice how their babies are frightened by loud noises or by a sense of falling. A mother may feel her baby's startled response to noises even before its birth, and the family members are amused when the baby tenses and clings harder when it is being carried down a flight of steps. As the baby grows, it becomes accustomed to these sensations, and its reactions become less and less intense. The baby is undergoing a psychological process called *habituation* whereby repeated experiences with a stimulus result in paying less attention to the stimulus.

Research tells us that babies develop the capacity to remember faces very early. Thus even an infant has the ability to realize that the face of a person approaching is one it hasn't seen before. Since it has also developed an emotional bond with the faces it does recognize, the stranger's differentness is frightening. Most of us have had the experience of having a friend's baby look at us as if we were the creature from the Black Lagoon, begin crying, and try desperately to hide itself in Mama's arms. This fear of strangers disappears in time (usually at about one year) through the same general psychological process, although some children maintain a general timidity toward strangers throughout childhood.

From infancy until school age, three categories of fear are present in children, each becoming less important as the child grows. First is the fear of noises and sudden movements associated with noise. The sudden, loud noise of thunder is frightening to most young children. Usually by eight or nine years of age, children have redefined it as exciting. They've decided it's fun to be scared . . . a little bit. The second category is fear of strange situations. Children become frightened when placed in unfamiliar circumstances where they don't know what to expect and do not have their parents nearby for support. Examples might be being left alone in a strange room with new people or getting lost at an amusement park. Thus most moms and dads spend a few weeks in the Primary nursery while Junior "gets acquainted." Fear of the dark also fits here because, in the absence of visual cues, even one's bedroom can become a strange place. This fear is often associated with the child's increasing ability to imagine frightening situations. One man described how important it was as a young boy for him to get to sleep before his father. His dad snored loudly, and, even though the boy knew it was his father, he also thought he could see lions and tigers coming into his room, growling around the posts of his bunkbed. Imaginary fears can develop from a fear into nightmares, which also occur in the dark. Thus, a six-year-old girl may not feel comfortable about going to sleep until she tells her parents, "Goodnight, sweet dreams," which reassures her that nightmares won't come. Small children often develop innocent bedtime rituals that help them feel more comfortable with their fears.

Some nightmares become what are called night terrors. Children with night terrors wake up screaming and crying and can't be comforted. That is because they are technically still asleep even though their eyes are open and they may be talking. Once they are gently and truly awakened, the dream is gone. Unlike most dreams, night terrors occur in the deepest stages of sleep. As a rule, children don't remember such dreams, and research suggests that they are harmless to the child (even if harrowing to the parent who thinks his child is delirious).

The third category of childhood fear is *fear of animals.* The sudden approach of a frisky dog or being carried in Daddy's arms up close to a horse's nose is enough to emotionally undo many young children. The suddenness or novelty of the experience seems to cause fright. If the animal were to move more slowly and if the child could choose its own pace for getting acquainted, he would feel much less afraid.

The intensity of these three kinds of fear generally declines over time, primarily because of repeated exposure to them and because of the help of caring adults who reassure the child. However, fears that have been increased by painful events (such as being afraid of a dog and then being bitten by it) may require a longer, more careful, repeated exposure and more emotional support if they are to decrease.

As a child becomes a toddler, he can experience a more serious fear called separation anxiety. This is an unreasoning fear of being separated from his parents, and it is often disguised as a fear of going to school, of being afraid to have his parents go out for an evening or weekend, or persistent worries about his parents dying. The child may develop headaches, become nauseous and vomit, or in other ways seem unable to stay in the situation in which he or she is separated from the parent. Parents can help the child deal with the fear in three ways: First, it is important that the parent be unafraid of the child's alarm. This will do much to help the child feel that the problem can be overcome. Second, it is important that the child be reexposed to the feared situation with encouragement and support. Sometimes it is necessary to build the exposure gradually, with increasing amounts of time spent before the parent returns. In each case the parent and others should continue to express confidence in the child's ability to overcome the fear. Finally, parents should look for opportunities to spend time with the child when the fear is not an issue. Reassured that he or she is loved and that his parents will not leave permanently—either physically or emotionally—the child's fear will diminish.

From middle childhood, children can become self-conscious. At this stage their fears revolve around people—family, friends, classmates, and even strangers. They fear criticism, rejection, being laughed at, and feeling foolish or inadequate. Such social fears may be expressed in a fear of public speaking or of schoolwork.

Like other normal fears, many people overcome these social difficulties by practice, by repeated exposure to the situation, and by learning confidence in their abilities. Others, believing that their fears have been confirmed by disastrous experience, choose to avoid the necessary events that would dispel their feelings. They may still lead healthy, fulfilled lives, but they will not enter certain social arenas.

Nearly all of us have experienced unreasonable fears. At different stages of life, our levels of intellectual and emotional development are associated with the kinds of fears to which we might have been susceptible. For most of us, the fear-arousing situations become more manageable and important as we grow through the influence of repeated exposure, support of family members, and our expanding capabilities. For some, however, childhood fears (especially those that have been increased by trauma) become excessive and persistent, limiting activities and opportunities. Such fears are classified as phobias.

Phobias

A phobia is an abnormal fear. It is characterized by irrationality, feelings of helplessness, and horror, and it seems to make normal, productive learning and living impossible. One person with a phobia wrote:

> Even walking to class, I was tense, with a feeling of dread knotting my stomach. I knew it was ridiculous to be so afraid of singing a solo. After all, the other class members had sung too, for the final exam. In the next twenty minutes I could find some distraction or logic to reduce my apprehension for a few moments only to have it rise again, stronger and more unreasoning than before. As it came my turn, I felt that I just couldn't do it. I wanted to do anything to escape from the feelings I was experiencing. But somehow any of the alternatives would be so humiliating. I knew I was trapped.
>
> Standing in front of the class, my knees actually shook so hard I had to hold on to the piano to make sure I wouldn't fall down. I felt that my face must be completely drained of any color, and yet I was sweating. As I began, I already had so much air in my lungs from breathing hard that I could hardly inhale any more. My heart must have sounded louder than my shaky voice.
>
> I don't know how I ever made it through the song. I was exhausted for the rest of the day. And now, even months later, I can get tense just watching someone else sing and thinking of my doing it. As much as I love singing, I don't think I'll ever be able to perform a solo. I don't ever want to have that feeling again. I know that it's silly, too, but that's how I feel.

This is a description of what might be called a singing phobia. Often a person experiencing such anxiety feels nauseous, dizzy, or weak and may have a sense of choking or suffocation. The heart beats rapidly, the skin perspires, the pupils are dilated, and the muscles tremble excessively. The extremes of such feelings are known as panic, and they may occur in a feared situation, real or imagined. Panic sometimes occurs without warning or apparent cause.

What are the differences between normal and abnormal fears? How do fears that many people experience and overcome become phobias for others?

One cause may be the intensity of the initial frightening experience. More important, however, are the reactions of the person to the experience. The person anticipates other such frightening encounters with increasing anxiety. For example, a person who fears flying may know that he needs to make a plane trip in several days. He begins to think about it and becomes nervous. The more concerned he becomes about his anxiety, the more the emotion increases. The closer he comes to the time for the flight, the more anxious he is. Then the final stage comes into focus—an actual decision to avoid flying. Having done so, the fear diminishes. The person has learned a means of escape, and the phobia is reinforced. This is what it means to be phobic. The person seems governed by emotions not appropriate to the real situation but which seem to be caused by the situation.

Such feelings may even be extended to additional settings, restricting the person's life and increasing his feelings of desperation about his situation.

Phobic behavior can be expressed in a variety of ways. Some people face the fearful situation over and over again, and the fear continues to grow. Also, some people who have animal phobias do not experience "anxiety in advance" as does the man who must fly or the woman who must sing. They may not anticipate the appearance of a snake in a park. So their emotions do not deter them from walking in the park.

Another illustration of a phobia is described as spontaneous panic. Victims of such panic attacks often report that they are feeling fine, occupied in normal tasks, when suddenly they feel heart palpitations, difficulty in breathing, nausea, sometimes an urge to urinate or defecate, and a sense of imminent death. Without clues to its cause, victims of panic attacks begin to avoid situations where they might have a reoccurence. These people are more afraid of the panic itself than they are of the setting, although the setting becomes associated with fear and becomes a place to avoid.

The first category is animal phobias. Professionals have categorized phobias by the nature of the symptoms. These fears are usually of one species of animal, although occasionally a person will express a fear of many kinds of animals. The most common are fears of snakes, certain insects, spiders, dogs, cats, and birds. Animal phobias often do not interfere with the lives of their victims as much as other categories because the victims can live away from the feared species. Of course, that is not always the case. One woman had such a fear of crickets that she would not leave her house during the warm months when she might encounter a cricket.

The second category is social phobias, where the fears are related to circumstances involving other people. As mentioned earlier, the person usually fears appearing foolish. Social phobias also range from being highly specific to general, from stage fright to being afraid to eat with or even talk with people.

Specific phobias constitute the third category. Usually these are fears of certain circumstances or settings: fear of high places (acrophobia), fear of closed places (claustrophobia), fear of flying, or fear of driving. About 20 percent of the people seeking phobia treatment have this kind of fear.

The fourth category of phobic symptom is agoraphobia. *Agoraphobia* literally means a fear of the marketplace. The symptoms are fears of being away from a safe person or a safe place. For example, an agoraphobic traveling away from home may eventually fear any kind of travel. A fear of driving on the highway leads to fear of driving in town, and then of driving at all. Being afraid of large department stores gradually spreads to any store, and so on. Being in the company of a loved one may lessen the fear dramatically, however. Some people who will not leave their homes alone can go anywhere if a family member or close friend accompanies them. This is interesting evidence that the situation itself does not cause the phobia, but this is a point agoraphobics rarely see. If they were to see it, they wouldn't be phobic anymore. Agoraphobics comprise the most frequently treated group (60 percent to 75 percent of the total) because their symptoms so severely limit their opportunities.

Over the past fifteen years, a great deal of clinical and research attention has been focused on fears and phobias. Several authors have described much of the apparent fear involved in phobias, especially among agoraphobics, as a *fear of fear*. People are accustomed to understanding themselves and having a greater or lesser degree of control of their feel-

ings. When they encounter a situation in which they experience extreme fear, one of the most frightening aspects of
that experience is the sense of not being able to control their
own feelings. As you might guess, that is especially the case
with those who experience panic, which seems to "come out
of the blue." Thus, what people are really afraid of is having
those uncontrollable feelings again. In addition, many people
are afraid of breaking down in front of other people. Their
nervousness about making fools of themselves increases
their anxiety as well as their attempts to avoid the feared circumstances. A study of fear and its effects in World War II
bomber crews found that the most intense fear occurred on
the first mission. The men reported that they were not so
much afraid of dying as they were of being so frightened
that they might behave like cowards! They were more anxious about controlling themselves than they were about the
object of fear. Once they found that they could perform
adequately under the stress, their fears dropped markedly.

Recently, therapists have noted that panic seems to
occur when the person is in very unpleasant interpersonal
interactions in which the person who panics has strange feelings that he has been unable to express or resolve. Women
who felt trapped in marriages in which they were not happy
but which they were afraid to leave were particularly prone
to panic. Most often, they had not connected the stress in
their life situations to the panic attack. In a small percentage
of the cases, panic had been experienced following severe
physical stress such as childbirth, adverse reaction to drugs,
hypoglycemia, or a major illness. Therapists soon found that
victims of the physical stress were more rapidly and successfully treated than those of more chronic, long-term, psychological stress.

Treatment

The procedure for overcoming phobias is much like that
for helping children overcome their fears—the fearful person needs to understand the nature of the fear, and especially his fear of fear. He needs to understand that fear,

while certainly not pleasant, is seldom dangerous, and that the way to overcome fear is to voluntarily enter the feared situation and remain there as long as he can until the fear dissipates. A lay counselor can explain that fear includes images that the person helps create. Or, rather than trying to stop the occurrence of the imagery, a counselor may simply encourage the person to imagine the feared situation while he is in a safe setting. Perhaps going together to the airport or piano or highway or a dark room may help. One claustrophobic man entered a darkened closet with a friend. He felt that he was becoming more and more alone, that everything was black, and that somehow he was floating away from life in the midst of his anxiety. When his friend touched his arm and urged him to remember where he was, he felt his fear immediately lessen, and he remembered that all he had to do was reach out and open the door to be free of the dark. Then he noticed for the first time that he could see light coming from underneath the closet door.

This supported exposure to the feared situation is the best way of overcoming phobias. In several formal treatment programs, the therapist goes with the client or with several clients to the actual settings or objects that may be fearsome. With encouragement and reassurance, the client approaches the feared situation and then attempts to remain without fear in the presence of the anxiety-arousing stimulus. Thus, a person who is afraid of heights (the acrophobic) is asked to climb a stepladder and stay there until the fear diminishes. The therapist is there encouraging the client, reassuring him, praising him for his successes, and verbally helping him to remain in the feared situation.

In some of the programs, the therapist sets up a progression from less fearful situations to more highly feared circumstances. A program developed by Bandura and his associates at Stanford University uses the additional benefit of what is called modeling. Here, the therapist shows the client how to enter the situation without fear. In the case of a snake phobia, for instance, the therapist approaches a snake inside a cage. Then he talks to the client and comes back.

Then the client approaches the snake and talks to the therapist. Next, the therapist will walk closer to the snake, talking to the client. Then the client will walk closer to the snake, and so on, until the client can actually stand to allow the snake to sit on his lap.

In some cases, the therapist finds that the initial fear is too severe for the person to approach the situation directly. As a preparatory step, the therapist may teach the client to imagine the events as though he were living through them. As the client becomes capable of imagining facing the feared situation and does so without excessive anxiety, then the therapist moves into live practice.

Often, in combination with such rehearsal or exposure, therapists will teach clients to talk to themselves, giving themselves encouragement and instruction. One woman with a severe snake phobia felt that the picture of a snake on a page began to come alive and move. The therapist helped her by having her say to herself as she looked at the picture, "Picture on page, picture on page." This statement helped the client maintain her sense of reality—the snake is only a picture. Similarly, when a client might be apt to say, "I could only climb three steps up the ladder today without becoming terribly frightened. This is terrible! I'll never be able to overcome my fear," the therapist might help the client to learn to say, "I climbed three steps up the ladder today. That's better than I've done for a long time. This is a slow process, but I'm going to make it." Or, instead of thinking, "Well, I really did well today, but what's going to happen tomorrow? Am I going to be able to continue my growth?" the client may learn to say, "Today was great. I really did well, and while I might do better or worse tomorrow, I'm on my way to overcoming this fear."

Another technique, called flooding, is used less frequently today, but it is simple to attempt. In this technique, the lay counselor instructs the person to imagine the feared situation, and then the counselor deliberately describes the situation in its most fearful terms. The worst possible events that could take place are described until the client has experienced the fear and its gradual dissipation. Although live exposure has proven to be more effective, where that is impractical this process can be helpful.

With complex phobias like agoraphobia, therapists have sometimes found it useful to refer clients to psychotherapy or marital counseling. Clinicians have noted that agoraphobics often experience panic as an eruption of emotional tension felt but not expressed. Spouses and sometimes other members of the family are asked to participate in the training to learn to understand the problem, to learn how they can help, and to learn what doesn't help. Occasionally the couple begins working on deeper relationship problems in the marriage.

What Can the Lay Counselor Do?

You may be asking, "What can I do to help?" or "How much can I do?" First, it is important to remember that people with phobias tend to be very sensitive individuals who want to please other people. They're very imaginative and usually think about the most terrible possible conclusion to a fearful situation. Thus, the person who wants to help must be caring and understanding and able to give reassurance and hope. If the lay counselor becomes frustrated, feels that the fear is silly, or feels that the person is weak, then he might be better off not to attempt to help at all. Similarly, because a phobic seems to know his fear is irrational and yet feels helpless to change the fear, the counselor needs to understand enough about the phobia to not take the phobic person's emotional inconsistencies as a personal rejection. On some days, the person may feel quite confident and make excellent progress. However, retreats or relapses are typical, and the phobic person needs a great deal of reassurance. In other words, the counselor must convince the phobic individual that he is "on his side" and that he will support the person regardless of his progress.

The psychological elements of agoraphobia and other fears that entail panic suggest that the nonprofessional should not attempt to treat such difficulties. However, a concerned, supportive person may help the phobic person with more specific fears. Helping the person understand his fear, providing encouragement, and reassuring him during treatment can be most beneficial.

The treatment of fears may be linked with a deeper understanding of our own spiritual beliefs. After all, fearfulness is a topic discussed in the scriptures. Most of those references suggest that the unrighteous and the wicked have every reason to fear God and his judgment; that each of us should prudently fear God in the sense of being aware of him and desiring in a reverent manner to live his commandments; and that the Lord has said that as we live his commandments we have no need to fear other people. Since many people fear rejection and criticism, the Lord's counsel helps provide comfort: "Fear not to do good, my sons, for whatsoever ye sow, that shall ye also reap; therefore if ye sow good ye shall also reap good for your reward. Therefore, fear not, little flock; do good; let earth and hell combine against you, for if ye are built upon my rock, they cannot prevail. . . . Look unto me in every thought; doubt not, fear not." (D&C 6:33-34, 35.) Drawing near to the Lord has its own calming effect—we are given greater perspective in which to understand what is really important and what is not. As we live God's commandments and look toward him and his kingdom, our fear of the responses of others will diminish. We will become less concerned about criticism and more confident about the rightness of our acts.

Perhaps, in a sense, some phobias are a crisis of faith after all. Perhaps God's admonition to look unto him in every thought has even more specific applicability. As a person approaches a feared situation, holding the image of a loving God in mind could be very beneficial. Similarly, understanding that we are God's children and that he wants us to succeed can give us confidence. Many of us have accomplished very difficult tasks beyond our ordinary skill because we have done it for God. We wouldn't even have attempted it for ourselves.

Each of us can choose to exercise faith and hope. Indeed,

God has commanded us to hope; therefore it must be within our abilities to choose to see things hopefully and to exert the energy and faith to overcome our problems and fears in spite of apparently insurmountable difficulties.

SUGGESTED READINGS

Bandura, A., R. W. Jeffery, and E. Gajdos. "Generalizing Change through Participant Modeling with Self-Directed Mastery." *Behavior Research and Therapy,* 1975, 13: 141-52.

DuPont, R. L. *Phobia: A Comprehensive Summary of Modern Treatments.* New York: Brunner/Mazel, 1982.

Mavissakalian, M., and D. H. Barlow. *Phobia: Psychological and Pharmacological Treatment.* New York: Guildford Press, 1981.

Rachman, S. J. *Fear and Courage.* San Francisco: W. H. Freeman and Company, 1978.

ABOUT THE AUTHOR

M. Gawain Wells, a native of St. George, Utah, is an associate professor of psychology and serves in the Comprehensive Clinic at Brigham Young University. He has published articles on children's feelings and has done research on religion and mental health. He has designed a diagnostic system for crisis intervention. He and his wife, Gayle, are rearing six children. Brother Wells has served in the Church as a high councilor, as a bishop, and in many teaching and administrative assignments.

23

Career and Employment Strategies
Lynn Eric Johnson

Sooner or later every family and most individuals face career and employment challenges, and many people will face them more than once. How they are resolved has a great bearing on everyone's future happiness and success. Yet most people do little to take full advantage of available career-assistance resources. You, as a lay counselor, can be a valuable resource for youth and adults who are seeking jobs, planning training programs, or upgrading present employment.

Counseling Guidelines
There are several guidelines to keep in mind when helping others plan their futures.

Remember that the person you are counseling has the responsibility to make his own decisions and to live by the consequences. Although you may want to take control of a situation, you generally should not. The person who must bear the consequences should make the decisions. You may be asked, "What do you think I should do?" But unless you feel inspired to share your preferences, it is usually safest to resist the urge to dictate another person's future. Turn the question around by asking, "What do you really want to do?" Ask appropriate questions, suggest issues to explore, offer assistance, and be optimistic and encouraging, but insist that the person make his own decisions.

Realize your limitations. There is much information available and there are professionals who are trained to use it. Don't be embarrassed to say, "I don't know the answer to that question. Let me help you find someone who does." This will save your time and also be of most help to the person you counsel.

Try to be aware of your biases and prejudices. Do your best to remain neutral. Encourage each person to make the most of the future.

Finally, the person should always pursue a career that matches his greatest personal interest. Even though opportunities may be few, if the person is enthusiastic and prepared, he can probably find an opening or create one. Encourage the person to make a thorough study of the true situation before rejecting a career choice near and dear to his heart. Enthusiasm, persistence, creativity, talent, and special training may make it possible to succeed in just about any field if a person can adapt properly.

The Changing Career Marketplace

We live in a time of rapid change. Employment specialists predict many changes in the job marketplace within the next few years. For example, technological subindustries will flourish. One such subindustry is telecommunications dealing with data and facsimile transmission. Others are office automation and data processing equipment, which facilitate the transmission and reception of messages over great distances. Future calls for qualified people to design, maintain, and service telecommunicating systems will be great.

Robotics is another exciting high-tech field that promises to provide ground-floor opportunities for many related occupations. Lucrative career possibilities exist for designers, technicians, and computer specialists, along with sales and marketing people.

Engineers will be in demand for the continuing development of synthetic fuels and defense projects. They will also be involved in the further development of microprocessors, fiber optics, satellite transmission, computer-aided design, and computer-aided manufacturing. *Peterson's Guide for Engineering Science and Computing Jobs* lists thirty-four engineering fields that recruiters are trying to fill. High demand areas include mechanical, computer science, electrical, electronics, industrial management, chemical, civil information science, engineering physics, and systems engineering—and there are many others. There will also be a demand for environmental, biomedical, fire protection, energy, ocean, ceramic, and plastics engineers.

Due to technological advancements and the increased average age of the U.S. population, the health-care industry will provide many new careers. In 1979, the number of persons aged sixty-five or older was 24.7 million, or 11.2 percent of the total U.S. population. By 1990, those who are sixty-five years old or older will number 29.8 million, or 12.2 percent of the U.S. population. Caring for these people will require geriatric physicians, psychologists, psychiatrists, support workers, social and recreation workers, physical therapists, employment specialists, and an army of clerical workers. Also, there will be a strong need for general practitioners, specialists, dentists, and technical medical-support workers such as emergency medical technicians, optometric assistants, electrocardiograph technicians, occupational therapists, dietitians, nutritionists, ultrasound technicians, nurses, and so forth.

Shorter working hours and new technological advances will provide more time for leisure activities. As a result, the service sector will grow faster than any other occupational group through the next few decades. Service careers will include travel agents, vacation assistants, hotel help, recreation pros, dude ranch staffs, tour guides, and multilanguage teachers. It is projected that people will be eating out more, so job openings will become available all the way from the local fast-food restaurant to the top of the giant hotel chains.

The growth of the entertainment industry will create additional jobs for artists and technicians along with marketing, advertising, public relations, and sales personnel. In the mid-1980s each month the cable industry alone continues to add 250,000 subscribers, 1,000 new jobs, and at least one more satellite service. Thousands of new openings are being created at the design, manufacturing, sales, and distribution levels of the computer and video-game industry.

Energy production will remain critical. The day is getting close when industry will decide to manufacture and distribute solar parts and accessories on a significant scale. This will open opportunities for engineers, architects, surveyors, insulation workers, welders, painters, general construction people, contractors, sales and marketing people, and so on.

Conservation-related careers may continue to emerge as government and industry pursue the effort to rid the environment of pollution and industrial wastes. Soil conservationists, scientists, technicians, and skilled and semiskilled workers will be needed.

Ergonomics is the study of the man-machine relationship. Specialists in this field seek to develop ways for men and machines to work more harmoniously and productively together. As technology progresses, this field will continue to expand.

Farming occupations will continue to decrease. Presently only one in thirty-six workers tills the soil. By the year 2000 only one in sixty workers will work on a farm. (However, there are many agriculture-related jobs, especially internationally, that will be available: researchers, agri-business, scientists, sales, and so on.)

The tedious jobs in industry are declining. Boiler tenders, core makers, eletroplaters, electrotypers, machine-tool operators, machine set-up workers, printing compositors, photoengravers, press operators, and production painters have all but been replaced by automatic, computer-controlled equipment.

Office requirements are rapidly changing. The use of computers has severely dampened future employment prospects for bookkeeping workers, cashiers, file clerks, keypunch operators, office machine operators, postal clerks, shipping and receiving clerks, and stock clerks. The message here is to upgrade office skills to deal with new techniques, equipment and services.

Liberal arts training in languages, philosophy, humanities, music, history, psychology, sociology, and similar fields can have special value for those in such fields because their training can be applied in a variety of occupations. Jobs such as bank officer, industrial psychologist, marketing researcher, and lawyer require an ability to reason and communicate. For these and many other similar management-type occupations, it pays to get a broad education. However, it is also strongly recommended that some business, computer, math, statistical, public relations, organizational behavior, economics, accounting, or other business-related classes be added to such training.

Assisting Youth

As a counselor, you may find the following guidelines helpful in counseling young people who are preparing for their careers:

1. Recommend that the young person pray about his various options.

2. Teach each young person to master three fundamental languages: English, mathematics, and computers. With proficiency in these areas, a person can adapt to various careers quite readily.

3. Encourage young people to get all the education they can. Girls, especially, may think they don't need much career training. The facts show otherwise. Most married women today work at least twenty-eight years outside the home, and those who don't marry, work forty-five years. Sister Camilla Kimball has advised the sisters of the Church: "I would hope that every girl and woman here has the desire and ambition to qualify in two vocations—that of homemaking and that of preparing to earn a living outside the home, if and when the occasion requires. An unmarried woman is always happier if she has a vocation in which she can be socially of service and financially independent. . . . Any married woman

may become a widow without warning. Property may vanish as readily as a husband may die. Thus, any woman may be under the necessity of earning her living and helping to support dependent children. If she has been trained for the duties and emergencies of life which may come to her, she will be much happier and have a greater sense of security."[1]

4. Discuss a proposed time schedule for the young person to complete the necessary education. Include in the schedule possible training locations (schools, colleges, and so on), programs, costs, deadlines for admission, requirements for admission, and possible career options after graduation. By thinking through their options young people can make better decisions about their best course of action. They may want to draw up a chart showing the various pathways and stages they might pursue in their education and career.

5. Help young people take advantage of all available information and planning resources. For example, school counselors have access to much information needed for career planning. Advisers at colleges can give firsthand information and answer questions about their institutions. School catalogs and other publications describe educational programs, opportunities, and requirements for particular schools, including dates, fees, tuition, and course descriptions. Textbooks, manuals, and other instructional materials can be examined in the bookstores of the colleges where they are used. And interest inventories and personality and aptitude tests can be given by counselors and advisers.

6. Point out that career options that were formerly reserved for one gender or the other are now open to both. Women have traditionally avoided mathematics and science courses, but these are very important now for men and women in almost any career.

7. Help young people list their most preferred careers and then gather information on each one.

8. Help young people investigate all financial assistance programs available. Perhaps the most complete compilation of these resources is a booklet called *Need a Lift?* It is

published by the American Legion, P.O. Box 1055, Indianapolis, Indiana, 46206. Other information about financial assistance can be obtained at each school being considered and from career advisers.

9. Arrange interviews for the young person with people working in jobs and careers the young person is considering. Ask the workers to describe their careers in detail.

10. Encourage young people to work hard. Parents can do this by supervising work at home; by helping young people obtain their first jobs; and by promoting positive work attitudes in family home evenings and other activities. Church leaders can foster work through charitable projects, campouts, and a wide variety of other activities.

11. Encourage careful financial management, including paying tithing, budgeting, careful shopping, and saving.

12. Help the young person prepare a portfolio he can use for resumes, job applications, employment interviews, and career advancements. Remember, facts sell, but generalities don't. This collection should include specific work experiences, including starting and stopping dates; name, address, and phone number of each employer; a description of work duties; letters of recommendation; news articles; diplomas; certificates of training; any pertinent creative works—articles, research papers, artwork, and so on; and photos of displays, handiwork, construction projects, or performances.

13. Discuss the future and help the young person evaluate what effect technology will have on his options as he decides what his best course of action will be.

What to Look For in a Career

Following are nine areas young people should consider as they choose a career. The *Occupational Outlook Handbook* and similar resources at libraries, counselors' offices, and places of employment can help young people as they think about these areas.

1. *Nature of work and working conditions.* What daily tasks are performed? Will the employee work with data, people, or things? Will he have regular hours, shift work, or

be on call at all times? Will the work environment be pleasant? What are the employee's opportunities for improving his skills? How much responsibility is involved?

2. *Interests required.* What things should the employee like to do?

3. *Abilities required.* What things should the employee be able to do well?

4. *Training and qualifications.* What high-school subjects should have been studied? Does the employee need training? Does he need an apprenticeship? Does he need a college degree? What classes are required? How many years of schooling are needed? Is union membership required? Is a state license required? Is approval by a professional organization necessary?

5. *Employment outlook.* How many workers are employed in this field nationally and locally? Is there a demand for these workers now? Is the demand increasing or decreasing?

6. *Salary, advancement, benefits, and security.* What is the starting wage? Will it probably increase? Are there paid vacations, compensation plans for illness and accidents, and a retirement program?

7. *Location.* Where must a potential worker go to do this kind of work? What are the living conditions there?

8. *Prestige and status.* Will the employee be recognized for his efforts? Will he be of influence? Is this job of high, middle, or low status?

9. *Overall satisfaction.* What are the pros and cons of the career under consideration?

Developing Interviewing Skills

You can help young people develop employment interviewing skills by helping them practice their posture, appearance, and responses to interview questions. According to Frank S. Endicott, who surveyed ninety-two companies, the following are the most frequently asked questions during interviews. Take the role of interviewer and ask the questions that will most help the youth you are counseling.

What are your future vocational plans? In what school

activities have you participated? Why? Which activities did you enjoy most? How do you spend your spare time? What are your hobbies? In what type of position are you most interested? Why do you think you might like to work for our company? What jobs have you held? How did you get them and why did you leave? What courses did you like best? Least? Why? Why did you choose your particular field of work?

What percentage of your college expenses did you earn? How? How did you spend your vacations while in school? What do you know about our company? Do you feel that you have received good general training? What qualifications do you have that make you feel you will be successful in your field? What extracurricular offices have you held? What are your ideas on salary? How do you feel about your family? How interested are you in sports?

If you were starting college all over again, what courses would you take? Do you prefer any specific geographic location? Why? Do you date anyone regularly? Is it serious? How much money do you hope to earn at age thirty? At age thirty-five? Why did you decide to go to this particular school? Do you think that your extracurricular activities were worth the time you devoted to them? Why? What do you think determines a person's progress in a good company? What personal characteristics are necessary for success in your chosen field? Why do you think you would like this particular type of job? What are your parents' occupations?

Tell me about your home life during the time you were growing up. Do you prefer working with others or by yourself? What kind of boss do you prefer? Are you primarily interested in making money, or do you feel that service to humanity is your prime concern? Can you take instructions without feeling upset? Tell me a story! (This is an open-ended question used to test creativity and ability to deal with a novel situation.) Do you live with your parents? Which of your parents has had the most profound influence on you? How did previous employers treat you? What have you learned from some of the jobs you have held? Can you get recommendations from previous employers? What inter-

ested you about our product or service? What was your record in military service? Have you ever changed your major
field of interest while in college? Why? When did you choose
your college major?

It is also a good idea for the potential employee to have
questions to ask the interviewer, especially if he offers the
applicant the job. The applicant should be sensitive enough
not to ask questions that would hurt his chances of receiving
a job offer. Following are some questions the applicant
might ask:

In your opinion, what are the most valuable traits a person can have for this company? What is the advancement
pattern you want people to follow? How are moving expenses
shared? What is the relocation pattern or requirement with
this job? Does the company want me to get additional schooling, and is there any financial assistance provided? What are
the special requirements for this job: travel, overtime, weekends? Are there any special financial provisions for these? How
are new ideas and suggestions received and rewarded? Are
promotions made from inside the company or outside? What
compensation is allowed for the use of my own tools, car,
home, computer, or supplies? How can I keep my retirement
program intact if the job is discontinued? How are relocation
decisions made? If for any reason I am laid off, what is the
severance pay arrangement? What reassignment assistance
is offered?

What provisions are there for pregnancy leave? Who has
the supervisory assignment to accelerate my development in
the company? Could you share some of the company's future plans with me and how I might be of help? What other
aspects of this job do I need to know? What special problems
or challenges can I help solve? What further information can
I provide? When will you be making a decision on this position? May I return at that time to discuss your decision?

Help the person you are counseling create a resume that
sells by using as many facts as are appropriate for a given
job. For young people, a one-page document is usually sufficient. (For adults, a three-page resume may be best, if hand-

delivered.) It should be tailor-made for the recipient and focus on solutions to the employer's greatest needs. One of the finest sources for resume examples is *Who's Hiring Who*, by Richard Lathrop, listed at the end of this chapter.

Stress the importance of follow-up. Far too often jobs are lost because the applicant does not send a follow-up letter, make a phone call, or, best of all, make a visit.

Assisting Adults

Adults can use many of the suggestions for young people given in this chapter, but they should also consider the following ideas.

They should develop a sound financial base. Salaries can be lost. Whenever possible, the sources of family income need to be diversified and expanded. A variety of financial resources should be considered, according to each person's or each family's needs and strengths. For example:

1. *Savings.* The average time a person is between jobs in America is ninety to one hundred and twenty days. Sufficient savings to provide for living expenses during this period can be very important.

2. *Food reserves.* Church leaders advise members to have a one-year's supply of food and other necessities on hand. During times between jobs, having food on the table helps stabilize family life and allows money in savings to be used for other items.

3. *Develop several sources of income.* In today's world, as in ages past, both spouses may need to work outside the home. Work on the job usually demands eight hours a day, five days a week. This leaves fourteen to sixteen additional hours each day. Allocating sufficient time for sleep and other necessary activities still leaves several hours a day to earn additional income. For example, a person may be a teacher by day and a tutor at night, or a musician on weekends. An accountant may be a tax consultant or develop real-estate rentals. Both men and women are able to do this.

4. *Create a financial portfolio of retirement savings, insurance, and investments.* Many jobs do not provide these,

and among those that do, coverage may be inadequate. Of course, employees should take advantage of the programs at their places of employment. However, additional preparation is strongly advised, especially in early adulthood, because when one leaves a company the company keeps most of these benefits, and the individual is left very vulnerable, usually at the worst time of life.

5. *Sketch out a time-table showing when major life events are likely to occur.* A simple set of boxes can serve the purpose, and the person can write in his projected life events.

Ages: 25-30	30-35	35-40	40-45

45-50	50-55	55-60	60-65

Some of these might include development of children, advancement at work, times when a wife returns to the work force, education, times of heaviest financial needs, times and types of diversified incomes, missions for family members, the onset of chronic illness in old age, and so on. Then, the person can plan how to best meet his future needs.

6. *Use all available resources.* In most communities, a number of resources exist to help anyone achieve his desired employment goals. In addition to the resources listed in the youth section, there are the following:

The Church's employment agencies and LDS Social Services. Each bishop has a directory that has information listing the addresses, phone numbers, and personnel involved in these programs. Wards and stakes are also encouraged to have employment representatives who are well informed about local employment opportunities. Further information may be obtained by contacting the Church's Welfare Services—Employment, Seventh Floor, 50 East North Temple Street, Salt Lake City, Utah 84150.

Private agencies. Virtually every city has private employment agencies that help people and employers get together. Each needs to be carefully evaluated in light of the individual's needs. A phone call filled with questions and answers about agency structures, services, specialties, track record, and fees (as much as ten percent of the first year's salary) should precede a visit. A second call to the Better Business Bureau to ascertain an agency's reputation is also recommended.

Vocational rehabilitation. Combined federal and state funds are available to help the disabled and handicapped obtain employment training suitable to their capabilities. Check under the state listings in the phone book.

Job Service. Again, federal and state funds are used to provide extensive services: job placement; testing for aptitudes and interests; training in job-seeking and interviewing skills; personal advisement; and the administration of various federal and state assistance programs. Check your telephone directory or in the *Occupational Outlook Handbook*, for sale from the Superintendent of Documents, U.S. Government Printing Office, Washington, D.C. 20402. This publication is also available at most libraries or from high school counselors. A number of other training programs and career opportunities are also described in this publication.

The Church. Church leaders and members are able to help each other in many ways. The person can contact Church leaders in various parts of the world by using the Church Directory.

Implementation

The implementation of a plan to obtain schooling or a job or to make career changes is probably the most challenging problem of all. The principles can be fairly easily learned, and the support systems are all in place, but many people are afraid to act.

How can a lay counselor help a person overcome his fears to achieve his desired goal? This will depend on the person, but there are some common elements helpful to everyone.

First, plan together what the person needs to do. Careful planning eliminates fear of the unknown. Make sure every aspect of the problem is considered and that a solution is prepared.

Second, break the plan into manageable steps and help the person start working on it. Too many people look at the whole job-finding process and are overwhelmed. Then, arrange times to get back together to review the completed steps and the one to come.

Third, help the person develop self-confidence through his successful completion of the initial steps. Work together to build a momentum of emotion and activity.

Fourth, establish time limits and a financial budget to help the person manage his resources and keep moving.

Fifth, counsel together less frequently as the skills and strengths of the individual develop. The goal is to help the person become self-sufficient, independent, and, in fact, able to help others.

NOTE

1. Kimball, Camilla. "A Woman's Preparation." *Ensign,* March 1979, p. 59.

SUGGESTED READINGS

Bolles, Richard N. *The Three Boxes of Life.* Berkeley: Ten Speed Press, 1981. This book discusses three periods of life—education, work, and retirement. In analyzing these areas, the author provides a structure to deal with the transition into each one.

————. *What Color Is Your Parachute.* Berkeley: Ten Speed Press, 1983. Successful job hunters were interviewed by the author, and he has attempted to distill their successes into four principles, including: keeping at it, knowing what you want, deciding where you want to work, and discovering who has power to hire you and showing them how your skills can help them. This best-seller is filled with practical, aggressive methods to get the job of your choice.

————, and Victoria B. Zenoff. *The Quick Job-Hunting Map.* Berkeley: Ten Speed Press, 1980. A brief approach to application of principles covered in detail in the book *What Color Is your Parachute.*

————. *Tea Leaves: A New Look at Resumes.* Berkeley: Ten Speed Press, 1976. A biting commentary on resumes and their uses and abuses. Makes many sound recommendations to improve your efforts if you must write one.

Crystal, John D., and Richard N. Bolles. *Where Do I Go From Here with My Life?* New York: The Seabury Press, 1974. This workbook deals with a system invented by John Crystal. It is useful for job-seekers and non-job seekers alike who want to better establish their goals and increase effectiveness in use of their talents.

Irish, Richard K. *Go Hire Yourself an Employer.* Garden City: Anchor Press/Doubleday, 1978. The theme of the book is how to become competent in the job hunt and how to make that competence carry over on the job. It explains how to identify contributions you can make to employers and to act on that information. The point is to make the applicant self-aware, confident, poised, and prepared to hire himself an employer.

Johnson, Lynn Eric. *Take Charge!* 576 So. 490 W., Orem, Utah 84057: Johnson International, 1984. A comprehensive textbook designed to help a person who is entering the job market, changing jobs, seeking advancement strategies, and conscientiously preparing now for later retirement. It is written particularly for BYU students but is adaptable for families, ward and stake employment specialists, and individuals.

Lathrop, Richard. *Who's Hiring Who.* Berkeley: Ten Speed Press, 1980. The author reports that in follow-up research, readers of this book claim to get more job offers and higher pay offers and take less time to find a job. The book explores the job market, conducts a self-inventory, and teaches how to make a qualifications brief, write effective letters, be effective in interviews, and negotiate salary and other benefits.

ABOUT THE AUTHOR

Dr. Lynn Eric Johnson, associate professor of counseling and personal services at Brigham Young University, received his bachelor's degree at Brigham Young University and his master's degree and Ph.D. from the University of Utah in educational psychology. Since 1961, Dr. Johnson has counseled young people in career and educational matters both at Brigham Young University and in workshops and BYU Education Weeks throughout the Church. He has published several articles for the *Ensign* and the *New Era*. Since 1979, he has been instrumental in developing an upper-division course to help university juniors and seniors prepare for the world of work, for which he has recently published the text titled *Take Charge!*

In the Church, Dr. Johnson has served as a bishop twice and as a branch president at the Missionary Training Center in Provo. He is currently teaching a Blazer A class. His previous callings include bishop's counselor, high councilor, stake Sunday School superintendent, stake Young Men's president, and West German Mission servicemen's coordinator.

He and his wife, Judy, are the parents of seven children.

24

Financial Counseling

Jerry Mason

Financial problems are generally acknowledged to be a major cause of divorce, suicide, and depression in our society. Often laymen and professionals assume that financial problems occur primarily because people are inadequately trained to manage money. Certainly many people would benefit by improving their money management skills, but often dysfunctional behaviors, more than inadequate money management skills, seem to contribute to peoples' financial problems. At times people find themselves in financial difficulties because of factors beyond their control, but in many situations problems can be prevented or reduced. The financial counselor is the "change agent" who helps individuals and families work through their financial problems as they make certain adjustments in the way they conduct their lives. Laymen, although lacking training and experience, can be effective in helping individuals and families resolve pressing financial concerns.

Effective financial counseling is commonly a three-part process. First, the counselor is concerned with helping the family arrest, at least temporarily, the financial crisis that has caused them to seek help. Until these pressures are at least partially relieved, the family will usually not be interested in anything else. Successful financial counseling, however, goes beyond crisis resolution. The second part focuses on identifying factors that contribute to the family's financial problems. The counselor helps the family clearly understand why their financial problems are occurring and helps them learn how to accept responsibility for their roles in creating them. The family members become aware of behaviors, attitudes, and financial practices that must be changed or modified if they are to adequately manage their resources. Planning is the third part of financial counseling and includes developing workable plans that will enable the family to gain control of their financial affairs. The family comes to realize that they can achieve realistic financial objectives as they learn to apply proven money management principles and practices.

Before discussing these financial counseling processes in detail, the following procedures or skills need to be mentioned. These recommendations may help you increase your effectiveness as a lay counselor.

1. Have the individual or family come to your office if possible. The family's home environment is usually not an ideal place because of distractions. Also, families who make an effort to come to you are more likely to take counseling seriously.

2. Meet with both spouses if the person seeking help is married. Counseling with just one spouse is not likely to be effective and can sometimes do more harm than good.

3. Ask the family initially to leave younger children at home. At a later session you may want to involve all family members.

4. Listen effectively and intently. Talk less than 50 percent of the time. Maybe you know more about financial counseling than the people seeking help, but you will learn more about their situation if you do not monopolize the discussion.

5. Do not judge. No one likes to feel condemned.

6. Ask questions effectively. Explain your need to know important information.

7. Acknowledge the fact that there are some things you don't know. Be honest; don't bluff.

8. Do not give tax investment or legal advice unless you

are licensed to do so. Refer those you are helping to professionals when necessary. The rule of thumb is: when in doubt, refer. You should be able to provide a list of at least three professionals who could help.

9. Maintain confidentiality. Keep everything you learn about the family in strictest confidence unless you have their permission to share certain information with a specific person. Conduct interviews in a private room with the door closed.

Part 1: Resolving Urgent Financial Crises

The following steps provide a systematic approach to crisis counseling: (1) establish rapport; (2) identify the crisis; (3) generate possible solutions; (4) resolve the crisis; (5) follow through; and (6) evaluate results. Adapt as necessary. When a crisis confronts the family, time constraints will usually allow you to meet with the family only one or two times.

Step 1: Establish Rapport

Put the family at ease so that they feel comfortable discussing the crisis with you. Remember, people frequently need to tell you many things that may seem foolish and embarrassing to them. Attempt to create an environment that encourages them to open up, or the effectiveness of your counseling may be diminished. The first few minutes in the interview are critical in establishing an effective counseling relationship. Therefore, be as warm and friendly as possible, and let them know that for the duration of the session, you have no other concerns but theirs.

Step 2: Identify the Crisis

At this stage you are not as interested in causes as in identifying enough details to effectively resolve the crisis.

Although excessive note-taking may be distracting, there is some specific information that is absolutely essential and that you must write down. For example, to whom money is owed; how much is owed; when it is due; expected consequences if payment is not made; and what attempts the family has made to try to resolve the problem.

As important as objective facts are, subjective information is just as essential. How do individual family members feel about what has happened? Your primary objective here is to gain an understanding of the problem as the family sees it. Let them describe the crisis. Make sure that you understand their view of the problem by restating it in your own words. Seek feedback until you clearly understand key aspects of the crisis. Try not to appear shocked by the circumstances that are presented. What they want and need is your help, not your criticism.

Even with the use of effective counseling skills, however, some families may resist exposing their private lives. There are many reasons why a family may not adequately explain their financial problems to you, reasons such as a lack of confidence in you as a counselor, their failure to understand their own problems, reticence to expose obvious individual shortcomings, and failure to take responsibility for the crisis. In addition, sometimes one spouse will resist revealing information that is as yet unknown to the other spouse. It is important to look for clues as to the hidden reasons why one partner may refuse to be open and fair in the discussions. But remember that at this stage in counseling you are still trying to understand the problem—you are not diagnosing the causes of the financial crisis. Be sure to mentally file useful bits of information for future use. By now you should have a pretty good idea of the parts of the crisis and how they fit together.

Step 3: Generate Possible Solutions

You are now ready to consider solutions. First of all, restate the crisis to make sure you have the big picture as the client sees it. Once the crisis has been adequately defined, a plan to resolve the crisis must be developed. Strategies that might be employed to resolve financial problems are of two types: quick fixes and term adjustments. Quick fixes are designed to defuse the present crisis but require no basic change in the way the family functions. As a result, problems are likely to occur again. On the other hand, term adjustments require the family to change certain behaviors

and also to systematically perform certain procedures over
an extended period of time. Term adjustments, sometimes
employed in crises, are typically associated with helping the
family deal with the basic causes of their financial problems
and will be dealt with in greater detail in part 2 of this chapter. Quick fixes are usually more common in crisis situations
and are therefore discussed here is detail.

A quick fix is needed when a family is faced with situations such as eviction from their apartment or home, loss of
utility service, or repossession of a needed personal asset,
such as a car or washing machine. Before selecting a quick-
fix strategy, however, you should devote a few minutes to
brainstorming other solutions. Write down all possible solutions mentioned by family members that may be useful.
Some combination of the alternatives listed below could
help reduce or eliminate the crisis:

1. Reduce living expenses.
2. Sell assets.
   a. Investments (stocks, bonds, and mutual funds)
   b. Personal property
3. Increase income.
   a. Get another job.
   b. Seek assistance from extended family.
   c. Seek assistance from Church and community
      organizations.
   d. File for entitlement program benefits: disability,
      veterans, Medicare, Social Security, and so on.
4. Renegotiate debt-payment schedules.
5. Seek additional loans (use with caution).
   a. Life insurance
   b. Credit union
   c. Bank
   d. Relatives
   e. Loan consolidation (not advised in most situations)
   f. Second mortgage on home (not advised in most
      situations)
   g. Pawnbrokers
6. Request legal assistance.

7. File for bankruptcy.
   a. Chapter 13
   b. Chapter 7

Each alternative needs to be examined from a cost/benefit perspective. It is important to accurately assess what the family must give up in order to obtain the desired benefit. In some cases the suggested cures could be worse than the illness. Often lay counselors, instead of recommending *a* solution, may be of more help by identifying several alternatives for the family to consider. The nonprofessional may have a limited knowledge of resources available to the family, but he can be effective in helping the family identify those resources. After all alternative solutions have been explored, work with the family to select the most desired ones. Help them identify which ones they think might be the wisest or most reasonable for them to employ. Try to obtain a consensus. Once the best solution has been identified, outline basic steps the family must follow to make it work.

Step 4: Resolve the Crisis

Families need to gain control of their lives by working through their problems. Counselors usually prefer not to interfere any more than is absolutely necessary. To keep interference to a minimum, you should review with each family member his responsibilities in resolving the problem. In some cases you may wish to write out instructions for the person or family and request that they periodically report back to you. When the person encounters an unexpected problem while trying to implement a strategy, you must jointly decide if it is more advantageous to adjust the original plan or to try something else.

Creditors usually prefer dealing with their customers instead of with a third party, but a financial problem reaches the crisis stage when a creditor refuses to talk with the customer. In such cases, consider referring the family to a professional financial counselor such as a consumer credit counselor who can contact creditors, government agencies, and employers.

If a creditor refuses to work with the family, if a community service program cannot provide needed service, or if the family does not perform their responsibilities as promised, the crisis may not be averted. This usually happens when the family waits until the last moment to seek assistance and it is simply too late to implement any solutions. However, if the problem is caught soon enough, you may be able to guide the family through the crisis.

Step 5: Follow Through

In order for the problem-solving process to be effective, coordination and follow-through are essential. Remember, the family may have created this problem by behaving irresponsibly. In addition, people who have experienced financial problems often become easily discouraged; they may have grown accustomed to being defeated. Therefore you should not be too surprised if family members do not adequately complete all of the steps as agreed. Be prepared to closely monitor their performance and repeat Step 4 if necessary.

Step 6: Evaluate Results

If the crisis has been successfully averted, you may wish to evaluate the solution that was implemented to determine its relative long-term effectiveness. Has the crisis been resolved permanently or is this just a temporary solution? Specifically, what must the family continue to do to ensure that the crisis does not reoccur?

The crisis has been resolved, but without additional counseling most families will again find themselves in financial trouble. If you and the family can still meet together, you have an opportunity to examine fundamental causes of financial mismanagement and institute new financial procedures that can permanently solve financial problems.

Part 2: Diagnosing Causes of Financial Problems

The second stage in financial counseling focuses on discovering and identifying factors that have helped create financial problems for the family. Initially, you must collect and organize essential information from the family. If you have not already obtained such data, now is the time to record names, addresses, and ages of the family members, as well as financial information such as income and expenditures. You may wish to develop a specific form to gather such information. (Check the references in the back of the chapter for assistance.) Ask the family to bring items such as recent pay stubs, checkbooks, and bank statements. Have them compile a list of balances owed to each creditor, indicating the number of payments they are behind. A list of important family financial goals is also useful. If possible, provide the family with a list describing the various documents to bring to the next counseling session.

After the family has brought in their financial information, it is useful to quickly construct both a net worth and a cash flow statement. The net worth and cash flow statements are valuable in helping you and the family obtain a picture of their current financial position. A simple net worth statement will be similar to the one on the next page.

Assets should be listed at their current market value (what each one could be sold for today). Liabilities are listed by the balances presently owed creditors. The basic formula for examining the net worth statement is: total assets minus total liabilities equals net worth. Any family with a negative net worth owes more than it owns. The size of the net worth is important. A family with a negative net worth or a small positive net worth has limited assets to use in solving financial problems.

A cash flow statement (see the form in this chapter) once completed may be useful later in setting up a preliminary budget. You should ask all family members to realistically estimate income and expenditures for the previous twelve months. Referring to last year's bills, check registers, and income statements can be helpful.

Net Worth Statement

_____
Name(s)

_____
Date

Assets
Cash   _____
Checking accounts   _____
Investments   _____
Retirement accounts   _____
Personal property   _____
Home   _____
Automobiles   _____
Business   _____
Other   _____
(A) Total assets $_____

Liabilities
Utilities (past due)   _____
Rent (past due)   _____
Charge account balances   _____
Judgments   _____
Credit card balances   _____
Taxes   _____
Installment loan balances   _____
Auto loan balances   _____
Education loan balances   _____
Mortgage   _____
Other   _____
(B) Total liabilities $_____

Net Worth (A−B) $_____

Cash Flow Statement

for the twelve months beginning _____

and ending _____

Income
        Wages (take-home pay)   _____
        Interest and dividends   _____
        Other   _____
  (A) Total income $_____

Expenditures
        Food   _____
        Mortgage or rent   _____
        Clothing   _____
        Utilities   _____
        Contributions   _____
        Insurance   _____
        Medical   _____
        Recreation   _____
        Personal   _____
        Transportation   _____
        Installment loans   _____
  (B) Total expenditures $_____

Income available for
saving or investing (A–B) $_____

When examining cash flow for the previous twelve months, use this formula: total income less total expenditures equals income available for saving or investing. Don't be surprised when income available for saving or investing is negative.

An examination of the cash flow statement holds many clues to the family's money problems. Discuss the following questions with the family: How adequate was total income [(A) on the cash flow statement]? What expenditures (B) appear to be excessive? Is too much income required to make debt payments? After the statements have been analyzed, you are ready to move on in the counseling process and learn about the family's basic financial problems.

Causes of Financial Problems

By now you know that the family is having financial problems in one or more of the following three areas: acquiring adequate income, controlling expenditures, or making debt payments. Now is the time to focus on all areas and to come up with possible factors that explain why problems are occurring in one or more specific areas.

By now you no doubt have some understanding of what the family does to contribute to their problems. As you review the procedures they follow in managing their money, be sure to identify things they do that appear to contribute to the family's financial problems. Such things as purchasing many items on time-payment contracts, overspending budget limits, and impulse buying are typical of the kinds of behaviors that lead to financial problems.

It is essential that family members assume personal responsibility for their financial mismanagement. If they are not willing to do this, you will probably find it extremely difficult to teach them sound money-management concepts. Typically, people will not change a behavior pattern unless they make a connection between their present actions and their current financial problems. Even so, recognition and acceptance alone are often not enough. In order for a money-management plan to be successful, each bad habit must be replaced with a new appropriate behavior. Review how the family acquires and spends its income. Identify habits that seem to contribute to the family's financial problems. When examining each of the three problem areas (inadequate income, living expenses, and excessive debt), focus on replacing bad habits with new patterns of behavior that contribute to sound financial management.

If you identify problems that you are not trained to handle you should refer the person to a professional. In referring someone for more extensive counseling, it is preferable to first get the individual's permission. Strongly recommend to the person that he contact the agency as soon as possible, and be sure to give the person's name, address, and phone number to the agency. In many cases, you may still work with the individual or family.

Sometimes you must refer a person or family to a specific specialist, but in such cases it is usually a government or private agency offering a unique service. If you live in a large city you may refer them to the local Consumer Credit Counseling service (CCC), which is prepared to help them work out a debt repayment plan with their creditors. The local CCC office also teaches effective budgeting skills.

A referral to appropriate legal services may be required in certain situations. Sometimes a family has been wronged by a creditor and needs to seek redress through the courts. In many cases, families are defendants in court actions. Most people experiencing financial difficulties are not aware of their rights under the law and do not understand "due process." Since you too may be uninformed, be certain to refer the person for legal assistance when it may be beneficial. (In larger cities, legal aid may be available at no or low cost to low-income families.)

Inadequate Income

If the family's income is inadequate, it may be helpful to explore some of the reasons that this situation exists. For example, do adults in the family lack the experience, training, or education necessary to secure satisfactory employment? Many times you will find that one or more family members will need to improve basic reading and writing skills in order to earn an adequate wage. Others may be unemployed or underemployed because they are disabled, retired, or have become a single parent with preschool children. Others may move from job to job and therefore lack seniority. Such people are highly vulnerable to financial stress, not only because of their low income levels, but also because they are usually the first ones let go during an economic downturn.

When income is low, retraining or additional education are often essential in helping a family become self-supporting. In the interim, however, many families may require assistance from relatives, the Church, or other social programs until they can support themselves. There are rarely easy, short-term solutions when a family's income is inadequate. Therefore, long-term planning should start as soon as possible.

Increasing Living Expenses

Inflation, moving expenses, purchase of a new home, and separation and divorce (which usually require supporting two households) can all contribute to increased living expenses. However, for many families, money problems are at least partially the result of poor budgeting and mismanagement in some areas. Perhaps one of the most common causes of overspending is impulse buying when purchases are based on spur-of-the-moment desires to acquire an asset or service. An even more serious spending habit is compulsive spending, when a person develops an almost obsessive need to make purchases. There are a variety of reasons behind such behavior, such as depression, feelings of inferiority, or revenge. People who are depressed sometimes make unneeded purchases in an attempt to lift their spirits. People with inferiority complexes often try to compensate for their perceived inadequacies by trying to "keep up with the Joneses." Revenge as a motivation often becomes manifest when one spouse attempts to "get even" by making a purchase in retaliation for a previously unplanned purchase made by the other spouse.

Other increased living expenses are the result of a lack of discipline with regard to saving for important future goals or for emergencies. This failure to defer compensation contributes to a variety of problems and is a major reason why many families lose control of their finances.

Often families simply do not realize what a high percentage of their income is already committed before it is even received. After subtracting taxes, payroll deductions, and debt payments from gross income, many families find that they have less then 40 percent of gross income remaining to cover living expenses. Part of what remains may also be committed to nonmonthly expenses such as car insurance and real-estate taxes, which are seldom budgeted for adequately. In some cases, the families do not have any particular plan for spending their income, and since their income and outgo are so closely matched, they often overspend. Budgeting can help people control where their money goes.

Excessive Debt

Many families find themselves in financial difficulty because they fail to determine if their budget can handle additional installment debt or credit card payments before making a purchase. As they increase the amount of debt payments they must make each month, a larger percentage of their paycheck is committed before it is received, making it increasingly difficult to balance the budget each month and almost impossible to save or invest.

Misuse of credit, especially the misuse of credit cards, is a major problem. Many families see credit as a source of money when they have exhausted other sources of income. Merchants encourage customers to charge. Many families ignore outstanding statement balances as they become accustomed to paying only the minimum due each month. As the outstanding balance on a credit card reaches its limit, they often request an increase in the limit, or they may apply for additional credit from new sources. Eventually payments to creditors exceed what the family can manage out of their income. This type of debt load, which can become excessive even when the income stream is maintained, can translate into a financial disaster should income be reduced.

As you have explored these three problem areas (inadequate income, increasing expenditures, and excessive debt) with those you counsel, it may have been easy for some people to readily identify their inappropriate behaviors, but for others, such insights were much more difficult, and some may not have had the slightest idea how they got into their financial difficulties. Once the causes of an individual or family's financial problems have been identified, you will need to shift your focus to changing their behaviors that seem to contribute to each problem.

Part 3: Teaching Sound Money-Management Concepts

This third section focuses on teaching sound money-management skills and will require family members to replace self-defeating behaviors with effective financial practices. An effective place to begin helping family members change their bad habits is to review the family's current financial decision-making process. For instance, have a family member recount how a recent important financial decision was made. Was the decision made on impulse? Was the decision's impact on other aspects of family life examined before the decision was implemented? Were alternative ways to implement the decision considered? What did the family have to give up in order to make this purchase? Could the budget accommodate the spending required to implement the decision? Is it common for one or more family members to be unhappy with the decision-making process? Understanding how decisions are made and implemented can provide useful insight into poor money-management behaviors. Based on such insight, you may more easily recommend new procedures that, if properly implemented by the family, are most likely to improve the quality of their financial decisions.

Defining Goals

Poor decision-making ability is often associated with ineffective goal determination. Ask the family to bring a list of financial goals to the counseling session. (Perhaps the entire family should meet with the counselor during this session.) If they fail to bring their goals, ask each family member present to make a list of goals; allow them two minutes to write them but ask them to not look at anyone else's list. Next, have them compare lists and try to reach a consensus on the most important *family* goals. Families who have never tried this exercise may be surprised at the contributions received from their children. The family who did not bring their children should go home and do this exercise again with all the family, and it should be repeated periodically, at least annually.

Most goals submitted will require revision. For a goal to be effective, it must contain three components: (1) a clearly defined target or end result; (2) the date when the goal is to be accomplished; (3) an action required to fund the goal. Compare the goal "buy a home" with "buy a $90,000 four-bedroom ranch-style home during the summer of 1990 by saving $250 each month starting next March." The first goal, "buy a home," is so vague that it is difficult to implement. However, the second goal clearly explains what it is the family wishes to achieve, when they wish to achieve it, and how they plan to fund it.

Funding future goals does not require that money be set aside today or even this year for any goal, but it does require that a plan be developed indicating when money can be set aside to fund important goals. Families who can see their way to start funding a goal in one, two, or even three years from now are a lot happier than those who think that they will never be able to achieve any important goals. Hope is an essential ingredient in money management. If a family cannot save, their financial future will seem, and often will be, bleak.

Developing Spending Plans

Families need to learn how to develop spending plans and perform necessary record-keeping functions in order to make sure that their expenditures are controlled and important goals are funded. However, family members often fail to consistently perform even the most basic budgeting procedures. For example, they are often not sure of the current balance in their checking account because they have failed to record checks in the check register. As a result, each month the bank statement is usually not reconciled with their check-register balance, which can, in some cases, lead to writing bad checks. This is just one example of the lack of an effective system for keeping track of a family's spending.

All families need to know how to develop and use spending plans. The following procedures are basic to any budgeting system:

1. Estimate income sources for twelve months.

2. Estimate expenditures for twelve months.

3. Compare estimated income with expenditures for each month. If income is less than expenditures for any month, figure out ways to increase income or reduce expenditures. Be realistic.

4. Set up a record-keeping system to monitor expenditures each month; make sure that they do not exceed actual income.

5. At the end of each month, compare actual expenditures with estimated expenditures. Make adjustments to future spending plans.

In instructing the family, do not assume that there is only one effective money-management system. Actually there are many, with no two families following the same one.

There are several excellent books listed at the back of this chapter that offer sound instruction on developing budgets and financial statements. If you find yourself needing to teach the mechanics of money management, they can serve as useful reference guides.

Restructuring Debt Payments

Many families have a difficult time balancing their budgets because they have so many credit obligations. Restructuring existing debt payments may be essential if some budgets are to balance. Adjusting debt payments requires the family, and possibly you, to contact the creditors. Before asking a creditor to modify a contractual repayment program, a financial counselor needs to become familiar with each creditor's policies; most laymen are not. You may wish to contact the various creditors for information on their policies, or if a Consumer Credit Counseling Service is available, you may wish to contact this service or merely refer the family to the agency. If one is not convenient, you or a member of the family will need to contact each creditor. Creditors are often willing to renegotiate payments if they understand the family's problem. You may wish to refer to Van Arsdale's book and the *Credit Counselor Training Handbook* listed at the end of this chapter, both of which provide excellent discussions on working with creditors.

This third stage in financial counseling will be successful if you have been able to motivate family members to replace their harmful behaviors with new actions and attitudes associated with sound money management principles and procedures. Although you may never see many of these families again, it is often useful to have a follow-up meeting after they have spent two or three months applying the principles and procedures you have taught them. Find out if they are gaining control of their financial affairs. Is there less pressure from creditors? Are they able to save for future goals? Do their budgeting procedures work? Does the budget balance at the end of each month? In what areas do they still need to improve? In most cases they should respond positively to most to these questions. You may not be successful with every person or family, but you should be reasonably helpful to many and extremely helpful to some.

SUGGESTED READINGS

Albrecht, W. Steven. *Money Wise: Money Management for Latter-day Saints*. Salt Lake City: Deseret Book Company, 1983.

Bailard, Thomas; David Biehl; and Ronald Kaiser. *Personal Money Management,* 4th edition. Chicago: Science Research Associates, 1983.

Credit Counselor Training Handbook. Credit Counseling Centers, Inc., 17000 E. Eight Mile Road, Southfield, Michigan, 48075, 1981.

Pulvino, Charles, and James Lee. *Financial Counseling: Interviewing Skills*. Dubuque, Iowa: Kendall/Hunt Publishing, 1979.

VanArsdale, Mary. *A Guide to Family Financial Counseling*. Homewood, Illinois: Dow Jones-Irwin, 1982.

Weirich, Jean Luttrell. *Personal Financial Management*. Boston: Little, Brown and Company, 1983.

Williams, Flora. *Guidelines to Financial Counseling*. Agricultural Experiment Station, Purdue University, West Lafayette, Indiana, 1980.

ABOUT THE AUTHOR

Dr. Jerry Mason, assistant professor of family sciences at Brigham Young University, received his B.S. degree from BYU, his MBA from Stanford University, and his Ph.D. in family economics from the University of Missouri. He is a member of the International Association for Financial Planners.

He has served in many Church callings, including ward executive secretary. He and his wife, Joyce, are the parents of six children.

The author wishes to express his appreciation to his colleagues Bud Poduska and Virginia Langrehr for their critical reviews and helpful suggestions.

25

Recognizing—and Avoiding—Bad Investments
John W. Hardy

Serious family and personal problems are often caused by financial reversals. Sociological studies have shown that many marriages fail because of financial problems in the home. Often Latter-day Saints have to be even more careful than others in managing their finances. They characteristically have larger families, which sometimes results in more financial stress. They sincerely desire to make financial contributions to the Church for the building of the kingdom of God on earth. Indeed, if Latter-day Saints are to succeed in having sufficient for their needs as well as having some savings set aside for times of emergency, they must manage their resources extremely well.

One resource that has been used for both good and evil is financial investments. As members of the Church, we are encouraged to save and invest money wisely. This is good advice, but too often we succumb to investment programs that are fraudulent. The cost of such unwise investments is not only financial; often those who get into tight financial situations reduce or eliminate tithing, budget, fast offerings, or other contributions as a way to get out of debt, and thus quickly lose needed blessings. How can members of the Church recognize bad investments and avoid them?

Why Do We Make Bad Investments?

Most fraudulent investment programs offer high returns in a short time. They are highly speculative but offer a quick road to riches. Why do Latter-day Saints sometimes invest in such ventures? One reason is that greed often subverts our good sense and caution. The truth is that greed is one of the major problems of humanity and will continue to be until each of us learns to control such desires.

Few people are immune to the temptation to make a fast dollar. We often are affected with a desire to "keep up with the Joneses." The Lord described some of the inhabitants of Zion in the early years of the Church as persons who "seek not earnestly the riches of eternity, but their eyes are full of greediness." (D&C 68:31.) The Lord has counseled us not to set our hearts upon the things of the world but to seek first the kingdom of God. If we do this, all else will be added to us. (See Matthew 6:33.) To avoid investment fraud, we must first avoid greediness.

Another reason Latter-day Saints succumb to fraudulent investment schemes is that many of us think, some quite falsely, that we are good judges of people and their intents and can easily judge between good and evil. We tend to be very trusting of other people.

In investment matters, many Latter-day Saints have a certain amount of naiveté. Perhaps their missionary attitude and desire to love all people causes them to be overly trusting. Even so, the Savior teaches us that we must be as wise as serpents in conducting our affairs. (See Matthew 10:16.) When we make an investment, we are not playing with play money. We are investing hard-earned dollars.

We need to go the extra mile in identifying the credentials of the person taking our investment dollar. We need to carefully study out in our minds the nature of the investment. If we feel uneasy or feel we lack the ability to analyze an investment, it may be worth the cost of paying a financial expert to give us independent advice about the investment before we invest.

A third possible reason why we make poor investments

may be the feeling that if we are righteous, God will bless us with riches. In other words, if we are good Latter-day Saints, our Father in heaven is bound to bless us financially with more than just sufficient for our needs.

Although God does promise to bless us if we are faithful in keeping his commandments, the promise isn't necessarily one of financial gain. Our Father in Heaven blesses us in many ways, and his blessings come as we obey the laws upon which those blessings are predicated. (See D&C 130:20-21.) For example, we receive certain blessings as we keep the Word of Wisdom. God promises to open to us the windows of heaven and "rebuke the devourer" if we pay tithing. (See Malachi 3:10-11.) Above all, our Heavenly Father blesses us with a celestial inheritance if we are faithful in keeping his commandments and the covenants we have made with him. Financial abundance, at best, is a mixed blessing; it is certainly not the greatest gift God has for us. (See D&C 14:7.)

While it is true that God can bless us financially, these blessings will probably come only after we have obeyed the laws upon which financial success is based. We will not get something for nothing.

Some people make one-sided promises with God when they invest in "fly-by-night" investments. They promise to pay their tithing or repent of certain sins if the Lord will bless their investments. Furthermore, if their investments fail, they often blame God for their own bad decisions. We need to be more careful that we do not mock God by such thinking!

Another reason we sometimes make bad investments is that we have a notion that if an investment opportunity is presented by a "good Latter-day Saint," then it must be a "sure thing." Sometimes we believe it is even a surer thing if the Latter-day Saint investment adviser is a stake president, bishop, or other Church leader.

Latter-day Saint investment counselors, like other investment counselors, have no crystal balls revealing the future of the economy next week or next month. At best, they can make only a professional guess about the future. A person may be an excellent bishop or stake president or Sunday School teacher, but he still is capable of making errors in judgment when giving financial advice. Do Latter-day Saint doctors, janitors, lawyers, teachers, clerks, or accountants sometimes exercise bad judgment even though they may have a Church calling? Of course they do.

We also need to be aware that there have been instances when Latter-day Saints have perpetrated investment frauds. Surely such people have traded their birthright for a mess of pottage! They will someday account for their theft; in the meantime, we must be wise and protect ourselves from them.

There are undoubtedly other reasons why Latter-day Saints become involved in risky speculative investments. Whatever the reason, it is unfortunate that we do.

Ultimately, we must bear the responsibility for what we do with our financial resources. It would be nice to be able to blame someone else if failures occur, but, typically, when it comes to investments, we do so of our own free will, and we must bear the consequences of our choices.

In fact, we cannot even count on the law to protect us in every instance from our misjudgments. Victims of fraud often find that lawsuits are fruitless because the investment money is already squandered and no recovery is possible. We must analyze potential investments carefully before signing a contract.

Things to Think About before Investing

How can people recognize and avoid highly speculative or fraudulent investment schemes? Here are a few guidelines to follow:

1. *Look for investments that have a reasonable as opposed to an exorbitant return.* Cornelius Vanderbilt, the American capitalist who became a multimillionaire, was once asked how he became so wealthy. His response was that he was satisfied with a *little* profit. He was not looking for an unreasonably large profit.

Vanderbilt's approach is a wise one, especially for new

investors. Certainly all investments have an associated risk, but some are safer than others. The higher the possible return on an investment, the higher the potential risk for failure. The lower the rate of return, the lower the potential risk for failure.

We know that banks pay a certain amount for passbook savings, and U.S. money-market certificates pay a certain range. If you are offered rates of return that are considerably higher than these cited, you should be aware that the risks involved are high. You should identify what those risks are before investing. There *are* high-risk, high-return investments that aren't fraudulent. If you are willing to take the risk, you could make a lot of money. On the other hand, you could lose a lot of money. If you contemplate such an investment, the least you should do is seek professional advice from two or three sources.

When offered an investment that claims an exorbitant rate of return, you may find it helpful to ask yourself, "Why doesn't Exxon, IBM, or strong local firms who are getting perhaps a 12-percent return on their present investments liquidate their assets and take advantage of this investment?" Some of these companies spend literally millions of dollars studying investment opportunities. Perhaps these companies do not invest in investments with exorbitant rates of return because these investments are too speculative, because there is too much risk involved.

2. *Ignore investment opportunities that are presented as having a secret approach to making money that cannot be disclosed to you.* The news media has cited bankruptcies for companies in which even the salesmen of the investment were unsure of how a return on the money was generated.

3. *Be aware of the liability you must assume in connection with a potential investment.* Do you have to sign a promissory note in addition to making your initial cash investment? While you may be told the promissory note will not be called because the success of the investment will pay off the note, if the investment fails, you will still be liable. The note can be called. If it is called, can you afford to pay off the liability? Do not take a chance.

4. *Beware of cosigning notes in connection with investments.* Sometimes an investment may require cash investment plus a cosignature on a promissory note. A cosigner assumes the liability on the note in the event of failure to pay
by the initial signer.

You need to recognize that by cosigning a note, you are
assuming a liability. Can you afford to pay off the liability if
called upon to do so? If not, do not cosign the notes.

5. *Obtain a full disclosure of information regarding the
investment.* Audited financial statements by a certified public accounting firm and a private-placement memorandum
prepared by a reputable law firm usually disclose the associated risks of an investment. Insist on being able to review such documents. If disclosure is refused, pass up the
investment.

6. *Don't be intimidated by the investment salesman.* The
use of fancy words and language about the investment may
make you feel embarrassed to ask questions. If the salesman
tries to "put you down" for being too inquisitive, perhaps he
is trying to hide something; and if he tries to interpret your
questions as an insult to his integrity, perhaps he has none.
Do not be afraid to ask enough pertinent questions to obtain
a thorough understanding of the investment.

7. *Seek professional assistance if you feel unqualified to
analyze a particular investment.* It is well worth the money
to pay a CPA or other reputable financial adviser for an independent opinion about the risks of the investment. Remember, it's your money that you are risking. Take the steps
necessary to be well informed.

8. *Do not borrow money to invest.* Sometimes the exorbitant returns promoted by speculative investments lure us to
borrow money for the investment. Borrowing money at 18
percent·to invest at 30 percent or better may sound like a
good investment, but if the high-risk investment fails, you
are left with a debt. You have lost the investment funds and
may be unable to pay off the debt you have incurred from
your regular earnings. If you do choose to invest in highly
speculative investments, do not invest money that you cannot afford to lose. Money that is normally used to buy food,

clothing, or shelter should not be used for investments, especially highly speculative ones. The court records are full of stories of families who have lost lifetime earnings through speculative investments.

9. *Beware of investments presented to you as the last chance for you to buy.* Why is the salesman in such a hurry? Do you know the whole story? If you feel you have to hurry into the decision, maybe you should let the salesman hurry on to someone else.

10. *Don't be afraid to say no.* If, after all your analysis, you do not feel the investment is right for you, then do not make the investment. You worked hard to earn your money; do not give it up for fear of hurting the salesman's or a friend's feelings. Instead, manage your money wisely. Think about how your family might feel if you were to lose your investment.

There are other ways to avoid losing your financial resources. We have considered here only how to avoid bad investments. The Church has given us other guidelines, and we would do well to review them often. Among them is the counsel to pay a full tithe, a generous fast offering, and other offerings; to properly budget our money; to live within our income; to plan major purchases, avoiding credit purchases; to work toward home ownership; to get out of debt; to have a savings plan; to provide financial security for times of disability and advanced age; and to take better care of our possessions. (See *Choose You This Day,* Melchizedek Priesthood Study Guide, 1980-1981, pp. 13-14.) We all need to take stock of our current financial situation and try to implement in our lives wise guidelines for financial management and success.

ABOUT THE AUTHOR

Dr. John W. Hardy, professor of accountancy in the Graduate School of Management at Brigham Young University, received his undergraduate education at BYU, his MBA at Indiana University, and his Ph.D. from the University of Texas at Austin. He is a certified public accountant in the state of Utah.

A high councilor in his home stake, he has previously served the Church as bishop and bishop's counselor.

He and his wife, Nancy, are the parents of five children.

Index